THE
PSYCHOTHERAPEUTIC
INSTRUMENT

And almost thence my nature is subdu'd
To what it works in. . . .
                              —*Shakespeare*

THE
PSYCHOTHERAPEUTIC
INSTRUMENT

Stanley L. Olinick, M.D.

NEW YORK • JASON ARONSON • LONDON

ISBN: 0-87668-403-7

Library of Congress Catalog Number: 80-620

Manufactured in the United States of America

To my family

CLASSICAL PSYCHOANALYSIS AND ITS APPLICATIONS

A Series of Books
Edited by Robert Langs, M.D.

SERIES INTRODUCTION

It is an honor and a pleasure to bring the work of Stanley Olinick to the readers of this series. Dr. Olinick has long been known and respected by his colleagues as an unusually gifted and perceptive clinician. His papers on the negative therapeutic reaction, empathy, the analytic work ego, and analytic paradoxes are known to many as clinical gems and modern-day classics. The present volume brings together his most important writings, a series of contributions that will provide a wide audience of practitioners an opportunity to share in his unusual perceptiveness and in his very special ability to broaden our understanding of the therapeutic interaction.

Olinick documents his insights with vivid case material that makes his contributions both unforgettable and eminently useful. His work reminds us once again of the importance of careful psychoanalytic studies in expanding our conception of the therapeutic process and its techniques, and in improving the work of all clinicians.

Robert Langs, M.D.

CONTENTS

FOREWORD

by K. R. Eissler, M.D.

Dr. Olinick has given us a veritable treasure of a book which ought to become indispensable for anyone interested in the scientific basis of psychoanalytic therapy and technique.

The Psychotherapeutic Instrument is devoted to the "middle game" of the psychoanalytic process, a term the author extrapolates from Freud's comparison of the beginning phase of treatment with the opening of a chess game, the rules for which are easily obtainable. It is quite different from the middle game, for which hardly any rules can be established. The center of the author's endeavor is the metapsychology of the analyst's "work ego," a designation Robert Fliess coined for the practitioner's analyzing functions.

The author unfolds a wealth of transitional events that are inherent in the steps from the reception of the patient's message to the analyst's interpretation. The global knowledge we have had of this most complicated course of inner events is now replaced by a detailed survey of intricate processes, "regression in the service of the work ego" being only one of many.

The author rightly conjectures that an understanding of the manner in which the analyst's inner processes are initiated, nourished, and brought to fruition will shed new light on the most elusive topic in psychology — the creative process. Indeed, an untried source of deepest insight into the creative process in general is opened here.

Once the psychoanalyst or psychoanalytic therapist has reached an understanding and knowledge of his own basic instrument, that is, his own psychic organization, a rational understanding and management of treatment becomes possible. The author is fully aware of the decline psychoanalysis has suffered in the public eye and of the various attempts to find salvation in psychotherapeutic modalities lacking any scientific underpinnings or in esoteric religious groups. His book stands as a valid contribution to the reaffirmation and demonstration that psychoanalysis is relevantly different from such attempts.

The author clarifies many concepts that enjoy daily use in the psychoanalytic jargon but whose meanings have become blurred and at times misplaced. Of the many, I mention here only empathy, whose rich world is presented in detail, and which he puts in its proper place. The author redefines a number of concepts in a constructive manner which ought to have a wholesome effect on future discussions among analysts, who often disagree on purely semantic grounds. Most sensitively, the author traces the possible infantile origins of the practitioner's interest in his métier, of his endowment, and of the corresponding pitfalls. His suggestions impress me as highly original and consequential to further research.

One feels throughout the book the author's power of artistic imagination tempered by admirable self-discipline and adherence to the scientific tradition of psychoanalysis. He himself steps modestly into the background; he lets theory and facts speak for themselves without *ira et studio* or the urge to persuade the reader. This adds greatly to the joy of reading this book, written in a precise, graceful language which, in addition to providing a huge body of new information and knowledge, offers a remarkable aesthetic experience.

PREFACE

The chapters of this volume state, explore, and resolve certain problems confronting the clinician in psychoanalysis and psychoanalytic psychotherapy. The central issue uniting these problems has several facets: while the issue itself is related to the art and science of knowing and understanding the patient for the purposes of treatment, we have long recognized in this post-Freudian age that the therapist must first of all know and understand himself. Historically, the training analysis was proposed for this reason; but even without formal psychoanalytic training, many psychiatric residents and postresidential practitioners seek analyses for themselves with the intention of clarifying and augmenting the basic instrument of psychotherapy—the therapist's own psychic organization. To know the psychology of the analyst or psychoanalytic psychotherapist is basic to a rational understanding and management of treatment, and this volume is, I trust, a contribution to the literature on that vital subject.

Consequently I offer here chapters on empathy that involve inquiries into pertinent aspects of the psychology of the analyst in the operation of this unique instrument. I have found it useful to employ Fliess's designation (1942) for the analyst's analyzing functions, comprehending these under his general rubric of "work ego"; I refer in this way to the therapist-at-work when informed by and operating in the context of psychoanalytic principles. Adapting a well-known phrase from Ernst Kris, I may speak of "regression in the service of the *work* ego." I refer in this way to the partial, temporary, and controlled regression of some of the analyst's analyzing functions in the course of his empathic operations, and in the service of the patient's analysis. In addition, there are chapters on the clinical and theoretical aspects of the psychology of questioning, on the negative therapeutic reaction, and on the meanings and uses of paradox and metaphor in psychoanalysis. I have elected not to rewrite the older papers, but rather to add introductions and postscripts. In one instance only (chapter 11) have I done any significant rewriting. I should like to think that my decision not to rewrite was dictated less by inflexible complacency than by a practical sense of the possibilities, as well as by the recognition that these papers have, through the years, been found useful by many colleagues.

A writer is successful in his endeavors to the extent that his own imaginative, innovative, and creative synthesis evokes a corresponding and parallel perception in the reader. This is to state the obvious. What is not so obvious is that a similar (not to say identical) process is bilaterally and mutually enacted in the psychoanalytic situation. I discuss this in more detail in chapter 12, with particular reference to Holland's work in the psychology of reading and its bearing on the theory of literature. The process of psychoanalytically oriented treatment is itself an imaginative, creative work. To understand another person in psychoanalytic breadth and depth is a creative action. The methodology of psychoanalysis and its clinical theory in no way constrict or restrict patient or analyst: quite the contrary. It may be that our growing understanding of how this creative process is initiated, nourished, and brought to fruition will shed further light on the creative process in general, particularly as this may relate to the "transitional" processes that are inherent in the analyst's prescribed posture of attentiveness to his analysand through "evenly hovering attention." But this is to abbreviate and impossibly abridge the several chapters on empathy and the work ego.

Psychoanalysis, since World War II having ridden a wave of popularity and popularization ill-suited to its private and rigorous methods, is now suffering a decline in public esteem. At the same time, its concepts and some of its methods are being preempted by a variety of treatment modalities, only a few of which are receiving scientific validation. There is a proliferation of treatment methods, ranging from the mechanistic and the pharmaceutical to the adaptation of certain Eastern cults and practices, all purporting to represent The True Way to Health, Happiness, Orgasm, and Success.

The dehumanization and curtailment of sensibilities that accompany an industrial, urbanized society confronted with glorifications of violence force individuals to search out any promise of salvation. There are some who continue to seek it in organized religion; but the majority of our younger people, I venture to say, seek out their religion and salvation elsewhere and otherwise. Psychoanalysis offers no salvation or rescue: it recognizes that living has always been fraught with difficulties, and will always be so. Perhaps this is best expressed in the now familiar words with which Freud closed his *Studies on Hysteria.* Speaking to a hypothetical patient who consults him, he says: "No doubt fate would find it easier than I do to relieve you of your illness. But you will be able to convince yourself that much will be gained if we succeed in transforming your hysterical misery into common unhappiness. With a mental life that has been restored to health you will be better armed against that unhappiness" (Breuer and Freud 1895, p. 305).

I am taking this way of affirming that psychoanalysis is a scientifically humanistic methodology and body of clinical theory and facts that continues to hold vast possibilities for expanded application to the relief of human suffering. It is my deep hope that the present volume may contribute to that goal.

In trying to express my indebtedness to the many who have made this book possible, I take heart from the fact that most writers, confronted with this obligation of love and gratitude, find that words are inadequate. My family — Vida, Philip, and Taya — have made it possible through their devotion, encouragement, and patience. To my patients I owe appreciative thanks, for having imparted to me their confidences, for having listened to me, and, above all, for having afforded me the opportunity to learn from them. To several of my colleagues I owe very much. They have been sources of support in the hard, daily work of analyzing, as I hope I have been to them. I have learned from them, and all of them have been friends, a word that barely indicates my indebtedness. I list only those who have been most closely linked with the chapters of this book. That I list them alphabetically is to indicate that we are all aware of the presence of envy and competition even among good friends: Dr. William L. Granatir, Dr. Kenneth A. Grigg, Dr. Warren S. Poland.

I wish finally, but not least, to thank my editor, Dr. Robert Langs, for his patience, encouragement, and many suggestions, and my publisher, Dr. Jason Aronson, for his confidence in suggesting this volume.

REFERENCES

Breuer, J., and Freud, S. (1895). Studies on hysteria. *Standard Edition* 2.
Fliess, R. (1942). The metapsychology of the analyst. *Psychoanalytic Quarterly* 11: 211·227.

Part I

THE THERAPIST AT WORK

Chapter 1

Empathy and Regression

THE "MIDDLE GAME" OF ANALYSIS

I am attempting here a review of certain functions of the psychoanalyst during what has been called the "middle game" of psychoanalysis (Freud 1913). The transactions of this main phase of analysis, as I define it here, possess a unique affective quality; and there is a special quality to some of the operations of the analyst during this period, making it in some ways quite different from the opening and closing phases.

On the part of the two participants, there is at times a sense of privacy, of exclusion of the outside world, of difficulty in reporting to outsiders, and especially of an empathic mutuality that lends a special clarity to the analyst's communications. The affective quality may be analogized to the spirit of a child's play or game. Thus, although it is an intensely absorbing and serious venture or ordeal, aspects of humor and enjoyment are present; it is performed in the service of the mastery principle, in order to master what has caused distress; it requires a controlled regression (Kris 1935, 1950) to perform its functions, and it does not require the original realities to be present in order to fulfill these functions (see also Waelder, 1933).

The delimiting of a middle game or phase of psychoanalysis is somewhat arbitrary, but allowing for a bit of leeway as to the beginning and end of the middle, it has value for classification and understanding. I propose that we consider it to begin when the patient evinces his first transference resistance, in a setting of having established a therapeutic alliance with the analyst (Sterba 1934,

Zetzel 1956, Greenson 1965). I would emphasize that the transference which has become resistance, besides employing displacement, projection and introjection, identification, and repetition (MacAlpine 1950), is often manifested in efforts by the patient to transform the analyst in accord with his transference needs. I refer to the acting out that is directed toward molding reality to narcissistic fantasy, thereby turning passivity into activity. Some writers, for example Nunberg (1951), prefer to regard this as a "readiness for transference."

By *therapeutic alliance* is denoted the therapeutic splitting of the patient's ego into an observing and an experiencing part, by a bond of identification with the analyst as observer and annotator (Sterba 1934, Zetzel 1956, Greenson 1965).

Middle game is a shifting and changing process, subject to progression and retrogression; but when these defining conditions have been met — when a transference resistance has been dealt with in a setting of therapeutic alliance — the prognosis as to outcome of the analysis has met one validating test.

We may consider the middle game over when (1) the patient has largely worked through his major resistances and conflicts, and (2) the attention of physician and patient is increasingly drawn to matters of separation and termination. I define the beginning from the side of the patient, with reference to the analyst in the context of identification and transference, and the ending in terms of patient and analyst both, in the context of separation.

CONTROLLED REGRESSION
AND TRIAL IDENTIFICATIONS

In what follows, in order to avoid certain ambiguities that accrue to the term *countertransference* (Gitelson 1952, Heimann 1950, Racker 1957, Spitz 1956), I shall employ the usage "psychology of the analyst" as referring to all of the reactions to the psychoanalytic situation, including those motivational factors that led the analyst into this field, and into work with this patient. I subsume under the term *eccentric response* the range of responses that are peculiar to him and that deviate from the appropriate. I exclude what is merely his individual stamp or style and is appropriate to the psychoanalytic situation.

A certain advantage inheres in the fact that it is the patient who initiates topics, who adheres to the basic rule or not, who actively transfers and resists. It is an advantage in one sense, in that the analyst is necessarily attendant upon the patient's expressions and communications. But it is part of the analytic paradox (see chapter 11) that while the patient enters into the contract willingly, permitting the analyst to assist him toward ego autonomy along a route of dependency and regression, he retains the initiative as to the themes and the resistances of the work. Inevitably, this will thwart the analyst's attempt to understand and, by imparting that understanding to the patient, to treat.

Consider then the psychology of the analyst as he experiences the continuing impact of hourly changes in the psychoanalytic situation, during which his ego must be kept open by means of self-imposed, evenly suspended attention, silences, minimal verbal and physical activity, and empathic observations, with intermittent concern for the day-to-day exigencies of the patient's living. Consider both the regressive allure and the regressive repulsion brought to bear upon those residual conflicts and needs related to his own central fantasies of rescue, nurturance, reparation, and curiosity.

This partially regressive openness and receptivity of the analyst renders him permeable, even vulnerable at times, to certain processes within the patient. These ongoing processes between and within the two participants are indispensable to the work; they are largely introjective and projective (see chapter 10, Loewald 1960, Malin and Grotstein 1966). It is part of the analyst's function of utilizing empathy or trial identifications (Fliess 1942) that he experience, even if preconsciously, the aggressive, erotic, and other affects that are projected and induced in him (Racker 1957). It is then his peculiar, hypercivilized function to return these to the patient, guilt-free and anxiety-free, often without words, but if with words, by employing the poetic art of interpretation. Nor is this all, for the art of interpretation is bound by compelling scientific, logical principles.

In general, such experiences by the analyst of the patient are distinguished by one or more of the following operations: (1) they are empathized directly from the patient, in a manner to be outlined; (2) they arouse in him his own eccentric response to what the patient is doing; (3) neither identical with the patient's experiences nor unique to the psychology of the analyst, they are induced in him by the patient's alloplastic efforts at resolving his transference conflicts. For familiar example, a patient having identified with the aggressor as a childhood defense may induce in the analyst, by means of aggressive behavior, the affects experienced at the hands of the original aggressor.

It is necessary that the analyst be enabled to respond to these experiences appropriately as to their origin, content, and form, in order to remain synchronized to and comprehending of the movement of the patient's associations, transference, and resistance. How are these experiences utilized by the analyst in the regular course of his work? They require, first, an observing ego that can draw upon what Hartmann (1939) calls "regressive adaptation" and Kris (1935, 1950) "regression in the service of the ego." I refer to the temporary and partial suspension of the usual forms of reality orientation in favor of an access to one's own subliminal or preconscious functioning. The analyst in this way obtains data about himself and his environment that he could not otherwise "re-cognize." In addition to this topographic regression, there may be available the analyst's past experience as well. Finally, less highly structured sensory representations may be noted, e.g., a visual image may condense within a single frame a complex evaluation of the patient (cf. Freud 1900).

I do not mean to imply that the analyst is regressed in any psychopathological sense. The presence of his observing ego, and the fact that his openness to what is within himself and the patient is thereby controlled and partial, make for a different effect, more in accord with what we see in creative work and problem solving (Kris 1950). During this controlled regression, the analyst gains a more direct knowledge of the other person than is otherwise available to him. It is in this frame of reference that the analyst's trial identifications are made.

Fliess (1942) defines empathy or trial identification as follows: "A person who uses empathy on an object *introjects this object transiently, and projects the introject again onto the object.*" Fenichel (1945, p. 511) refers to such trial identifications as repetitions of "archaic types of perception in general." I am employing the equivalent term *regressed* for "archaic." The developmental background for this aspect of the analytic work ego will be outlined presently.

The subjective experience of empathy is one of direct, nonmediated knowing. The feeling is of certainty, though one may not at the moment be able to specify either the derivation of one's information or the manner in which it will be imparted to the patient. The feeling of certainty will be the greater, depending on the extent of one's validated experience with this aspect of functioning. The experience enters awareness as a completely verbalized logical statement, as an affect, or as sensory (usually visual) imagery. Considering the quality of mutuality that empathy may carry with its feeling of certitude, it would seem appropriate to conceptualize empathy as involving the regression of an ego-system or systems to the point of intrapsychic fusion of self-image and object-image, momentarily and reversibly (Jacobson 1964, Greenson 1960, Kris 1950). Some regression is always necessary in order for empathy and identification to take place. Moreover, regression under the aegis of an observing ego is necessary in order to recognize the contents of empathy and identification — that is, for there to be awareness of what is otherwise subliminal.

REGRESSION IN THE SERVICE OF THE OTHER

In this view of the complexities of transactions that are integrated within the middle game, Freud's descriptive metaphor of the mirror (Freud 1914, Loewald 1960, Stone 1961) does contain many of the analyst's functions of reflecting back to the patient; but it is with an altered perspective, freed of guilt and anxiety. As we have seen, the analyst both observes and experiences in parallel with the patient. He also evaluates what of his own experiences with the patient needs to be reflected.

We are brought then to the following ancient questions: How does one person know the other's thoughts and feelings? How does one person influence another to feel what he is feeling? How does it come about that the analyst is permeable to processes within the patient?

It may be said, first, that it is one of the basic functions of the human being as a social animal to experience his fellows. It is essential to survival, and it is one of the first things he learns as an infant (Spitz 1965, Scott 1958, Knapp 1963, Lorenz 1966). Second, it is a specifically psychoanalytic function for which the analyst has been trained, though the training in respect to these questions has not always been explicit. Finally, the patient in some measure forces it upon the analyst. This too, from either side, is learned in infancy and early childhood, in a manner now to be outlined.

A basic aspect of acculturation or humanizing has to do with earliest nurturing conditions — the manner in which the infant or toddler, within the mother–child dyad, experiences and learns the bilaterally ongoing influencing of each other to the end of mutual satisfaction (Spitz 1965, Mahler 1965). On the elucidation of these early processes depends not only the understanding of the analyst's work ego as it utilizes empathy and intuition, but indeed the understanding of anyone's full recognition of "the other one" as a person. In general, one may say that a condition for successful nurturing, whether maternal, pedagogic, or psychotherapeutic, is immersion in the needs of the other one, to the end that the other will in turn be immersed in the nurturing person. Infant and mother, and later, child and parent of either sex are participants in a circular process, the responses of each more or less reflecting the needs of the other (Mahler 1965, Geleerd 1965). It may be that some of the regressive processes of pregnancy serve to prepare the mother for participation in these developments, as of course do also the various other biological and psychological sources of motivation to nurturing (Spitz 1965, Bibring 1959, Benedek 1949).

Immersion in the needs of a regressed or undeveloped person necessarily entails a regression, whether as parent, teacher, or therapist. Such regression in the service and interests of the other's development is controlled, partial, and reversible. It is concerned not with the patient's immediate gratifications but with his ultimate ones; not with the myriad secondary effects of frustration but with the development of tolerance for frustration.

It should be clear that the phrase *in the service of* is elliptic, condensing within itself the fact that the regressing, nurturing person is thus "serving" because he is so constituted as to be unable to do otherwise. His motivations impel him, in the service of his own equilibrium, to perform in this manner, in this context, and with this other person. Stated differently, the analyst "serves," through the use of empathy as a by-product of a controlled regression, to comprehend the patient and to impart this understanding to him. This is accomplished through verbal and nonverbal interventions, or feedbacks — interpretations, silences, tone of voice, presence or absence of affect, etc. The feedbacks are aspects of the introjective-projective transactions that proceed between and within the two participants (see chapter 10).

That the nurturing person has himself once been nurtured is a potent force in rendering him nurturant at present. On the other hand, he may by now have learned to do his nurturing differently than he had initially experienced it.

In the course of this controlled regression in the service of the other, the analyst, as we have seen, is to a greater or lesser extent open to the patient, to his needs, influences, projections, and inductions. A curious phenomenon may now ensue, one neatly encompassed by Coleridge's phrase, "a willing suspension of disbelief." For the moment, one may be caught up with the patient's wishes and feelings, in a way not dissimilar to our suspension of disbelief in the presence of vividly realistic acting on the screen or stage. This effect depends on the readiness of an observer-participant to yield to the regressive pull of identifying with the narcissistic and successful reliance of an actor on his own abilities within the role played. In a similar way, the power of the child in the patient is considerable, and this child's demand for and expression of narcissistic omnipotence, unless grossly dystonic, can mesh with the analyst's own residual needs. One may hear a parent say, for instance, that "he wants it so much, it seems terrible not to give it to him." Freud (1914) understood well the possible effects of regression on sublimated drives when he wrote in his discussion of transference-love:

> When a woman sues for love, to reject and refuse is a distressing part for a man to play; and in spite of neurosis and resistance, there is an incomparable fascination in a woman of high principles who confesses her passion. . . . It is . . . perhaps, a woman's subtler and aim-inhibited wishes which bring with them the danger of making a man forget his technique and his medical task for the sake of a fine experience.

Under the psychoanalytic conditions of "regression in the service of the other," there is a partial, controlled suspension of disbelief in the patient's transference operations. The patient's intent is to make the past real and actuated in the present, either as it once was or as he would like it to be. The analyst does not confirm the transference by responding to this behavior as appropriate; rather, he experiences the effects of the transference upon himself, if only momentarily, in order to understand it in a way other than abstractly intellectual. The transference experience is emotionally real to the patient, even when his observing ego may know different. Similarly, though not identically, it is momentarily real to the analyst, even as his work ego knows different. The suspension of disbelief, resulting from those operations of the work ego that I am referring to as "regression in the service of the other," is conducive to an intimate comprehension of the patient that is both instant and usable. Experiencing the patient in this fashion is recognized by the work ego as dystonic, and the affects are consequently employed as signals leading to a reality-oriented appraisal, on the model of signal-anxiety (Freud 1925) or other signal-affects (Zetzel 1965). By means of empathy or trial identification, and a selective receptivity to the patient's alloplastic inductions, a setting of mutuality is established out of which an effective, mutative, transference interpretation may be made (Strachey 1934). In such a context and in clinically experienced hands, even some of the analyst's eccentric responses can be brought to serve as affect-signals.

Some of this can be illustrated by an example from a querulous patient. He had been showing clinical improvement when he began to complain that it was difficult to keep his appointments, that he wanted them changed, that his work requirements were increasingly stringent, and moreover that he was now enjoying his work to such a degree that he would prefer not to leave his office for the analyst's. He complained also of the fees, of the diminishing value of the therapy, and of the analyst's seeming disinterest and boredom.

In view of the patient's clinical improvement, including the fact that his presenting symptom had been homosexuality and that in the course of treatment he had had transient heterosexual relations for the first time in his life, and since he was currently engaged in maneuvers with a responsive young woman, the analyst was entitled to entertain doubt and curiosity regarding the complaints; moreover, he wondered why he should be feeling a guilty and irritable discomfort at the patient's continuing resistance.

The patient's complaining came to be understood in terms of his angry denial and projection of his guilt feelings concerning his impending oedipal success with the young woman. This success carried with it the implication of defeating the analyst as the other man.

If now the analyst could be made to feel guilty, deprived, and angry—these 'being feelings the patient had long been struggling with—and if the analyst could be induced to experience what the patient had also struggled to make his parents feel, then the patient, freed of bad feelings, could feel absolved of responsibility for incestuous and parricidal feelings and impulses. More than that, he could feel vindicated, good, and lovable.

It was necessary for the analyst to be open to the patient's affect and to employ this as his own affect-signal, in order to know what needed to be clarified and interpreted. It could then be progressively clarified to the patient that, in effect, transference had become a resistance: that he was "working" the analyst instead of working with him; that he was creating a transferentially projected diversion in which the analyst was the bad, guilty one, and the patient the maligned, innocent one; and that he was making the analyst feel something instead of feeling it himself. Clarification and interpretation of the patient's guilt feelings and their sources could then follow, in a new phase of working through.

There had in fact been a suspension of disbelief: the patient's acting out resulted in the analyst empathizing guilt in temporary collusion, or trial identification, with him. This guilt was recognized as a signal of processes within the patient.

It is true that the analyst had known this cognitively, but such abstract, theoretical knowing has little operational relevance. With empathized or induced affect, one has a sign that, other things being equal, it is timely to intervene with clarification, confrontation, and/or interpretation. If it now be asked whether the analyst in such an instance has the same conflicts as the patient, in order to be able to form the trial identification as described, the answer would be: "For the moment, yes; but only as applicable to the therapeutically oriented regression and suspended disbelief of the patient-doctor dyad."

The reverberating effects of such regression may be prolonged and may result either in the appropriate reality orientation and therapeutic intervention, or in the eccentric response. It seems to me that either reaction is secondary to the effects of the analyst's regression and his consequent affective contact with the patient. If now the empathic observations and the resultant interventions are congruent with the "therapeutic and scientific conscience" of the analyst and with the overall contextual understanding, the regression may be said to have been in the service of the other (see Fliess 1942, Menninger 1958).

To return to our earlier questions, we need not ask: How do we come to comprehend each other, to empathize or be intuitive, to influence or be influenced? Rather we ask: What interferes with these processes, natural as they are and essential to living, humanizing, and at least potential in everyone? The answer lies in the infant's and child's utilization, under the censures and nurturance of the adult, of his own capacities for learning to adapt to what is required of him, in the mutual, interdependent relatedness that may lead either to normal development or to pathology (Mahler 1965, Geleerd 1965).

THE ANALYST'S MOTIVATIONS

That a mother should immerse herself in her child over a period of years is largely taken for granted in our present child-orientated culture, though in many periods of history and in many cultures this has not been the case (Ariès 1962, Olden 1952). But that an adult man or woman should devote his energies to years of arduous study in order to spend his days and hours with a small handful of patients in what has been called an impossible profession (Freud 1937, Greenson 1966) is a phenomenon that has baffled our colleagues and at times ourselves. It is no explanation to refer to scientific curiosity, humanistic dedication, and the like: these are not unique to psychoanalysts. The uniqueness, it seems to me, lies in the degree to which the psychiatrist is willing and expectant of regressive immersion in the service of the other, as distinguished from service without such regression. The resultant closely integrated dyad is analogous in intensity and extended influence to the early mother-child unit, in so far as it establishes an emotional setting for development and maturation, giving to the patient the opportunity to resume ego development.

Despite the individual stamp or style of the analyst within the accustomed scope of his work, there are underlying common denominators of psychodynamics — more clearly discernible in situations where the fact of an eccentric response may expose underlying fantasy. I suggest that a powerful motivation for the psychiatrist dedicating himself to the psychoanalytic relationship is the genetic effect of a rescue fantasy having to do with a depressive mother, the latter having induced such rescue fantasy in her receptive child. By "depressive" I intend to connote a character prone to depression and in whom we discern oral dependency, narcissistic hunger, and feelings of deprivation as the factors prominent in evoking the reciprocal and complementary fantasies.

For such relatedness of mother and child to be formative, it must be early, though the necessary duration is not clear (see, for example, A. Freud 1954, 1963, and Ferenczi 1923, 1933, especially 1933, p. 165). It seems that depression or sadness alone is not sufficient; in addition, the maternal character must be at least in certain aspects alloplastic. Often there is an effort by provoking guilt to force the other to rescue, such enslavement also confirming one's lovableness. Perhaps these factors help incidentally to explain the often powerful "helpless appeal" of some depressive persons.

To be sure, no amount of rescuing or healing, however successful, is going to satisfy a therapeutic ambition and master a conflict whose wellsprings are in a child's rescue fantasy. It is the internalized conflict and the introjected object that must of course be mastered. Nor do I mean to say anything so naive as that the analyst's work ego is "nothing but" a child playing at rescue. Nevertheless, there is a tendency in human beings to return endlessly to the reactuation of unmastered basic conflicts of childhood, the settlement of which is necessary to simplification and efficiency in living. There are many forms of the riddle of the Sphinx and, as Oedipus sadly learned, she is a ghost not easily laid.

It must be said that the process of rescuing, as distinguished from the fulfillment of fantasy by the definitive act or by the convincing illusion of rescue, may temporarily alleviate guilt or anxiety. By cathecting an activity, and so replacing the object (Sandler and Joffe 1966), the practice of therapy may come to replace or substitute for the internalized conflict and object. But such marriage to one's work has a neurotically compulsive basis, and it is subject to the usual changes of fortune of the compulsive defenses.

CONCLUSIONS

The middle game of psychoanalysis has been defined, and scanned for the delineation of some of the basic operations of the analyst.

His empathic skills are facilitated by exercise of what Kris, in the context of creativity and problem solving, referred to as "regression in the service of the ego." Such regression within a nurturing dyad may result in "the service of the other." Its vicissitudes point the way to understanding of motivation in choice of profession and selection of patients, as well as of decompensation into non-therapeutic misalliance.

The distinguishing factor for the psychoanalytic psychiatrist lies in the degree to which he accepts regression in the service of the other, as contrasted with service lacking such regression. This factor in turn reflects the genetic effects of a rescue fantasy in a family unit uniquely marked by a depressive mother.

Such behavior as I have described here, on the part of one adult with another, is in Western society often regarded with disdain and distrust, though also with envy. Be that as it may, the analyst's motivational sources are in their way no stranger than those of other colleagues in the service professions. His rescue fantasy, or St. George complex, is sublimated, or integrated, into character. He is subject to regressive decompensation, but he and his patient are safeguarded by the techniques of his work, his own training analysis, and his own integrity. It is my view that the controlled regression of the analyst during the middle game is one of the defining conditions for his work and for the psychoanalytic situation.

REFERENCES

Ariès, P. (1962). *Centuries of Childhood*. New York: Knopf.

Benedek, T. (1949). The psychosomatic implications of the primary unit: mother-child. *American Journal of Orthopsychiatry* 19: 642–654.

Bibring, G. (1959). Some considerations of the psychological processes in pregnancy. *Psychoanalytic Study of the Child* 14: 113–121.

Fenichel, O. (1945). *The Psychoanalytic Theory of Neurosis*. New York: Norton.

Ferenczi, S. (1923). The dream of the 'clever baby.' In *Further Contributions to the Theory and Technique of Psycho-Analysis*. London: Hogarth Press, 1950.

_____(1933). Confusion of tongues between adults and the child. In *Final Contributions to the Problems and Methods of Psycho-Analysis*. New York: Basic Books, 1955.

Fliess, R. (1942). The metapsychology of the analyst. *Psychoanalytic Quarterly* 11: 211-227.

Freud, A. (1954). Discussion remarks: problems of infantile neurosis. *Psychoanalytic Study of the Child* 9: 71.

_____(1963). The concept of developmental lines. *Psychoanalytic Study of the Child* 18: 245-265.

Freud, S. (1900). The interpretation of dreams. *Standard Edition* 5.

_____(1913). On beginning the treatment. *Standard Edition* 12: 121-144.

_____(1914). Observations on transference-love. *Standard Edition* 12: 157-171.

_____(1925). Inhibitions, symptoms, and anxiety. *Standard Edition* 20: 87-174.

_____(1937). Analysis terminable and interminable. *Standard Edition* 23: 216-253.

Geleerd, E. (1965). Two kinds of denial. In *Drives, Affects, Behavior,* vol. 2, ed. M. Schur. New York: International Universities Press.

Gitelson, M. (1952). The emotional position of the analyst in the psychoanalytic situation. *International Journal of Psycho-Analysis* 33: 1-10.

Greenson, R. (1960). Empathy and its vicissitudes. *International Journal of Psycho-Analysis* 41: 418-424.

_____(1965). The working alliance and the transference neurosis. *Psychoanalytic Quarterly* 34: 155-181.

_____(1966). That 'impossible' profession. *Journal of the American Psychoanalytic Association* 14: 9-27.

Hartmann, H. (1939). *Ego Psychology and Problems of Adaptation.* New York: International Universities Press, 1958.

Heimann, P. (1950). On counter-transference. *International Journal of Psycho-Analysis* 31: 81-84.

Jacobson, E. (1964). *The Self and the Object World.* New York: International Universities Press.

Knapp, P. H., ed. (1963). *Expression of the Emotions in Man.* New York: International Universities Press.

Kris, E. (1935). The psychology of caricature. In *Psychoanalytic Explorations in Art,* chap. 6. New York: International Universities Press, 1952.

_____(1950). On preconscious mental processes. In *Psychoanalytic Explorations in Art,* chap. 14. New York: International Universities Press, 1952. Also in *Psychoanalytic Quarterly* 19: 540-560.

Loewald, H. W. (1960). On the therapeutic action of psychoanalysis. *International Journal of Psycho-Analysis* 41: 16-33.

Lorenz, K. (1966). *On Aggression*. New York: Harcourt, Brace.

MacAlpine, I. (1950). The development of the transference. *Psychoanalytic Quarterly* 19: 501–539.

Mahler, M. (1965). On the significance of the normal separation-individuation phase. In *Drives, Affects, Behavior*, vol. 2, ed. M. Schur. New York: International Universities Press.

Malin, A., and Grotstein, J. S. (1966). Projective identification in the therapeutic process. *International Journal of Psycho-Analysis* 47: 26–31.

Menninger, K. (1958). *Theory of Psychoanalytic Technique*. New York: Basic Books.

Nunberg, H. (1951). Transference and reality. *International Journal of Psycho-Analysis* 32: 1–9.

Olden, C. (1952). Notes on child-rearing in America. *Psychoanalytic Study of the Child* 7: 387–392.

Racker, H. (1957). The meanings and uses of countertransference. *Psychoanalytic Quarterly* 26: 303–357.

Sandler, J., and Joffe, W. G. (1966). On skill and sublimation. *Journal of the American Psychoanalytic Association* 14: 335–355.

Scott, J. P. (1958). *Animal Behavior*. University of Chicago Press.

Spitz, R. A. (1956). Countertransference: comments on its varying role in the analytic situation. *Journal of the American Psychoanalytic Association* 4: 256–265.

———(1965). *The First Year of Life*. New York: International Universities Press.

Sterba, R. (1934). The fate of the ego in analytic therapy. *International Journal of Psycho-Analysis* 15: 117–126.

Stone, L. (1961). *The Psychoanalytic Situation*. New York: International Universities Press.

Strachey, J. (1934). The nature of the therapeutic action of psychoanalysis. *International Journal of Psycho-Analysis* 15: 127–159.

Waelder, R. (1933). The psychoanalytic theory of play. *Psychoanalytic Quarterly* 2: 208–224.

Zetzel, E. R. (1956). Current concepts of transference. *International Journal of Psycho-Analysis* 37: 369–376.

———(1965). Depression and the capacity to bear it. In *Drives, Affects, Behavior*, vol. 2, ed. M. Schur. New York: International Universities Press.

Chapter 2

Interpretation and the Psychoanalytic Work Ego

The work ego of the experienced psychoanalyst manifests a relatively stable autonomy of function that varies from person to person and within the same person in accordance with his general stability of organization. This autonomy operates very effectively in certain instances of interpretation and other therapeutic interventions. Examination of such instances leads us to the present clinical description and discussion of a special group of interacting functions of the analyst's work ego.

Work ego as a concept of the analyst-at-work refers to "the temporarily built-up person who [functions] under the circumstances and for the period of his work" (Fliess 1942, p. 225). It is not to be confused with any aspects of role taking. It is definable in terms of its functions; and of course it implies a personality that manifests the special traits, motivations, and talents that have already been abundantly discussed in the psychoanalytic literature (e.g. Greenson 1961; see chapter 1). Specialized training is intended to sharpen and enhance these qualities.

The work ego operates in a matrix of empathy—in Fliess's terms, "trial identification"; of curiosity about human nature; and of what has been called "diatrophic presence"—"the healing intention to maintain and support the patient" (Spitz 1956, Gitelson 1962). We shall demonstrate that an open communicating network of other functions enters into its operations, e.g. cognitive and affective informational feedback in the therapeutic alliance and a special

With Warren S. Poland, Kenneth A. Grigg, and William A. Granatir.

monitoring by the superego—ego-ideal systems. We shall also review certain actions and objectives of ''regression in the service of the ego'' (Kris 1950), as this is observed in the function of interpreting. The timing of interpretations is a resultant of multiple vectors in the work ego. Regression, for instance, functions as a signal in the context of specially adapted observing and experiencing. At such times it occurs in the service of a problem-solving, empathic understanding, in parallel with the patient's regressive experiences.

PRIMARY DATA AND PROCESS

The primary data from which the work ego operates are the analyst's and the patient's psychic processes. Freud wrote (1923, p. 239):

> Experience soon showed that the attitude which the analytic physician could most advantageously adopt was to surrender himself to his own unconscious mental activity in a state of *evenly suspended attention,* to avoid so far as possible reflection and the construction of conscious expectations, not to try to fix anything that he heard particularly in his memory, and by these means to catch the drift of the patient's unconscious with his own unconscious.

He was referring not to the content of the patient's free associations, nor to the content of the analyst's attention, but to the *drift*—the course or direction—of the parallel, matching, communicating processes *in the analyst.*

By *process* we refer to the ''dynamic change in the matter, energy and information of a system over time . . . [it] includes function—regular recurrent changes or reversible actions . . .'' (Peterfreund 1971, p. 141). *Content* is cross-sectional, historically static, and unyielding except to other content, while process changes and can be changed. The codependence of verb and noun partly expresses this distinction. The verb denotes action, process, and function, while the noun names the person, thing, or quality that acts or is acted upon. Content is verbally communicable but cannot be empathized. What may appear to be the direct empathy (''telepathy'') of content must be presumed to be an effect of introjection and primitive parallel regression, wherein the dyad's patterns and processes closely coincide. When this occurs the result is an uncanny experience that may be useful as a signal of the movement of processes within the patient.

Content may indeed be "information about," and as such it may be clarified, and connections and interpretations made. It is primarily processes, as these are organized into reality-oriented relatedness, defenses, resistances, conflicts and transferences, that are resonated to by the work ego, and through which the day-to-day psychoanalytic work is performed. Our concern here is with process as a primary source of data, including genetic data. We are not advocating the use of present, "here and now" experience in order to avoid or obscure genetically significant experience.

A standard content interpretation might be that the analyst has become a substitute for the patient's mother. In process terms one might say, "You are relating to me as if I were your mother," or "You want from me what you wanted from your mother." The emphasis then is on relatedness, action, wishing. The content interpretation could be a functional one, but only if it is tacitly understood to be an elliptic statement, referring indirectly to the processes that are entailed in the mother transference.

With a patient's dream, what is presented is manifest content; but the analyst works toward the clarification of dream thoughts and wishes. These are process and function.

Confronted with hostility in the patient, the analyst might interpret this as content, "You are angry," which would seldom be enough. Either patient or analyst would subsequently amplify this *what* of content to the *how* of process, e.g. as it relates to other factors of a hierarchy and pattern of conflicts, defenses, adaptations, impulses, and affects.

In the analyses of some patients, it may be long before the work ego can be occupied more with process than content. Middle game processes—those involving transference neurosis and therapeutic alliance—may be slow in developing or transient in character. Also, patients whose difficulties are predominantly in the oedipal, three-person mode are less prone to regress so intensively and globally as those whose pathology is mainly preoedipal and narcissistic. When the patient's regression affects the therapeutic alliance, this becomes taxing to the work ego, which must permit its own empathic, regressive processes. Eccentric counter-responses may then occur.

In fact, the work ego draws sustenance from an effective therapeutic alliance. In the relative or absolute absence of the alliance, the work ego can still function, but it is hampered. The affective-cognitive informational feedback from a functioning psychoanalytic dyad is necessary to optimal working conditions.

In the case of retarded or defective feedback, alternative nutriment and sustenance may be obtained from discussion with colleagues. Psychoanalytic supervision is based on this fact; it is a strong argument against the use of audiotapes and prepared written records and reports in supervision, lest this important process be hampered.

The following clinical material will illustrate these ideas.

Vignette I

A patient who had sought treatment some months after the death by suicide of her husband was speaking of experiences of disappointment at the hands of her husband and her father and of her frustrations vis-à-vis her analyst. An erotized transference had been developing. Despair and a half-submerged, angry grief were the tone of the session. The analyst found himself distracted by somnolence, sadness, and a sense of the impossibility of working with this woman: she was in a hopeless state; her loss had been frightening, dreadful, and irreversible; restitution was out of the question. The work had been progressing for no more than a few months. How could it now be terminated without further trauma to her? With these dimly perceived thoughts and feelings, he now became aware of his continuing silence. But then, as though automatically, he found himself saying thoughtfully aloud, "You have been disappointed by all the men who were important to you, and now you expect disappointment from me." To his momentary surprise this simple restatement of her sad reproachfulness was met by a change in the tone of her associations. The patient's mood, following the analyst's, lifted to one of collaboration in pursuing this theme in an objective way.

What had happened? We emphasize the analyst's verbal responses, an autonomous assertion of his work ego. He offered nothing new in the formulation, except perhaps in giving additional weight to the patient's expectation of disappointment from him. In the act of restating, his own mood lifted, and this change was followed by the patient's reorientation. Only later did he recognize with distinctness the determinants in his own life of the identification[1] with the patient. His own activity, as opposed to the passive resignation and defeat previously characterizing the dyad, served as a model for the patient in her therapeutic splitting and the reinforcement of her observing ego. This was, to be sure, a temporary effect: in subsequent hours she returned again and again to the passively aggressive, grief-laden manner. A potentially dangerous situation, though, had been averted and partly worked through. A transference resistance was interpreted in a preliminary way in a setting of therapeutic alliance; middle-game processes had begun (see chapter 1).

It would superficially appear that the analyst had identified with the patient's loss, grief, and disappointment. However, the regressive pull that he experienced from her on this and subsequent occasions was that he was to be the object of restitution for her losses. Her efforts were in the direction of continuing to experience disappointment, both to receive punishment and to keep alive the possibility of gratification from the new object in the person of the analyst. The analyst had partly identified with this object, thus responding in a complementary way (Racker 1957) to her process of defense — to a transference resistance that entailed gratification and frustration, pleasure and pain, simultaneously as subject and object, in the pattern she had experienced with parental figures. His further response was regressively to identify her content as his own, and this approach to fusion was manifested as somnolence. An instant later, he became aware of his efforts at mastery of guilt and anxiety, and finally of the definitive verbal activity of his work ego.

His verbal intervention had a salutary, defining effect upon his own analytic position. The conscious ruminations had been to repudiate responsibility for dealing with the patient's disappointment and despair — how to terminate his work with her. But his response to her indicated that his work ego, functioning in an autonomous,

---

1. For reasons of expediency we view the analyst's reactions as a continuum, from trial identification (empathy) at the one end through more regressed phenomena of counter-identification and overidentification. Differentiation is made on the basis of evaluation of the degree of ego discrimination and mastery. We deliberately avoid the term *countertransference* because of its multiple and at times ambiguous connotations.

diatrophic manner, was accepting the patient and the trials that her problems would present to both of them. Making no promises to offer more than understanding, he committed himself to analytic work. Therein he also claimed the patient for the analysis.

These actions of the work ego had been preceded by a rumination of concern for the patient's welfare, here reproduced approximately as, "How could [the analysis] now be terminated without further trauma to her?" *Primum non nocere* is a cautionary, admonishing principle with which all practitioners of the healing arts must be imbued. It is a superego injunction, reinforced by society. Closely related to the functioning of the work ego, it may have received something less than its due of psychoanalytic attention (but see Fliess 1942). In the extreme of its range of variations, it may become distorted, e.g. in the direction of scrupulosity or in the opposite direction of disregard of traditional standards. In the clinical instance under consideration, it operated benevolently (Schafer 1960).

The effects of superego and ego ideal upon the work ego were further manifested. The analyst described his experience to a study group within the same twenty-four hours, without prior rehearsal and with some puzzled concern. The description, a nearly accurate recall of the events as here described, was difficult, but he succeeded in conveying a sense of the affect-tone of the experience. The group's acceptance was reassuring.

A later attempt at describing the experience to a small group of candidates in an institute seminar did not meet with similar success: their response was passively accepting of the vignette as illustrative of a point under discussion. The analyst was left with the impression that while this was attributable in some measure to the student-teacher hierarchy, there was also the factor of a lessened transmission by himself of the immediacy and affective validity of the experience. It was like a piece of wit that requires a special setting to be effective, or a dream that has already been told and analyzed. He became aware that some internal working through of the material had resulted in a change in its value for communication.

In part, this had come about through the first group's tacit confirmation of his ideals and their actualization through his work with this patient. Also, during the analytic session, a residue of archaic superego had already been mastered, thus liberating effective work ego function. The analyst had then been free to reflect back to the patient without guilt or anxiety or sadness, something of her anachronistic, misguided functioning.

Vignette II

A thirty-one-year-old woman had four years of successful analysis before she was married. She sought a second analysis when troubled by intense anger at her husband who, she felt, abandoned her by withdrawal to work after the birth of their son. The hour reported occurred in the middle of the third year of the second analysis.

For the entire session the patient proclaimed in loud, forceful, angry terms her "Declaration of Independence." She was tired of always having her husband's quirks understood and all her own involvements scrutinized. In some ways the words were manifestly reasonable because she was a woman who had hyperanalyzed everything she touched. However, there was such a forceful head of steam that the analyst felt angry, then overwhelmed, then hopelessly futile. He felt exhausted, as if without the energy to withstand the patient's forcefulness or even to follow with much conscious attention her long harangue. Most of the hour he withdrew into a half sleepy reverie, and for the entire hour he was silent. This was especially striking as this was a patient with whom such hour-long silence had been rare. The analyst felt as if he had neither the heart nor the energy for such battle: he thought he would deal with the issue another day when he felt more up to it.

As the patient was leaving, she turned toward a bowl of roses and in an imperious tone proclaimed that they were pretty flowers. To the analyst's surprise, he responded softly, "They're called 'Peace.'" He was surprised he had said anything at all and more surprised that his voice was without sarcasm or anger, but rather sounded calm, unchallenging, and accepting. The patient burst into laughter; she left smiling.

The subsequent session with the patient demonstrated the usefulness of the intervention in interpreting her sadomasochistic rage and its transferential nature. Further repressed material then became available.

Here, as in the first vignette, the work ego was reintegrated by processes leading to a partial interpretation that in turn led to a reestablishment of the therapeutic alliance on a higher level of ego integration. The intervention arose out of an affective-cognitive context of futility and anger in the analyst, empathically reflecting the patient's own feeling tone. This in turn was a defensive screen against her recognition of her positive feelings. The analyst's experience occurred in a prolonged trial identification that could not be interrupted or curtailed until the patient was available, through her own observing functions, to permit the reestablishment of the therapeutic alliance.

The patient's behavior in the face of the imminent separation at the end of the hour elicited the analyst's diatrophic response. His identification with her manifest defenses could then appropriately give way to what had now been preconsciously worked through. The patient's sadomasochistic rage was a narcissistic transference resistance that had induced in the analyst parallel defensive processes of futility, anger, and somnolence. The parallelism of processes continued until the analyst responded to the patient's seeking of positive relatedness; this she attempted through something she sensed to be close to him, his flowers. His intervention—in Balint's sense of "recognizing" (1968)—was as though he held a mirror to the patient, saying in effect, "Peace. There are better, more pleasant, more effective ways of dealing with frustrations. Join me."

This was not a complete interpretation. Without the ultimate working through to a genetic insight, this would not lead to structural change. Yet this instance represented a vital stage in the development of such insight.

The initial thinking through and reporting of this incident to the study group was apologetic in nature. The analyst felt threatened by guilt and shame, particularly over the apathy and futility he had experienced. Much of that hour had involved a prolonged trial identification with the patient, including the aspect of futility, the affect of sadness, the superego tension of reproachfulness to the self at failure to measure up to the "challenge." The analyst had to work through preconscious material induced by the patient before he was able to attain the autonomy from conflict that permitted an intervention. In thus permitting this resonance *without defending against trial identification,* the analyst was then able to define the issues of the transferential repetition of relational processes. The intervention came with a combination of spontaneity and softness that revealed that mutative work was being done in the service of the therapeutic alliance.

Vignette III

A twenty-seven-year-old woman had sought analysis four years previously because of frequent periods of depression. She had described her parents, both professionals, as ungiving, nonfeeling people who were frequently away from home during her childhood. The father spent thirty minutes on the toilet every morning—his own prescription for preventing hemorrhoids. This ritual was in lieu of breakfast, and consequently the patient seldom had a meal with her father since he was also almost invariably late for dinner at night.

Great difficulty in associating freely had always been present in the analysis, particularly in regard to feelings, both negative and positive, toward the analyst. Prior to the exchange to be recounted the patient had been able to reveal her hostile fantasy of paying her bill in bags of pennies—70,000 of them. On this day the analyst was three minutes late in beginning the hour. The patient had previously complained when a session ran over time because of her difficulty in getting to her own next appointment. On lying down she testily inquired, "Well, what do we do about the *five* minutes?" The analyst responded with what he thought was a fairly neutral, "What would *you like* to do about them?"

"What are the possibilities?"

"We could continue at the end of this hour. We could begin early or run late at the end of an hour next week. Or (with a smile in his voice) I could refund you—uh—350 pennies."

Both laughed, and the analysand recalled having gone home to visit her mother and sister the previous weekend—the first holiday since the death of her father. While going through old papers and photographs, the mother found a picture of the patient sitting on a pottie and being held by her grandmother.

"Mother asked if I knew why my grandmother was holding me. When she said I was too young to sit on it by myself, my sister and I almost fell off our seats! Then mother said, 'Well, you know how your *father* was—always having BMs on schedule.'"

"And now you can't stand being five minutes late," the analyst spontaneously responded. The patient burst into laughter, and the heavy, uncooperative mood of the hour seemed to be transformed into one of alliance.

The analyst was late, thereby placing pressures on the patient that she could not realistically meet. Because of previous experience with his patient, he had partially identified with a rebellious reaction to a superego imago representing her father. She joined the analyst in concentrating on the content of the reality situation, during which time the analyst, though consciously pleased that she had been able to express her anger fairly directly, felt at the same time challenged by her implicit accusation of negligence and her prior complaints of his incompetence.

The analyst now, in an attempt to react to the external reality, suddenly found himself responding with humor (Poland 1971), which arose from the operation of his work ego. The emphases on the *content* of what was transpiring shifted to a clarification of the *processes* involved. The analyst had been able to bring his own conflictual areas into the light of his observing ego, thereby allowing him to focus on the patient's need for him to respond like her father. The work ego's regression and reintegration served to reestablish the alliance on a new level of ego mastery.

In this trial identification, there had been a resonating of processes. Without such parallel and partial regression, it is not possible to recognize the patient's operative processes. Stated differently, the two observing egos regress—the work ego for the purpose of empathy, the patient's observing ego for the purpose of transference gratification. The work ego then responds both to the threat of its own dissolution and the threat to the therapeutic alliance as a signal; it returns to an observing, information-processing function. This reintegration, a response to the anxiety of regression, culminates in a verbal intervention directed to the psychic reality of the patient.

Vignette IV

The patient, a twenty-six-year-old married man in the second year of analysis, was working through the recall of a period in his life at the age of four or five, when his father had deserted the family. It was a particularly difficult hour among a series of difficult ones, in which he was in a state of great tension and anger. In this session he was alternately crying and berating the analyst in a very hostile way, thrashing about on the couch and cursing the analyst. The analyst felt very tired, but at some point noticed a strange physical sensation in his arms, related to tenderness, but not quite a tender feeling. He said to the patient, "You are wanting me to take you in my arms." The patient relaxed on the couch and said, "Yes." After a moment of silence he began to talk about his affection for his father and his yearning for an affectionate relationship with an older man.

In this example the patient was reacting as if the analyst were his disappointing parent. The hostility served two functions: to protect himself from the projected hostility anticipated from the analyst as well as from his own anxiety about his repudiated and repressed longings. The analyst was able to perceive and accept both projections, although the situation was wearing on him. Identifying with the patient, he regressed in a state of fatigue. He then perceived the positive side of the ambivalent situation in his empathic experience of the physical sensation of tenderness.

The analyst had withheld the interpretation of the homosexual conflict and ambivalence in the patient's feelings about his father because of concern about the patient's readiness to receive such an interpretation. The complete reconstructive interpretation of this side of the patient's attitude to his father and his analyst was only begun with this piece of confrontation.

The physical sensation experienced by the analyst was an empathic clue that affective experience was now available to complement prior cognitive knowledge of the dynamics. The work ego was operating autonomously, following the principle of multiple function (Waelder 1936).

THE FUNCTIONS OF THE WORK EGO

The interventions in these clinical vignettes clearly were not full interpretations. They were partial statements directed toward working through and the development of complete interpretations. They reflected the discipline of the analysts' work egos, thus differentiating them from "wild psychoanalysis," where interventions are in the service of the analyst's unresolved conflicts or narcissism.

It will be useful to review the functions of the work ego as they have been depicted in the clinical vignettes.

1. An initial covenant or agreement leads to the therapeutic alliance, where the varied and many aspects of the patient's conflicts are examined in the special psychoanalytic context.

2. The situation facilitates or induces processes of transference regression. The analysand now employs less recounting of content in the genetic and anamnestic modes and turns more to remembering through reliving, repeating, and recreating. Working through is, of course, an important aspect of this complicated set of processes.

3. The analyst, through his work ego, functions in the context of "diatrophic presence" (Spitz 1956, Gitelson 1962). Through the inevitable and necessary, though partial and controlled, regressive immersion in the needs and other processes of the patient, he will experience a regressive pull induced by the patient's own regressive processes. The preconditions for this parallel experience lie in the work ego's function of trial identification, or empathy; this in turn is contingent upon a regression in the service of the work ego. Success-ful nurturing or diatrophic functioning requires some degree of regressive experiencing of the regressed other as oneself and oneself as the other (see chapter 1). Introjective-projective processes operate at this level, and deviant counter-responses may occur.

4. The work ego, through its self-observing function, responds to a signal of regression and passivity with a resurgence of its function of scanning and collating primary data. In the course of this reinte-gration, observations and judgments are made, and ultimately these may be consciously and cognitively formulated into an interpre-tation. In some instances (e.g. vignettes I and II) the formulation may have taken place outside of awareness. In other instances a postponement of intervention may be judged necessary in order to accumulate and organize further data (see discussion, vignette IV). The timing of an interpretation is an acquired art that involves the synthesis of empathic and cognitive processes. Partial and sponta-neous interventions of the kind described are then further elaborated in the course of subsequent working through. The psychoanalytic process, like the creative process, always operates against resistance; psychic pain is an inevitable part of both activities (see Eissler 1951). The experienced analyst or analysand knows, also, that these pro-cesses work in their own time and pace; patience and tolerance must be extended to preconscious working through toward insight.

5. The work ego draws sustenance from the therapeutic alliance and from the analyst's superego–ego-ideal systems, as these have become modified through psychoanalytic working through and special training. At this level additional pathological processes may be incurred. The systems may be strengthened or weakened with resultant distorting and degrading of the psychoanalytic situation and its purposes.

6. The work ego's interpretation serves to reestablish the therapeutic alliance and to initiate or reinforce the recognition and working through of transference resistance. The full process by which an interpretation is arrived at also reintegrates the work ego itself, in both its experiencing and observing functions. Optimally the processes and functions in both members of the dyad complement and augment each other for the purposes of the analysis. The usual functioning of empathy and other introjective-projective functions requires that there be a parallelism of processes. The work ego must continually evaluate and clarify processes that signal a primitive mingling of the patient's content with the analyst's own. This leads to an eccentric counter-response, if not recognized. These functions of the work ego are often silent. We become aware of them only after the fact (cp. Freud 1915).

For the analyst to communicate these subjective and often highly personal reactions to his fellows in a systematic, meaningful way requires a stable, sublimated exhibitionism in a self-system that is soundly integrated or which at least has the quality of a firm and unbreakable resolve, perhaps to the point of oppositionalism. It also requires a real or imagined interlocutor who, in terms of sympathetic and empathic listening, is to the analyst *in some ways* as the analyst is to his patient. We are referring to the supplementary assistance to the work ego through the superego–ego-ideal systems. This may be made available through consultation with colleagues. We include cognitive as well as emotional processes.

We hope to have made it clear that it is not solely the analyst's personal and subjective responses in the usual sense that are responsible for the exigencies of clinical psychoanalysis. Rather, many of the thorny problems of psychoanalytic practice are inherent in the processing of primary data by a specialized and specifically trained group of functions. While it is true that the problems and solutions of the work ego are often obscured by eccentric responses, one should not overlook the additional obscuring effect of the intangible quality of the material, of the primary data with which one works. Bion comments (1970, p. 70):

> Anyone who has made careful notes of what he considers to be the facts of a session must be familiar with the experience in which such notes will, on occasion, seem to be drained of all reality: they might be notes of dreams made to ensure that he will not forget them on awaking. To me it suggests that the experience of the session relates to material akin to the dream . . . the dream and the psychoanalyst's working material both share dreamlike quality.

DISCUSSION

The subsequent analyses of the patients described in the foregoing examples were in varying degrees favorable and progressively unfolding. Nevertheless, we anticipate criticism of the analysts' interventions. The transference resistances that evoked or induced these interventions, it may be said, could more usefully and less dangerously have been interpreted in the mode of the burnished mirror (Freud 1912) with no personal involvement, but with classic commitment to and anxiety-free concern for the welfare, security, and ultimate well-being of the patient. The diatrophic function of the analyst, that is, would have been cleanly operative.

While that situation represents a model to be approximated, human facts make it neither possible nor necessary. Indeed, the work ego functions more often as described here than is generally recognized or acknowledged. To be sure, we have centered upon an extreme of the range of variations within which the work ego processes its data, and this has enabled us to discern or to deduce more clearly what otherwise happens in a silent but similar way. The meaningful distinction lies in whether the work ego masters its regressive pull. We are referring to a quantitative factor of degree of regression, one that is more prominent in work with those patients who are designated as borderline, narcissistic or character disorders.

Usually the work ego's regressive forays in the service of its empathic functions are momentary, partial, and quickly mastered.

Often, however, a more lasting regression and trial identification—or a series of them—will occur. They represent necessary delays in a dyadic problem solving that is a continuing and integral part of the psychoanalytic process (cf. discussion, vignette II). The work ego in its empathic functions must experience the "drift of the patient's unconscious." The work ego as a problem-solving system may require time in which to perform these functions, as well as the recognition and use of time as one of the dimensions of its primary data. Were it otherwise, we should be viewing the analyst as capable of instant omniscience. The ideal or model situation is one in which the work ego is sufficiently integrated to master its trial regression and to respond to the matching or paralleling of processes as affect-signal and not for surrender to affective discharge. The parallelism of processes in the two participants is a *sine qua non* in the steplike, hierarchic development of the analysis.

Before an analyst can interpret, he must be able to tolerate a trial regression in the service of the ego (Kris 1950), or of a process (Khan 1969), or of the other (see chapter 1). This regression and its concomitant trial identification facilitate the review of primary data in the service of the patient's needs within the psychoanalytic situation. The work ego is consequently subject to the pull of the patient's own regression. Here the monitoring functions of the superego–ego-ideal systems, as these have been modified by motivations toward and training in psychoanalysis, are the built-in safeguards for a methodology that is flexibly devised to assist the development of a curative process.

The work ego, that is to say, encompasses functions that define and delimit the actual operation of analyst *qua* analyst, under the aegis of superego and ego ideal. Such experiences as we have described are utilizable as affective and cognitive signals essential to an operational comprehension of the patient's condition. They cannot be artificially devised, nor should they be; they are not artifacts with pernicious effects. Rather, this way of experiencing primary data represents a necessary and spontaneous course between the Scylla and Charybdis of affective intuition and cognitive mastery (Fenichel 1941).

There are certain common denominators of the work ego's actions cited in each of the clinical examples: (1) They represented deviations from the pattern of the immediately preceding sessions. (2) The resolution occurred unexpectedly, with surprise in the analyst. (3) The analyst's verbal intervention was preceded by a varying period within the session of a sense of futility, an affect of sadness, and reproachfulness toward the self for failure to live up to the challenge of the patient's condition; a sense of somnolent depletion of energy was noted. (4) With the intervention there ensued a shift of affective tension toward greater alertness and a return to the usual analytic stance; an affect-signal had been appropriately responded to. (5) There followed in subsequent sessions, if not within the same session, a more usual rate and type of movement and an improved therapeutic alliance. (6) The analyst's return to the usual functions of a work ego whose final common pathway is interpretation, presented to the patient a useful and acceptable model for identification that strengthened the observing ego and permitted the ongoing working through of a transference resistance. (7) The patient's return to the usual work was in sharp contrast to the previously dominant theme of a hostile transference resistance. (8) The analyst's state of mind could be characterized as one of regression in the service of the work ego, in the presence of an ambiguous and obscure problem of some intensity.

Scanning the temporal sequence and progression of these items, one should not be surprised that they tend to follow the well-known pattern of creative problem solving: i.e. laborious data collecting and collating; a conscious search in vain for the solution; a period of retreat from the work, sometimes into sleep and dreaming; and the emergence of the solution, to be followed by renewed conflicts and solutions.

SUMMARY

(1) The primary data of the work ego are the processes of the analyst as they parallel those of the patient. (2) The work ego operates relatively autonomously. (3) The work ego exercises diatrophic functions. (4) The work ego within the therapeutic alliance regresses with and observes the patient and itself, thus enabling the paralleling of processes. (5) The work ego responds to its own regression as a signal. The degree of tolerable regression varies; it is monitored and controlled by the diatrophic functions and in turn by aspects of the superego–ego-ideal systems. Mastered regression is

in the service of the work ego's function of empathy. (6) The work ego is motivated and trained to seek knowledge of the other person by means of empathic regression in the service of the other. The analyst through his work ego has learned to experience his own internal and internalized processes as a way of learning about the other. (7) The verbal intervention of the analyst represents a final common pathway of the work ego in its multiple functions of scanning and collating the primary data, evaluating and mastering its own regression in the service of empathy, and reintegrating itself through those functions that have come to be called the therapeutic alliance. (8) We have attempted to define a unitary model of the intrapsychic and interpersonal processes involved in certain functions of the work ego.

POSTSCRIPT 1979

That the subject is a difficult one should be clear. The phenomena that are being explored are more readily apparent when the problems are "noisy"—when resistance and especially countertransference and other eccentric reactions of the analyst are involved. (See Postscript, chapter 10, for a discussion of these terms and their distinctions.) Usually the work ego operates silently, and its inner functions are barely, if at all, perceptible, except through their results and consequences. At best, one can examine these matters only after the event; when the work ego has operated effectively, one has meager data to work with. When the sequence of events has permitted discerning the usually preconscious or unconscious workings, they are not infrequently unsatisfactory examples of the highest form of the art. Nevertheless, we can learn from such occurrences, and moreover, a psychoanalysis does not founder on the basis of isolated instances of less than perfect management.

Clinical vignettes, also, are useful only in a limited way: they are illustrative but they cannot be expected to furnish complete documentation. Inevitably the brevity that recommends them will raise questions that cannot be answered except with impractically long and full case presentations.

In a word, the chapter illustrates, among other matters, the fact that it is difficult to clarify these important psychoanalytic issues. However, it cannot have escaped notice that we anticipated criticism, that this must arise out of the nature of the subject and sources of data, that we thought the venture worthwhile, and concluded that the benefits outweighed the risks.

Kanzer (1975) and Langs (1976) have pointed out certain methodological weaknesses along the lines that I have discussed above. I believe that our basic clinical impressions of the mode of operation of the work ego are valid. It is, after all, accepted methodology in all of medicine to deduce and infer the natural or ordinary state of affairs from examination of the extreme ranges, to establish the rule by testing the exceptions.

REFERENCES

Balint, M. (1968). *The Basic Fault*. London: Tavistock.

Bion, W. (1970). *Attention and Interpretation*. New York: Basic Books.

Eissler, K. (1951). An unknown autobiographical letter by Freud and a short comment. *International Journal of Psycho-Analysis* 32: 319–324.

Fenichel, O. (1941). *Problems of Psychoanalytic Technique*. Albany: Psychoanalytic Quarterly.

Fliess, R. (1942). The metapsychology of the analyst. *Psychoanalytic Quarterly* 11: 211–227.

Freud, S. (1912). Recommendations to physicians practising psychoanalysis, *Standard Edition* 12: 109–120.

_____(1915). The unconscious. *Standard Edition* 14: 159–215.

_____(1923). Two encyclopaedia articles. (A) Psycho-analysis. *Standard Edition* 18: 235–254.

Gitelson, M. (1962). The curative factors in psychoanalysis. *International Journal of Psycho-Analysis* 43: 194–205.

Greenson, R. (1961). Panel report: The selection of candidates for psychoanalytic training. *Journal of the American Psychoanalytic Association* 9: 135–145.

Kanzer, M. (1975). The therapeutic and working alliances. *International Journal of Psychoanalytic Psychotherapy* 4: 48–68.

Khan, M. (1969). Preface to *The Hands of the Living God*. M. Milner. New York: International Universities Press.

Kris, E. (1950). On preconscious mental processes. *Psychoanalytic Quarterly* 19: 540–560.

Langs, R. (1976). *The Therapeutic Interaction.* 2 vols. New York: Jason Aronson.

Peterfreund, E. (1971). *Information, Systems, and Psychoanalysis.* New York: International Universities Press.

Poland, W. S. (1971). The place of humor in psychotherapy. *American Journal of Psychiatry* 128: 635–637.

Racker, H. (1957). The meanings and uses of countertransference. *Psychoanalytic Quarterly* 26: 303–357.

Schafer, R. (1960). The loving and beloved superego in Freud's structural theory. *Psychoanalytic Study of the Child* 15.

Spitz, R. A. (1956). Countertransference. *Journal of the American Psychoanalytic Association* 4: 256–265.

Waelder, R. (1936). The principle of multiple function. *Psychoanalytic Quarterly* 5: 45–62.

Chapter 3

Empathic Perception
and Its Adequate Verbal Equivalent

> . . . the rose was to be found in its own eternity
> and not in his words . . . we may mention or
> allude to a thing, but not express it; and . . . the
> tall, proud volumes casting a golden shadow in a
> corner were not . . . a mirror of the world, but
> rather one thing more added to the world.
>
> —*Jorge Luis Borges*

THE DATA OF INTROSPECTION
AND EMPATHY

The nature of psychoanalytic data is unique among the sciences. Indeed, it has been categorically stated that the facts of consciousness cannot be used in scientific method (Ashby 1954) and that there can exist no science of the unconscious mind (Planck 1949). That these prestigious scientists are mistaken is a painful example of the fact that our data are readily misunderstood or misperceived by the untrained observer or commentator, no matter how able a scientist he is (cf. also Lashley's comments in Colby and Lashley 1957). Recognition and knowledge of the observational data of psychoanalysis are prerequisite to the subsequent understanding of psychoanalytic theory—a banal truth, but only if one is already familiar with and accepts these data. How to communicate them, or whether they can be communicated, warrants more attention than it has so far received within psychoanalysis itself.

In this chapter I shall discuss the problems inherent in the communication of the observed data of psychoanalysis. It will be necessary to comment also on both the nature and the manner of perception of those data. The transmission of content in the traditional psychiatric usage of that term and in the sense of verbatim or condensed transcription of what has been said usually offers little problem. The inherent difficulties are mainly those of transmitting the phenomena of ambiguous, often obscure, regressive processes, as they occur within the psychoanalytic situation. Unfortunately many clinical reports have the ambiguity of sounding as though an intellectual, nonregressed situation is being described, even when this has not been the case. Some of this difficulty is to be found in the usually overlooked problems of language and in the confusions of reality and fantasy. This is expressed in the epigraph from Borges and in a statement made by Otto Fenichel (1941): "I was once reproached with the use of the words, 'something like,' . . . as indicating that I do not take unconscious fantasies seriously. I deny this. Its use means that the unconscious fantasies are *vague,* and therefore can only be reproduced in words inexactly, always with the addition of 'something like.'"

Such data concern not only the patient's regressive processes but also the parallel, limited, and partial *signal* processes of regression as these are noted through the operations of the analyst's work ego (Kris 1952, also see chapters 1 and 2). Early mental organization as the nodal point of this regression need not concern us as limiting the applicability of the psychoanalytic technical instrument, so long as the patient is functioning within a therapeutic alliance. That is, I shall be trying to elucidate the communication to a third person of clinical processes that are open to introspection and empathy (Kohut 1959, Waelder 1962, Loewenstein 1965, p. 55). This involves an analyst working with a patient whose ego is sufficiently intact that he can at least some of the time be self-observing and self-reporting.

ADEQUATE VERBAL
EQUIVALENTS FOR EXPERIENCE

In his classic monograph *Remembering,* Bartlett (1932) reported experiments in which subjects were asked to read selected folk tales and then to reproduce this material at successive intervals of time. It was striking that the picturesque stories thereby lost their special style and content. They were conventionalized, made commonplace and flat, and became devoid of any force and beauty. At best, they might show something of the personal style of the narrator-subject. Errors of fact were frequent, though the general theme of the original story was preserved.

It is largely in this sense of themes, patterns, and processes that the findings of one analyst can be duplicated in another analysis. This suffices within the discipline. Audiotapes and videotapes may additionally be useful in directly transmitting the raw data, but this does not resolve the problem of reporting the experience itself. The affective quality even of a patient's silence may in fact somehow be partially registered and communicated through the audiotape, but, to borrow a phrase from Aldous Huxley, what is the "adequate verbal equivalent" for this experience? Is there no other way to transmit it?

The psychoanalyst's skills are primarily developed in oral communication and its nonverbal concomitants. Auditory and introspective channels are emphasized, and other sensory modalities are minimized or virtually eliminated. However, imagery, memory, fantasy and imagination exist largely in visual terms. Consequently, the subjective recording and the objective reporting of intrapsychic and interpersonal events of the psychoanalytic situation are handicapped by the necessity of operating in modalities that are relatively unnatural and unfamiliar. Even for the experienced analyst, for whom these may have become familiar and well-trodden ways, to find an "adequate verbal equivalent for experience" is not easy.

It is even more arduous and difficult when the organizational complexity of "writing it down" is superimposed. If we take a clue from the admonitory connotation of that phrase, to "write it down" often has the force of a superego injunction. This may particularly be so in writing for the critical scrutiny and information of other scientific workers.

The confidentiality of what is heard and reported by the analyst need not always be a problem, for the external circumstances of the patient can often be disguised. But what may be called, clumsily, the eavesdropping usage of auditory perceptions is an aspect of curiosity that is homologous to the voyeuristic drive derivatives. In its sublimated form this is an important element of the analyst's work ego. The exceptional position of the auditory sphere in the formation of the superego (Isakower 1939)—the fact that conscience, self-observation and reality-sense are organized around early auditory perception—contributes a special concern to matters of gossip, confidences, and communication on the part of the analyst. Although the strictures of our society regarding the inviolable rights of human privacy seem nowadays to be changing in the direction of the primacy of the group over the individual, there nevertheless remains the sense of something that must be kept secret and private. This finds a responsive chord in the analyst. To reveal the secrets overheard in his consulting room, although to trusted colleagues and with all efforts to preserve the anonymity of the patient, often requires the overcoming of irrational scruples of conscience. This is the more so when, additionally, the analyst's own private responsiveness is part of the revelation.

Traditionally, analysts renounced the didactic use of the witnessed interview—the one-way screen, the audiotape or the open demonstration in front of a class. Such renunciation is less frequent now, yet I question whether any analyst employs these methods without some private discomfort.

SOME PROBLEMS REPORTING

The elusiveness of remembering and reporting both dreams and analytic sessions has frequently been compared (Lewin 1955, Stein 1965, Bion 1970). In reporting such experiential data—in seeking "adequate verbal equivalents"—analytic writers often resort to the general comprehension within the profession of the clinical and metapsychological vocabulary and syntax that is our *lingua franca* and model of human nature. This technical, esoteric language expresses a theory that becomes a prism through which subsequent experience is refracted. The language shapes our realities, even while our external world shapes our language. For the most part, this language does no violence to the clinical facts; at least not for one who has himself been in contact with these facts through psychoanalytic introspection and empathy.

The hazard is that the distinctions may be lost between the data of observation and the subsequent, inferential steps of discernment of clinical connections and of conceptualization (Waelder 1962,

Loewenstein 1965). The elusiveness of the data often leads to an emphasis on cognitive, intellectual elements and aspects, and there results a blurred distinction between content and concept (Zetzel 1956). This is automatically or preconsciously corrected by analysts of experience, in accordance with their own recognition and recall. For the colleague who is not psychoanalytically oriented and for the relatively inexperienced psychoanalytic candidate—and I omit here the sophisticated layman, whose clinical ignorance presents an additional set of problems (Waelder 1962)—there emerges a skewed and clouded version of the basic data.

The successful transmission of clinical data of the middle phases of analysis also depends greatly on the reader's or the auditor's having had the experience of something similar himself. For oral more than for written transmission of data, a special factor becomes prominent. This is the capacity and willingness for empathy, in Fliess's sense of trial identification (1942), but now with the reporter rather than the patient.[1] Minimal cues take their significance from the fact of the auditor's familiarity or extensive verbal contact with the speaker. Members of the same study group, for instance, will automatically develop a system of verbal shortcuts for communicating and registering the transactions of a segment of clinical psychoanalysis. An emotional milieu of trust, confidence, and mutual support is of the utmost importance. Not unlike the psychoanalytic situation, this milieu is conducive to partial identifications.

A speaker at a scientific session of a psychoanalytic society will be responded to differently by the audience when he reads his prepared text and when he answers questions from his discussants. Even so talented a writer as Freud rarely read from a prepared manuscript but presented his ideas and findings extemporaneously. It is as though the written word were an embalmed affect as compared with the living, spontaneous affect of the spoken word. The latter seems to permit and foster a greater degree of intimate sense of knowing the data.

Finally, and not least, the psychoanalytic dyad itself develops its own allusive language, based on many partial or trial identificatory sharings, which are difficult to transmit to a third person. Each of

---

1. Strictly speaking, these partial or trial identifications are actually introjections. They are temporally limited and do not lead to structural changes. Their precursors are patterns that are rooted in early childhood.

these elements of the "experience of something similar," leading to the intimacy or inwardness of partial identifications, contributes to the finding of "an adequate verbal equivalent for experience"; more of this later. The difficulties will be greater in the instance of the writer and his reader, and not only because of the lessened intimacy. We must now *presume* a degree of congruence of the reader's and writer's personal style of conducting analysis, their theoretical persuasions, their selection of patients, and the extent of their clinical experience. We must also note their unfamiliarity with each other, their emotional distance, and the probable competition with or mistrust and fear of the outsider or stranger.

TRANSITIONALISM AND EMPATHY

The results of Bartlett's experiments could have been predicted by psychoanalytic supervisors or the readers of clinical reports. As supervisors know, clear reporting is rare; the most vivid clinical reporting does not necessarily come from the most gifted of analysts-in-training, nor from the culturally best educated. Often the gifted candidate is the one who struggles with the clouded recognition that the material he is bringing for supervision fails to reproduce the subtle, fleeting nuances of his dyadic experience with the patient. It is possible through diligent application to improve one's skills, but an "adequate verbal equivalent for experience" is attained by only a few. As though to compensate for this deficiency, and demonstrating in exaggerated form the inevitable and indispensable element of trial identification in the psychoanalytic process, the supervisee may unwittingly enact the less accessible aspects of the patient's role — those aspects that are anxiety provoking and not otherwise assimilable — in words, verbal tone and manner vis-à-vis the supervisor (cf. Searles 1955). When this is called to his attention, the supervisee may respond in a nonplussed or sheepish way, temporarily off balance because of confusion of self boundaries and superego tensions of guilt or shame. Remarkably, supervisors can nevertheless usually detect and verbalize the essential processes that have eluded the student.

That they can do so, and that a participant listener can usually correctly discriminate between what is reported and what is the reporter himself, involves complicated and rapid exercises in semantics and in the perception of one's own self boundaries, as well as those of the other two persons. It is in this series of covert and obscure gradients of distinction between the self and other selves that the clear statement of the adequate verbal equivalent for the experiencing of the other person's processes is to be sought.

The image of temporarily and partially blurred boundaries of self is one that is often evoked in discussing states of regression. Shifting patterns of self are highly significant to psychoanalysis, resulting in part from patternings of introjection and projection that are basic modes of transaction within the psychoanalytic dyad. Through them the patient is enabled to reduce his subjection to his transferential past. They include, for example, the ego-splitting and partial identifications that form the therapeutic alliance (Sterba 1934, Bibring 1937, Zetzel 1956, 1958). To be sure, the analyst's interpretations are special and basic, helping to define psychoanalysis as a rational psychotherapy. However, the effectiveness of interpretations depends on more than the soft voice of the intellect. On the analyst's side of the dyad, these patternings are conditional upon a partial and temporary regression in the service — variously considered — of patient, of psychoanalytic process, of psychoanalytic work ego (see chapters 1 and 2). In turn, this permits the operation of a discriminating introspection and empathy (Kohut 1959). The analyst, operating through a conflict-free work ego, has learned to experience his own internal and internalized cognitive and affective processes as a way of knowing his patient (see chapter 2). There is an awareness of the other and of oneself as momentarily and transitionally similar.

The introjective–projective transactions are frequently preconscious and fleeting, so their dominant functions and effects may be overlooked. The analysis can still progress satisfactorily, and the basic data can be inferred. Inference, though, is a pallid substitute for the immediacy of empathic, transactional experiencing, and it is a poor basis for the translation of these processes into a language that is congruent, apposite, and therefore informative to a third person.

I am trying here to clarify an adult phenomenon of passage between illusion and reality, of an "intermediate area of *experiencing*," of "transitionalism" as Winnicott (1953) has expounded it with reference to infancy. In the infant's progress toward functioning within the reality principle, the separation-individuation from the mother involves several factors. I need mention here only the beginnings of mental activity and the "growing sense of process," the latter entailing "remembering, reliving, fantasying, dreaming; the integrating of past, present, and future" (Winnicott 1953). These are analogous and cognate to the experiences of the analysand. In the regressive aspects of the middle phases of psychoanalysis, transitional objects and phenomena appear. Illusion, disillusionment, and "weaning" are experienced. Concerning these often shared experiences, it is true that to name them is sometimes to lose them. Phenomenologically some experiences are sharply defined, and some are "seen" only with peripheral vision. The inherent problems of communicating essential processes of a psychoanalysis are to be found in the adult counterparts of these transitional phenomena — i.e. in the unfinished, residual psychic work of infancy and childhood. We are indebted to Winnicott and others for reminding us that "this intermediate area of experiencing" is retained in imaginative living and in creative scientific and artistic work.

In this sense, language that is otherwise communicative may itself be used as a transitional phenomenon of varying degree, ranging from clearly denotative to vaguely allusive. When allusive, words and sentence arrangement may be important primarily as a kind of indispensable, parallel accompaniment to the meaning that is being negotiated, an *obbligato* that is not to be omitted. Lewin (1955) and others (Eissler 1951, Balint 1968), in addition to Winnicott, have touched on these facts and circumstances. In describing the analyst as "soother," Lewin likened this "deep effect" to the musical, citing Eissler's comment about the treatment of schizophrenic patients: at one stage the intellectual content of what the analyst says is far less important than his voice and manner. Balint described something similar in his discussion of therapeutic regression, basic fault, and "the unobtrusive analyst."

The less accessible aspects of the patient are often transitional processes of inner and outer reality, related to themes of separation-individuation and to gradients of distinction between self and other selves. Even so relatively advanced a set of developments as oedipal conflicts must contain these earlier processes. Because the referents are mainly preverbal, it is arduous to translate them into language of secondary process, and perhaps it is not always entirely possible. I venture the suggestion that this may be a problem to be solved with the Delphic ambiguity of allusion. It is worth noting that much of the truth, beauty, and clarity of Freud's writing lies in the evocative imagery of his allusions, similes, and metaphors.

ENACTED EQUIVALENTS OF EXPERIENCE

Enactment is a special mode of communicating these processes. I am not recommending its practice; in any event few can successfully do it on a voluntary and conscious level. Nevertheless it can be extraordinarily effective in transmitting meaning. For instance, a supervisee has identified with his frustrating interlocutor, the patient, and has then induced in the supervisor what has been induced by the patient. With each partial identification, or introjection, with each bit of empathic regression, there has been a partial loss of the subjective sense of self, of the gradients of distinction between self and other, together with a fleeting but as yet inarticulate perception of what is pertinent to the moment of psychic action. The presence simultaneously or eventually of a critically reflecting, observing ego is essential in order to grasp and transmit the meaning. Only then can verbal facility be mobilized by analyst and patient. It is now that, occasionally, appropriate written words may be found to describe what has happened (see chapter 2).

Vexing as this is for its less tangible qualities, enactment in the service of communication is often contributory to successful case presentation and clinical teaching. Its prehistory is as primitive as the origins of emotional expression and dramatic action. One may think of Freud's formulation of "acting out" (1914) as a substitute for remembering and talking out; yet enactment may express the utmost refinement and social tact. In this sense, enactment includes vocal tones, gestures and postural tensions, and the entire range and repertoire of drive, affect, defense, conflict, autonomous function, and scenario of transference. Beyond the content of the free associations, it is the patient's enactment within the framework of transference that transmits to the analyst the data that are necessary to the functioning of his work ego. Verbalizations for these phenomena are achieved laboriously and often outside of awareness, drawing upon the synthetic functions of the ego. For both analyst and analysand, the roots are preverbal and nonverbal and stem from infancy and childhood (cf., e.g., Fernandez 1973, Condon and Sander 1974).

Enactment makes manifest what has been hidden, and as such it is the matrix of communication and of the literary, dramatic, and plastic arts. The psychology of the actor or writer and his audience, of the patient and his analyst, and of the supervisee and his supervisor possess elements in common. Each of these is dyadic in a respectively dramatic alliance, therapeutic alliance, and supervisory alliance. There is in each member of the dyad a specifically willing participation in an illusion, whether theatrical or transferential. That the three contexts do shade off into one another, and have done so within recorded history since Aristotle's comments on *Katharsis* and the Greek tragedies, is suggestive of the many transitional elements in common and of the heuristic usefulness of these analogies for understanding communication.

Shall we be forced to conclude that there are no adequate verbal equivalents for these middle phase experiences — that we must be referential and allusive, relying finally on subliminal cues in action, in vocal tones, even in pheromones? After all, it is one of the tendencies of language to dilute meaning rather than to concentrate and refine its communication. Words and phrases that are commonly used are likely to change in their connotations over a period of time — a fact abundantly attested to during the relatively brief span of psychoanalytic terminology. The defenses against the unconscious are institutionalized in verbal forms that have become conventional structures, adaptively and defensively directed to "civilizing" rather than to psychoanalyzing. Perhaps one must paraphrase for the communication of the psychic experience in psychoanalysis what Freud (1899) said of childhood memories — that memories *relating* to our experience may be all that we possess.

CROSSING THE FRONTIERS OF SPEECH

The analyst cannot always reproduce clearly the experience of the psychoanalytic situation because of the noncognitive, transitional, subjective, and regressive nature of much of his data, and in addition because of the anxiety often generated by his regression in parallel with his patient (see chapters 1 and 2). Freud (1900) made an analogy between the patient's state during free association and that before falling asleep. Similarly the analyst's state of evenly hovering attention parallels the patient's, so each member of the psychoanalytic dyad is idiosyncratically subject to the compelling circumstances that Lewin (1954, 1955) described for the patient in his studies of the relationships of sleep, narcissistic neurosis, dreams, and regression. The analyst's difficulties in recalling and/or reproducing the situation for communication to coworkers are similar to the situation of the dreamer who has forgotten his dream because he wishes to be weaned and to awaken (Lewin 1953).

Isakower (1939) suggested that "going to sleep itself is a case of 'crossing the frontiers of speech': the ego behaves just as though . . . it was obliged to leave behind its linguistic belongings." The psychology of the dream has little in common with the grammatical and logical connections of secondary process. The same is true of some of the regressed intrapsychic and interpersonal transactional processes that are the observational data of the middle phases of psychoanalysis. Perhaps here we have the phenomenological basis for, as well as a genetic root of, the usual absence of an adequate verbal equivalent. It is during partial identifications, in "transitionalism," in the obscure gradients of distinction between self and other selves, that the verbal equivalent for experiences in psychoanalysis is to be sought, though often in vain.

While the patient may temporarily take leave of his observing ego, the analyst's work ego must be continually functioning. That it does so is attested to, for example, even by the fact of the analyst's parapraxes, those phenomena of partial and limited regression. These almost always express vicariously, like an interpretation, something that is striving for utterance in the patient. Even while partially and temporarily regressed, processes are operating in the service of the analytic situation and the patient, and consequently of the analyst's function as awakener and interpreter (Lewin 1953, see chapter 2).

It must be remembered that the analyst's experience of parallel regression in trial identification is not always unpleasurable. It may even have a serendipitous therapeutic or reality-orienting effect on the analyst. However, superego elements of shame and guilt and experiences of self-diffusion may contribute to the difficulties of transmitting the supposedly tainted observational data.

STRATEGIC MISUNDERSTANDINGS
VS. BENEVOLENT SKEPTICISM

I have reviewed the reasons why, in matters of communication that are profoundly relevant to the science and art of psychoanalysis, the possibility of misunderstanding is great. Because of this possibility, the ongoing repetitions in the psychoanalytic and psychiatric literature of so much that has been said and resaid before is necessary and useful. The discursiveness of spoken language has its usefulness in that it increases the possibility of the information being transmitted and received. Its written counterpart is more unwieldy but no less necessary. Nevertheless, it has not been successful to any notable degree in the transmission of much of the observational data of psychoanalysis.

Predictably this problem is not solvable by any unitary approach. Beyond the complex individual and social factors that I have reviewed as affecting the analyst-reporter, there remain the imponderable ones of his native skill and talent, as well as the resistance of the auditor or reader.

There are few analysts who have the capacity, not to say the talent or genius, to engage in all four of the following arduous cognitive-affective operations: (1) to experience the range of the patient's communications in a cogent way; (2) to be able to recall these experiences, together with the congruent and parallel processes in oneself; (3) to be able to collate and to transmit these dual and dyadic experiences in such a way as to be comprehensible to a sympathetic listener or reader; and (4) to overcome the resistances and/or prejudices of the listener or reader—what Lionel Trilling (1955) has aptly termed their "strategic" misunderstandings.

Since Lewin's formulations (1954, 1955), we are accustomed to thinking of the analyst's functions as including those of arouser or soother. People do not take kindly to being awakened before they are ready; the surge of unexpected popularity of psychoanalysis during the past thirty years has been in some ways unfortunate because of the predictable counterclaims, if not counterblasts, that it has called forth. On the basis of public relations, one could argue that we should have been more soothing than arousing. Still, the analyst is infinitely more careful with what he says to his patients than is often assumed.

In meeting the issues of transmission of data to those who are strategically misunderstanding, one can barely hope to be able to circumvent the resistance and that the working through will not be excessively stormy. The weight of authority may be invoked for purposes of circumvention, as may the evidence of multiple validation and verification of the data. It is no longer feasible or sufficient to recommend the traditional recourse to psychoanalytic treatment or training, for this will have appeal only for those who scarcely need it in order to be convinced. In addition, however well this has worked to open up comprehension and experience among most of those who tried it, it has been subject to the charge that it results in an emotionally induced loss of objectivity.

As a partial measure in the management of a problem that will always be with us, I should recommend the multiple authorship and editorship of psychoanalytic papers. Though multiple authorship, like the action of some committees, might produce an ungainly hybrid, attention to the limitations that I have outlined could result in something more nearly approaching an "adequate verbal equivalent for experience." Specifically the oral reports of analysts within the protective and intimate circles of their own study groups are often most communicative of what really happens and of what data are processed in the psychoanalytic situation. It must be acknowledged that the analyst is a less than perfect instrument, and that his awareness is sometimes limited. In these aspects of clinical reporting, one's colleagues may be profoundly valuable in assisting the clarification and communication of the basic data. These reports, transcribed by audiotape and/or writing, could be submitted to critical, written comment by the other members of the group, who would evaluate them with specific attention to their validity, clarity, and verifiability (see chapter 2).

There is sadness and exasperation in these matters, akin as they are to the ultimate separateness and aloneness of human beings. These have been noted in the past by philosophers and poets and in recent years by the more imaginative investigators of early childhood development (e.g. Winnicott 1953, Mahler 1972). There are inner experiences that all of us have but of which only a few can speak and write intelligibly. For many, perhaps most, there is unwillingness and inability even to know of these experiences. To disturb the sleep of man is presumptuous enough; to ask him to remain awake and to remember can be sheer effrontery. For science to face such tasks becomes an irony and a challenge, the alternative being a retreat to the sadness and resentment of shackled separateness. The practitioner-investigator in psychoanalysis is open to these paradoxes and ironies throughout his professional life. Like the mathematician he can talk meaningfully of his work only with his colleagues; with others he must rely upon their benevolent skepticism—upon their willingness to learn and upon his own ability to clarify. These are the hardships and rigors of scientific curiosity. They are made more poignant at a time in history when values are rapidly changing, when the forces of antirationalism are again being strengthened.

REFERENCES

Ashby, W. R. (1954). *Design for a Brain.* New York: Wiley.

Balint, M. (1968). *The Basic Fault.* London: Tavistock.

Bartlett, F. C. (1932). *Remembering: A Study in Experimental and Social Psychology.* London: Cambridge University Press.

Bibring, E. (1937). Contribution to symposium on theory of therapeutic results of psycho-analysis. *International Journal of Psycho-Analysis* 18: 170–189.

Bion, W. R. (1970). *Attention and Interpretation.* New York: Basic Books.

Borges, J. L. (1964). A yellow rose. *Dreamtigers.* New York: Dutton, 1970.

Colby, K. M. and Lashley, K. S. (1957). An exchange of views on psychic energy and psychoanalysis. *Behavioral Science* 2: 231–240.

Condon, W. S. and Sander, L. W. (1974). Neonate movement is synchronized with adult speech: interactional participation and language acquisition. *Science* 183: 99–101.

Eissler, K. R. (1951). Remarks on the psychoanalysis of schizophrenia. *International Journal of Psycho-Analysis* 32: 139–156.

Fenichel, O. (1941). *Problems of Psychoanalytic Technique.* Albany: Psychoanalytic Quarterly.

Fernandez, J. W. (1973). Analysis of ritual: metaphoric correspondences as the elementary forms. *Science* 182: 1366–1367.

Fliess, R. (1942). The metapsychology of the analyst. *Psychoanalytic Quarterly* 11: 211–227.

Freud, S. (1899). Screen memories. *Standard Edition* 3: 299–322.

———(1900). The interpretation of dreams. *Standard Edition* 4/5.

_____(1914). Remembering, repeating and working through. *Standard Edition* 12: 145–156.

Huxley, A. (1956). The education of an amphibian. In *Tomorrow and Tomorrow and Tomorrow*. New York: Harper and Row.

Isakower, O. (1939). On the exceptional position of the auditory sphere. *International Journal of Psycho-Analysis* 20: 340–348.

Kohut, H. (1959). Introspection, empathy and psychoanalysis. *Journal of the American Psychoanalytic Association* 7: 459–483.

Kris, E. (1952). *Psychoanalytic Explorations in Art*. New York: International Universities Press.

Lewin, B. D. (1953). The forgetting of dreams. In *Drives, Affects, Behaviour*, ed. R. M. Loewenstein. New York: International Universities Press.

_____(1954). Sleep, narcissistic neurosis, and the analytic situation. *Psychoanalytic Quarterly* 23: 487–510.

_____(1955). Dream psychology and the analytic situation. *Psychoanalytic Quarterly* 24: 169–199.

Loewenstein, R. M. (1965). Observational data and theory in psycho-analysis. In *Drives, Affects, Behaviour*, vol. 2, ed. M. Shur. International Universities Press.

Mahler, M. S. (1972). On the first three subphases of the separation-individuation process. *International Journal of Psycho-Analysis* 53: 333–338.

Planck, M. (1949). *Scientific Autobiography*. New York: Philosophical Library.

Searles, H. F. (1955). The informational value of the supervisor's emotional experience. In *Collected Papers*. New York: International Universities Press, 1965.

Stein, M. H. (1965). States of consciousness in the analytic situation: including a note on the traumatic dream. In *Drives, Affects, Behaviour*, vol. 2, ed. M. Schur. New York: International Universities Press.

Sterba, R. (1934). The fate of the ego in analytic therapy. *International Journal of Psycho-Analysis* 15: 117–126.

Trilling, L. (1955). *Freud and the Crisis of our Culture*. Boston: Beacon Press.

Waelder, R. (1962). Psychoanalysis, scientific method, and philosophy. *Journal of the American Psychoanalytic Association* 10: 617–637.

Winnicott, D. W. (1953). Transitional objects and transitional phenomena. *International Journal of Psycho-Analysis* 34: 89–97.

Zetzel, E. R. (1956). Concept and content in psychoanalytic theory. In *The Capacity for Emotional Growth*. New York: International Universities Press, 1970.

_____(1958). Therapeutic alliance in the analysis of hysteria. In *The Capacity for Emotional Growth*. New York: International Universities Press, 1970.

Chapter 4

Work Ego and Observing Ego: The Treatment Alliance

COMPLEXITIES OF THE TREATMENT ALLIANCE

In the development of a psychoanalytic situation, there must evolve that special form of collaboration between analyst and analysand that, with the transference, is indispensable to the therapeutic process. The collaboration goes beyond Freud's description of the analytic pact (1940, p. 174)—"complete candour on the one side and strict discretion on the other"—though the pact is clearly essential as a starting point. It has been viewed by some analysts as an alliance that is basically transferential; e.g., the "rational transference" of Fenichel (1941), the "therapeutic alliance" of Zetzel (1956), and the "mature transference" of Stone (1961). More emphasis is placed by others on careful attention to the non-transference realities of the "working alliance" (Greenson 1967). There is a considerable literature that has been extensively reviewed, and I need not elaborate on it here (see Sandler et al. 1973, Kanzer 1975), except to note that not all practitioners of psychoanalysis adhere to one or the other of the polarities I have outlined. In practice there is sufficient variation in the kinds of collaboration or alliance, even with the same patient at different times, that one must conceptualize in terms of a continuum, rather than of a bipolar model.

Alliances are based upon a continuing dynamic ebb and flow of reality factors and transference. They disconcertingly vanish into the transference at times of resistance; regression claims them, and only careful attention to the analysis of transference and resistance may release them again. Yet even during times of obdurate resistance, there is some part of the psychoanalytic patient that attends and listens to what is happening. Analysands will often tell us, for instance, that months earlier we had offered an interpretation that they had rejected, but that now they recognize as having always been valid. Not always does this represent the effects of a premature interpretation. Rather, a considerable period of working through has been necessary before the patient can rediscover the issues beset-ting him. The fact is that, even while the alliance seems to be in abeyance, some agency within the patient is preconsciously active—monitoring, viewing, testing, and evaluating.

We arrive at a well-known empirical observation, one that has been known to analysts for many years, though it has been variously described and labeled. Sterba (1934) formulated the "splitting" or "dissociating" of the analysand's ego into an observing and an experi-encing part: two sets of functions that are facilitated and enhanced through the analyst's task of interpreting transference and resistance and the analysand's tendency to identify with the analyst.

However, the identifications frequently take bizarre turns. In what must be recapitulative enactments of personal history, the patient often will identify early in the work, not with the analyzing functions of the analyst, but with such extraneous items as his mode of dress or speech or other personal mannerisms. When a candidate reports to his training analyst that he has been intervening with his own patients in the manner and even the words that the analyst employs, we are well advised to regard these actions as, at best, tentative first steps in a dependent mode, still defensively regressive rather than progressive. These identifications are developmental steps in the analysis to which I shall refer again.

It is almost superfluous to state that there is a misnomer in what has been referred to as observing functions of the ego. Introspection, attention, memory, judgment, evaluation, and many other complex psychic actions are also connoted; we are dealing with a network of multiple, synergistic combinations. Moreover, in a progressing analysis additional connections are opened. These observing func-tions are in the process of developing in a manner and direction presently to be discussed.

In the absence of these developments—the therapeutic splitting into observing and experiencing functions—analysis cannot proceed.

At the same time, these are reciprocal systems, for neither can the functions of the observing ego progress favorably unless the analyzing of the resistances continues.

It must also be said that the term *therapeutic splitting,* as employed in this context, is misleading (Calef 1972). It does not have the connotations derived from the work of Klein (Segal 1964) or of Kernberg (1975): the observing functions are not a consequence of pathological defenses. In fact, they do not result from regressive defenses, but rather are autonomous, neutralized, sublimated, aim-inhibited functions, which are additionally enhanced by aspects of the relationship with the analyst.

The self-observing functions of the ego are ideally superordinate and autonomous in a hierarchy of functions. This does not obviate the fact that they are subject to reinstinctualizing and deinstinctualizing — they come and go; they may be covertly or overtly operating. Moreover, the observing functions have to begin from some pre-analytic locus; their presence constitutes one of the criteria of analyzability; at the least, the patient's ego must be sufficiently intact so that he can be effectively self-observing and self-reporting. This is a precondition for analysis, but we also expect that analysis will materially strengthen, deepen, and broaden the functions. In assessing the potential for self-observation in a diagnostic interview, we may find that there is an immoderate admixture of superego with ego functions, but we expect that analysis will modify, transform, or otherwise change the locus of the observing functions. Such transformations are possible on the basis of shared boundaries, processes, and developmental roots (Loewald 1962).

THE OPERATING FACTORS
IN THE OBSERVING EGO

I have so far described some complexities of the treatment alliance and some positive contributions of the patient to the alliance. In speaking or writing of the therapeutic, working, or treatment alliance one condenses many clinical phenomena as well as many sources of confusion. The terms have inescapably tended, as have other terms with large, global applications, toward misunderstandings and misapplications that must be constantly guarded against.

In everyday usage, and in some published communications, "alliance" has tended to become descriptive, indicating little more than that the patient was or was not task oriented and collaborating. This is no improvement over the thinking that historically preceded introduction of the terms and emphasized the necessity for taking note of reality factors, human sympathy, and the development of the transference (Freud 1911–15).

The operative factors in the alliance are subsumed in the term *observing ego*. We must take note of the continuous rise and fall of these factors in the course of an analysis, resulting from both the continuing transferential shifts and the day-to-day attitudinal changes in analyst and patient. The psychoanalysis proceeds on the basis of careful attention to a myriad of small details of the patient's reporting and free associating and of the analyst's internal responses, combining gradually into larger patterns of meaningful experience through the process of analyzing. The therapeutically desirable changes in the patient during this endeavor are also cumulative, and consist of minute shifts and movements (Joseph, reported by Naimann, 1976) that represent the opening of new connections and perspectives. Often these small changes can be recognized as imitations or as identifications with the analyst's point of view toward the emerging material. This mental set is influenced by the analyst's presence, his interventions, his sensitive curiosity, his introspective and empathic listening, his interest, non-possessiveness, consistency, steadiness, and his ability to impart his understanding at appropriate times and in appropriate ways through the technicalities of clarification and interpretation. The patient's unconscious reactions to the analyst comprise a significant part of his developing capacity to analyze.

It is hardly solving the problems of alliance to say that the observing, analyzing functions of the patient are built on identifications with the analyzing functions of the analyst. I have already called attention to the primitive and defensive forms that the identifications take, frequently in a pattern that bears little or no resemblance to analyzing functions. But I affirm that, by an accretion of small changes and shifts of pattern and attention resulting from the ongoing analytic work, the identifications with the analyst-object can become internalizations of the analyzing functions of the analyst. The intersubjective or interpersonal becomes intrapsychic and structurally differentiated. The object attachments to the analyst, arising from transferential, neutralized, as well as more realistic bonds, are gradually transformed into an alliance that, while still subject to regressive changes, moves in the direction of augmented analyzing functions.

It is extraordinarily difficult to give clinical vignettes or reports of such changes. Much of what happens in analysis is not directly available to clinical observations and description (see chapter 3). What we "see" clinically is often analogous to the individual frames of a motion picture; the motion is added by means of silent processes of inference and of empathy within the observer. We "see" the just noticeably different consequences of inner shifts and changes of functions, as compared with what had been manifested a moment, an hour, or a month before.

Clinical Vignette 1

In the sixth month of his analysis, a resistant, passively aggressive patient with inhibitions in his awareness and expression of anger began one day to speak more emphatically of matters that he had formerly spoken of in a flat, barely audible monotone. His chief presenting symptom had been anxiety about public speaking, and our early work had been concerned with clarifying this problem and its ramifications. Anxiety developed frequently during the sessions and was dealt with by the patient by means of brief periods of silence during which he struggled for self-control. Interventions at these times were directed toward further clarification, but from time to time interpretations were of his fear of his own anger. He would accept interpretations thoughtfully, perhaps especially so when the question would be raised: Anger toward whom? No other immediate effects could be noted.

That oedipal conflicts were involved was slowly made clear, but it was not until several months after the session referred to above that the patient was able to link his anxieties to sexual problems — specifically, to premature ejaculations with his wife — as well as to fear of his own anger, and of his father's and my anger. This became explicit and was first integrated into a coherent whole with the analysis of a manifestly incestuous dream about his mother.

In the course of the session in which he began to speak more emphatically, he mentioned his misperception of me as sharing qualities of his father's appearance and personality, a phenomenon that he had noted to me in the earliest sessions. Although that fact in itself had indicated some early functioning of an observing ego, he now spoke of it differently, not only more emphatically but in a manner that was less defensive and more objective.

The change in behavior and attitude was, therefore, more an expression of a reasonable observing ego that had been partly emancipated from the regressive pull of the transference. It was not that by deliberate, conscious intent of patient and analyst some state of mutual adjustment had been reached so that now the patient trusted the analyst. Nor was the fresh quality of the session the result of interpretation and working through. In fact, the transference had temporarily yielded to another set of forces—the incremental changes in ego functions that led to internalization of the analyzing functions of the analyst's work ego. That is, the analyst's aims and interventions *in the direction* of interpreting transference resistance had enlisted and augmented the patient's preanalytic tendency to be self-critical, self-observing, and curious about himself.

The change did not, of course, prove durable; it yielded by the time of the next session to transferential forces. Such "transference improvement" is brought about by the strengthened analyzing functions of the so-called observing ego. Insight in this patient at this time was dependent on the operation of a set of ego functions that were observing, evaluating, and reality-oriented, and that were based in part on identification with the work ego. This combined set of operations was mostly preconscious, even unconscious, until the final common pathway of a more emphatic, objective manner of expression.

I am of course not suggesting that the internalization of the analyst's analyzing functions and the resultant emergence of a stronger observing ego are alone curative. Curative factors are multiply and synergistically determined. I do, however, think it necessary to reassert that there are transferential as well as reality elements in any progressing analytic alliance, insofar as there is an effective working dyad. There is no incompatibility between these points of view; each deals with the same phenomena but from different perspectives.

THE WORK EGO AND
INTERNALIZATIONS BY THE PATIENT

It is artificial to discuss either member of the analytic dyad in isolation. The experiences of psychoanalysis, as distinguished from conceptualizations about psychoanalysis, are of two linked persons. The clinical data are derived from intersubjective transactions, from the time of establishment of an observational stance by the patient in the presence of a beginning transference; from the time, that is, when we can begin to speak of the "middle game processes" (see chapter 1).

Nevertheless, for the sake of expediency I must proceed to extract from the dyad the functions of the analyst-at-work, what has been called the "work ego" (Fliess 1942). I shall draw on two previous studies (see chapter 2, also Olinick 1975), and I shall comment on the issues of internalization by the patient of these analyzing functions of the analyst's work ego.

1. The functions of the analyst-at-work are relatively autonomous from drive and conflict, freeing the work ego for such tasks as evenly suspended attention, introspection and empathy, clinical judgment and inference, etc. The patient, on the other hand, moves only gradually and by spurts and starts toward full autonomy and neutralization of his so-called observing ego functions and the capacity to perform free associations. The observing, reasonable ego functions arise, as we have seen, from some preanalytic locus. This locus or starting point must include trustful dependency and curiosity about the self, enhanced and in part initiated by psychic discomfort. Perhaps these words will of themselves connote something of the vastness and complexity of the task of developing the analyzing functions. Psychic pain—a powerful motivation to psychoanalysis—is both a prerequisite to and a result of the functions of self-observation. Our patients are dependent, but conflictedly so, and barely trustful; curious, but not adaptively so; and their distress and discomfort further their regression. Clearly, no one function can be singled out without reference to others.

2. The analyst is motivated by an altruistic concern, a healing intention to maintain and support (Spitz 1956, Gitelson 1962, see

chapter 1) that has been desexualized, aim inhibited, and neutralized. It has often been pointed out that the patient's harshly critical superego functions are mitigated in favor of his identifications or internalizations of the analyst's attitudes toward him. There is, we have seen, a pressure toward identification, augmented by the abstinence rule and what Stone (1961) has referred to as "separation in intimacy": the analyst is not available as the object of gratification of transference wishes, even while he is paradoxically available in terms of his proximity, reliability, durability, and nonpossessiveness. There is also pressure toward identification on the basis of some aspects of the regression (Greenacre 1954, Stone 1961, Sandler et al. 1969). The analyst is not a model for the patient's values, only for his analyzing, except that when we speak of the mitigation of superego we come not only to the matter of new identifications but to new evaluations of oneself and new values.

There is inherent in the psychoanalytic situation, congruent with the doctor-patient relationship and the transference regressions, a dominant-submissive axis of relatedness in the analytic dyad that is variously responded to by the patient, for example, with exaggerated polarizations, with identifications with the aggressor-frustrater, or with reasonable acceptance of the fact that one must be dependent before one can develop a realistic emancipation. The various identifications and other anaclitic defenses and transference resistances require interpreting and working through, thereby further assisting in the gradual augmenting of the autonomously observing, analyzing ego functions. The axis of relatedness only gradually changes into one of mutuality-separability (see chapter 11).

3. The analyst's work ego draws upon the full range of his emotional and intellectual capacities. Problem solving is a prominent set of functions. The empathic processes are an integral part of the clinical inferences and judgments that enter into the problem solving and comprehension of the patient (see chapter 2). The work ego is self-observing, self-critical, and open to regressive processes in the self as a source of information about the other person. A myriad of small increments of information about this mode of working is introjected, assimilated, and internalized by the patient, with varying degrees of successful integration. In the analyst, reintegration from such regression by the work ego takes place by means of an

automatized response signaling a return to the prior state of oscillation between observing and experiencing. The observing, analyzing functions of the patient "learn" to operate in a similar mode. Such reintegration is facilitated in each member of the dyad by the presence of the other member of the alliance, each member constituting a nodal point in an informational feedback loop.

EMPATHY AS A
PROTOTYPE OF INTERNALIZING

The developmental theme of the analysis is that internal integration by the work ego is contingently, over time, paralleled by the patient's observing ego. It is necessary to trace out the integrative, internalizing changes in one member of the analytic alliance by recognizing the parallel, though not identical, changes in the other. Loewald (1960) has discussed the metapsychology of some of these processes: "The patient and the analyst identify to an increasing degree, if the analysis proceeds, in their ego-activity of scientifically guided self-scrutiny. . . . This identification does have to do with . . . new object-relationship . . ." (p. 19).

I do not wish to leave the impression that the "new object-relationship" is an end in itself. It is part of a continuing circular process, a means to an end of intrapsychic restructuring, resulting in augmented parallel analyzing functions of both work ego and observing ego. These in turn facilitate the continuing technical interventions and reintegrative working through.

The understanding of empathic processes in the analysis, therefore, offers us a set of clinical patterns for understanding some fundamentals of intrapsychic change in the psychoanalytic collaboration and for recognizing the growth of parallel functions of work ego and observing ego in the developing analyzing functions of the latter.

Empathy as a mode of understanding the other person is a trial identification (Fliess 1942). It is based on controlled, partial, regressive substitutions for lost or failed object-relatedness (Greenson 1967). Empathy is not curative; it is not a skill or talent possessed by everyone, though when present it can be refined and augmented; it is not a latter-day royal road to the unconscious; it is, above all, not be confused with sympathy.

Empathy is a phenomenon of two persons transacting; it entails processes both between and within each of the participants. It is a way of learning to know the other person by means of a rapid collating and organizing of apparently disparate data into a harmoniously corresponding system. To accomplish this, as I have said, the empathizing analyst must enable an integration of his own external and internal perceptions. He does this by utilizing his regressive thoughts, reveries, and perceptions as they emerge during his evenly hovering attention; he associates to them in the context of what he already knows about the patient, consciously and otherwise, and discerns through clinical judgment and experience whether this meets the objective test of veracity and validity. By means of the empathic experience, the analyst is able to evolve in a creative way a working model of the patient out of seemingly incongruous internal and external perceptions. To do so, the analyst has taken into himself a strange object, coordinated it with his own endogenous psychic events, and through these internal and internalized actions has brought order out of seeming disorder and strangeness.

It is thereby imprecise to speak of having introjected or identified with the patient, for the full empathic process is one that also calls on the integrative and synthetic functions of the ego. Therefore, only as a curtailed description may one say that empathy is a trial identification; the work ego accomplishes more than identification. It is correct to say, however, that through the utilization of empathic processes, as outlined above (also, Olinick 1975, and see chapters 1, 2, and 3), the work ego is integrative in both the intrapsychic and interpersonal spheres. Stated differently, the empathic experience is integrative to the analyst insofar as it is a function of an autonomous work ego. It is otherwise a seductive and/or threatening experience for both participants that can be neither durable nor therapeutic. It is nevertheless true that for limited periods of time, in the presence of empathy, the two participants are often — not always — persuaded that they work well together and belong together. This is so because empathy as a regressive experience relies on qualities of the transitional processes (Winnicott 1953). These processes between inner and outer reality partake of both intrapsychic and interpersonal functions; they operate between primary and secondary process, having their origin in the period of separation and individuation from the mother-child matrix of infancy. As factors in progressive development, the transitional processes have much that is valuable and durable. They may lead to the developing of sound relationships, reality orientation, imaginative living, and creativity. This is not so when they are fixated at a regressive level, nor when they are exalted as mystically unique, as is done in some of the currently popular cultlike gropings toward "therapeutic encounter."

The utility for patient and analyst of these regressive and transitional processes—their integrative potential—must depend, first, on the fact that the psychoanalytic situation inherently does not permit a self-centered isolation. Not only are the parallel regressions controlled, transient, and partial, but they occur in a task-oriented, two-person group. The standard methodology, sympathetically conducted, is basic to these statements, and Eissler's criteria (1953) for the application of technical parameters are highly useful guidelines.

Also, I suggest that the depth and extent of the regression may be set in part by the upper developmental limits of the transitionalism, that is, by that which was developmentally a beginning capacity for social relatedness. This touches on the subject of analyzability in relation to the degree of developmental arrest and fixation—a subject the full discussion of which goes beyond the scope of this paper. However, two additional clinical vignettes will be discussed presently, in order further to clarify these clinical problems. Here I should like to indicate in general terms some of the matters that must be considered:

1. The degree and extent of developmental defects can be discussed methodically in the abstract, but their actual, early appearance in the consulting room often requires a quantitative evaluation of mutability on the basis of meager data. Limitations as to analyzability are caused by multiple factors. Still, incapability to internalize means inability to analyze; and genetic issues lead the list of factors interfering with the capacity to form a reasonable observing ego with its evolving analyzing functions. Nevertheless, because it is a quantitatively determined factor, and because other factors are also involved, it is within clinical experience that in such instances the analyzing functions can in varying degrees be improved by the analytic process. (See clinical vignettes, below.)

2. Analyzability can be evaluated during the initial interviews and/or the early months of analysis on the basis of the patient's ability

to observe and report about himself, particularly about what he is able to observe of himself during the sessions. In chapter 1 I proposed that the prognosis as to successful analyzability is enhanced when it has been possible to deal collaboratively with a transference resistance — that is, in a setting of alliance with an observing ego that was augmented in its operations by means of identifying with and internalizing the work ego's analyzing functions.

3. An essential set of factors is the appropriate matching of analyst and analysand — that is, some patients are not analyzable by certain analysts, but can proceed successfully with others. It sometimes even appears that multiple analyses with more than one analyst are necessary for some patients, but this is a *post hoc ergo propter hoc* explanation, and is difficult, if not impossible, to substantiate. By "appropriate matching" I refer to an ability on the part of the two participants to communicate meaningfully, not only verbally but also empathically, by means of mutual identifications the existence, integration, and comprehension of which need initially be a task of the analyst and not of the patient. As we have seen, such identifications are essential to the evolution of the observing ego's analyzing functions. Only a period of analysis can demonstrate the presence or absence of a useful "matching," though the extremes of such correspondences — effectual or ineffectual, on a continuum — can sometimes be detected during initial interviews.

To recapitulate, psychoanalytic regression contributes in the ways outlined here to the expansion and resilience of ego functions through the organizing of the psychoanalytic situation and through the agency of continued analyzing by work ego and observing ego. The ongoing introjective-projective processes and mutual identifications (Loewald 1960) lead through regression to an ultimate autonomous stability. The analytic collaboration gives affective support and nutriment to each of the participants; that is, the range of cognitive and of empathic identificatory processes serve as informational feedback loops.

Depending on the degree of successful completion of the integration by the empathizing work ego, two courses are now possible. The analyst may be left with a "bad" internal object, insufficiently assimilated, with consequent malaise. Or he may be left with a feeling of accomplishment and effectively assertive action. Failure of integration on the part of an analyst who is appropriately striving to understand and to impart his understanding must be experienced by him as an incompleteness, a failed gestalt that has not attained closure. This is responsible for many of the temporary moods of discouragement and fatigue that are among the occupational hazards of our profession.

With completion of the task of integrating, the anxiety of discovery or uncovering has been surmounted, an anxiety based on the dim, mostly preconscious precognition that all discovery is rediscovery and therefore subject to the anxiety of derepression. Other residual or active affects and impulses have been reined in and their energies deployed constructively. This is a means of effecting a higher psychic organization, superordinate to, but not replacing, what has been prior in time and structuring. A model for action is thus made available to the analyzing functions of the patient.

An ailing patient is in conflict between giving in to his suffering, even to the extreme of finding perverse satisfaction in it, or of surmounting and mastering it. The analyst's imparted understanding, as described, given in a mode of organization to which the patient can adapt and modify himself, for example, as in moving between primary and secondary process, offers the way to mastery. In a manner comparable to the analyst's learning to know his patient through introspecting his own internal and internalized experiences, the patient learns to know himself through having internalized a working model of the analyst's analyzing functions. This becomes a means to further self-knowledge through the opening of additional intrapsychic communications and connections.

These are not consequences of desensitizing and deconditioning, nor entirely the results of transferential working through. These are special effects from the regressive substitutions for object-relations that are evinced in the well-known identifications of the psychoanalytic situation; these identifications lead to the neutralized, "sublimated," integrative internalizing of the analyzing functions.

The following two clinical vignettes may throw more light on some of these processes. In both instances the development of the alliance and parallel analyzing functions was greatly restricted, but for that reason the rudimentary workings could be more clearly discerned. Generally, with progressing analysis of transference resistance, the observing, analyzing functions operate smoothly and silently, and their development is almost imperceptible. (See clinical vignette 1.) In a psychotherapy where the transference is not or cannot be analyzed, the weight of the treatment falls on an alliance that is basically transferential, consisting of the frail and, ultimately, resistant and limited development of observing ego functions. Both patients described below defended against transference development and analysis; both developed a fragile observing ego based on identification as defense, with limited analyzing functions and correspondingly limited therapeutic results. If there is a degree of successful interpretation and working through of transference resistance—possibly in vignette 2, more probably in vignette 3— some internalization of analyzing functions and greater stability of treatment alliance may result.

Clinical Vignette 2

The patient was a young unmarried professional woman who referred herself for "analysis" because of her agitation and depression during the breaking up of a three-year affair with an older married man. She had not, she said, expected him to marry her, but she had been devastated when she learned from him that he was dating another woman.

On a schedule of four sessions weekly, using the couch, her acute symptoms quickly abated; but it was obvious that any psychoanalytic work would be superficial for a prolonged period. This was to be a holding operation interspersed with occasional, tentative inquiries into her narcissistic resistances. Much of her early improvement could be attributed to her willingness, in the warmth of the transference, to become aware of her self-directed rage and to explore in a limited way some of the early determinants of her present relationships. These explorations were, however, barely collaborative, and the data so collated were shallow and stereotyped.

She resented being categorized by what she called "Freudian formulas"; she insisted upon her uniqueness, though she did not deny others their equivalent uniqueness. She affirmed that she knew herself better than the analyst could ever hope to, and that it was manifestly unfair that he sit there "judging" her. She was given to flights of temper, to withholding of information, and to provocative rudeness, while at other times she was charming and intelligent.

The analyst was perceived in the transference as the indifferent brother; and above all, as the sullen, brooding, silent, angry father who had drunk himself into withdrawal, hepatic coma, and death. His death had occurred about five years earlier, and her grieving had been severely limited.

During the first year of treatment, she went through several months of frenzied dating and sleeping around with various men; she maintained for the most part a cheerful facade, although she was often hurt, and as often hurt her partners. After a brief affair with a second married man, this one with an active, jealous wife who threatened violence, her sexualized defenses against transference centered about a young man who might have become an interested partner had not the intensity and quality of her demands led to his withdrawal. She became vaguely aware that something about him reminded her of the analyst, but she chose not to pursue this topic any further.

Otherwise, she assiduously avoided any references to the analyst, having decided with annoyance that he would not budge from his position as an unknown person who shared nothing with her except his unwanted, unilateral "judgments." She now ensconced herself among her several young women friends, and professed herself to be uninterested in men, sex, and marriage.

Any alliance was an ephemeral happening, and any observing ego was warped to observe the analyst critically as the projected imago of her bad introjects. Gradually, this situation moderated, until one day, to the not complete surprise of the analyst, she spontaneously began to recount the ways she had improved in her living and her work. She expressed shyly her gratitude for what she had been able to accomplish. She was aware that the analyst might not know this from what she had been telling him prior to this session. Her gains were in fact considerable; she was less impulsive and more self-composed, but she was still far from being a well-integrated person. She now spoke pleasurably of her expectation that she would always be "in analysis," much as diabetics require constant medical supervision.

The analyst was not pleased with this prospect, but he recognized the narcissistic, transferential determinants. He found within himself some feelings of tender caring, overshadowed by curiosity as to whether this position of hers could be turned to her analytic profit. I mention this latter development because it may have portended some beginning, inappropriate, therapeutic zeal on the analyst's part. For this patient the danger of such a development would be that it presented a threat to her sense of uniqueness and independence. Her narcissism was strong enough to demand aggrandizement from the analyst, but vulnerable enough to feel hurt and humiliated when he did not confirm her independence and grandiosity. This, together with the intensified conflict between her dependent and grandiose needs, may have led to her coldly and angrily leaving treatment in order to take a position in another city. This was a move that she had been intermittently considering for some time, but now she announced it in conjunction with her claim that the analyst was inadequate to her requirements.

These are retrospective explanations. The final several weeks of treatment were obscured by a resurgence of the patient's defenses, as though she had committed herself to a threatening degree of intimacy and closeness and was now pulling away. The analyst's empathy was blocked in the face of the diminishing signs of a collaborating observing ego. Her reporting of her introspection was never a prominent feature of the work and was now completely absent; also, the analyst was kept almost completely ignorant of intercurrent events in her life. Her work and social activities seemed to have maintained their previous level.

There had been little possibility for interpretive work on the transference; but there had been, nevertheless, some beginnings of a change of function in her self-observing, self-controlling abilities. These changes were first manifested in her work. She became more steady and reliable in relationships with colleagues by virtue of an increased ability to view herself objectively. She was more committed to the organization for which she worked and, correspondingly, found greater opportunities for advancement. It is not infrequent, early in an analysis, to recognize such improvement in work; it is, I think, not necessarily a consequence of a developing transference neurosis with its attendant disentanglements outside the analysis and its focusing of the neurosis onto the person of the analyst. There was no evidence of such trends of a transference neurosis in this patient. Rather, as in many, perhaps in most, patients the work improvement is traceable to identifications with the analyst as a representative worker. With this patient, the changes were modeled after the analyst's inquiring, objective, supportive attitudes, as well as based upon whatever of such functions had been preanalytically her own. Throughout this period of clinical improvement the patient remained self-centered and self-involved in that the ultimate value for her was whether her own needs and fantasies were uncompromisingly fulfilled. Independence on the part of another person in whom she might become interested was threatening and intolerable to her. The impelling force of her self-announced, extraanalytic improvement in living and of the increase in certain observing ego functions was to be found in her investment in others—in this instance, the analyst—as enhancements of herself. Self-aggrandizement was to be reached for but not attained through the agency of another person—by transference, from each of her parents in turn—but this agency could exist only at a distance and to the degree that she could permit and control. At all times her objectivity about herself entailed unstable identifications and, at best, incompletely internalized functions. To discuss this material further in terms of mirror transferences (Kohut 1971) would take us too far afield.

Clinical Vignette 3

This patient had some of the qualities of the young woman described in the previous vignette; but she was older, more mature and resilient, and more desperate for help. The psychic pain that brings patients to treatment is, as I have already said, a prerequisite to, as well as a result of, functions of self-observation. In this patient it gave powerful momentum to the work, although it substituted dependency for a more healthful alliance. Her desperation impelled her through some difficult periods during our attempts at a collaborative venture.

She was in her third marriage, with two grown children and one young child. Her decompensation into recurrent agitated depressions had begun two years earlier, after her mother's sudden death. In treatment her depression soon lifted, revealing the workings of recurrent masochistic crises. These were the negative therapeutic reactions of superego resistance, disallowing success, enjoyment, or self-understanding, except at the cost of great suffering. Her physical attractiveness was fading, and while this caused anguish, it fell into the service of her punitive superego, and it did permit the compensatory use of a considerable intelligence.

The analyst, she announced, was for her a surgical instrument, an "iron lung," definitely not to be personalized. Transference was derided or otherwise denied and rejected, though its manifestations were clear enough to the analyst and, as time went on, to the patient. At the same time, she admired his clearsightedness about her problems and his capacity for imparting his understanding to her. She developed a considerable skill in duplicating his points of view about her, and she became quite adept at quickly recognizing the beginning signs of her negative reactions. Slowly, her crises became much less intense and limited in duration. Her gains were reduced, of course, by the fact that she rigidly guarded against working on her transference by "using" the analyst defensively and dependently, rather than for working through her resistances and increasing her ability to internalize his analyzing functions. The unacknowledged transference was an erotized one, replicating the relationship with her father. He had been charming, erratic, and seductive; after the parents' divorce when the little girl was barely out of infancy, he had visited her only sporadically. In and out of her sessions, she too was charming, often erratic, and seductive; she frequently cancelled or missed appointments. She admired and idealized him intensely, even to having a photograph of him as a young man on her bedside table. Her identification was with her father as the idolized aggressor-frustrater.

At the same time, her relationship with her mother had been mutually dependent, and her resentments were deep-seated and secret. The early analytic work centered on this; the early "transference improvement" entailed a considerable liberation from the superego introjects and injunctions that stemmed from transactions with a mother who was herself emotionally erratic, demanding, possessively exploiting the patient, and preoccupied with gambling and money, and men as sources of money.

It was as though, through the analyst, she had secretly found and created her "good" father as the longed-for antidote to the poison represented by her mother. Through the analyst, she could secretly replace mother with father, which her mother had prohibited, and thereby mourn them both, and mitigate her superego mandates.

A "transference improvement" such as this is not always to be discounted, for it may be all that a patient is capable of, at least for the time being. It was this patient's need to please, a part of her positive transference derived from her relationship with both parents, that contributed to the motives and structuring of the alliance and to the identifications and limited internalizations of analyzing function. The latter were limited in extent and number because the forces of the transference were largely pregenital and narcissistic and resistant to that essential renunciation of infantile aims and objects that permits developmental advance. With this patient, sexually overstimulated by her attractive father, by a grossly seductive uncle, and by the presence of her mother's lovers, all was sexualized except sex itself. She kept herself closely guarded, as though life itself were threatened. In fact, the deaths of close relatives, in childhood and adulthood, reinforced and contributed to this narcissistic defense.

CONCLUSIONS

I have outlined here the development of those internalizations of function that constitute or contribute to the analyzing functions of the patient and that evolve from the preanalytic functions of self-observing. These are the operative functions of the variously named forms of treatment collaboration or alliance. Their development, preanalytically and during analysis, is complex in form and content; they have been generally denoted by the inadequate, narrow term *observing ego,* a term implying only the kind of introspection employed by the analyst. Perhaps a more fully descriptive term would be *operative ego, analyzing functions,* or even, clumsily, *on-serving ego;* these have the advantage of suggesting more of the specifically effective transformations. But names represent only some of our concerns in this intricate subject. It is as inescapable for psychoanalytic explanations as it is for psychoanalytic case reports that the formulations are far more simplified than are the raw, natural data.

Among the effects of the controlled regressions and the internalizations of analyzing function are an increased resilience and expansion of certain ego functions. The desexualized, nondefensive processes are identical with those that occur in the usual, "normal," extratherapeutic development (Loewald 1960, 1962). The resultant autonomy from the drives is equivalent to active mastery and renunciation of pregenital drive and transference object. It is common analytic observation that pregenital motivations toward treatment alliance result in resistance (vignettes 2 and 3) rather than in effective working through (Calef 1972). Insight and increased efficiency of functioning are manifestations of augmented operations of the observing ego and increased capacity for constructive oscillation between observing and experiencing. These sequences represent a network of interacting factors that contribute to the superordinate analyzing functions of the postanalytic personality.

The so-called therapeutic, working, or treatment alliance is more than a contract or collaboration; it is a matrix for the playing out of the vicissitudes of transference, and for intrapsychic change. The effective operative agent in the patient is the vectorial resultant of having internalized work ego functions into observing ego. These latter gradually evolve into durable executive functions. Thus a set of processes in the patient increasingly parallels certain functions of the analyst's work ego and becomes an agent of intrapsychic change, through the regulated work of analyzing transference and resistance.

REFERENCES

Calef, V. (1972). A theoretical note on the ego in the therapeutic process. In *Moral Values and the Superego Concept in Psychoanalysis,* ed. S. C. Post. New York: International Universities Press.

Eissler, K. R. (1953). The effect of the structure of the ego on psychoanalytic technique. *Journal of the American Psychoanalytic Association* 1: 104–143.

Fenichel, O. (1941). *Problems of Psychoanalytic Technique.* Albany: The Psychoanalytic Quarterly.

Fliess, R. (1942). The metapsychology of the analyst. *The Psychoanalytic Quarterly* 11: 211–227.

Freud, S. (1911–1915). Papers on technique. *Standard Edition* 12: 85–173.

_____(1940). An outline of psycho-analysis. *Standard Edition* 23: 141–207.

Gitelson, M. (1962). The curative factors in psychoanalysis. *International Journal of Psycho-Analysis* 43: 194–205.

Greenacre, P. (1954). The role of transference. *Journal of the American Psychoanalytic Association* 2: 671–684.

Greenson, R. (1967). *The Technique and Practice of Psychoanalysis.* New York: International Universities Press.

Kanzer, M. (1975). The therapeutic and working alliances. *International Journal of Psychoanalytic Psychotherapy* 4: 48–68.

Kernberg, O. (1975). *Borderline Conditions and Pathological Narcissism.* New York: Jason Aronson.

Kohut, H. (1971). *The Analysis of the Self.* New York: International Universities Press.

Loewald, H. (1960). On the therapeutic action of psycho-analysis. *International Journal of Psycho-Analysis* 41: 16–33.

_____(1962). Internalization, separation, mourning, and the superego. *The Psychoanalytic Quarterly* 31: 483–504.

Naimann, J. (1976). Reporter, Panel on the fundamentals of psychic change in clinical practice, 29th I. P. A. Congress, July 1975. *International Journal of Psycho-Analysis* 57: 411–418.

Olinick, S. L. (1975). Position statements, panel on the fundamentals of psychic change in clinical practice. *International Psycho-Analytical Association Newsletter* 7: 26–28.

Sandler, J., Holder, A., Kawenoka, M., Kennedy, H. E., and Neurath, L. (1969). Notes on some theoretical and clinical aspects of transference. *International Journal of Psycho-Analysis* 50: 633–646.

Sandler, J., Dare, C., and Holder, A. (1973). *The Patient and the Analyst: The Basis of the Psychoanalytic Process.* New York: International Universities Press.

Segal, H. (1964). *Introduction to the Work of Melanie Klein.* New York: Basic Books.

Spitz, R. A. (1956). Countertransference. *Journal of the American Psychoanalytic Association* 4: 256–265.

Sterba, R. (1934). The fate of the ego in analytic therapy. *International Journal of Psycho-Analysis* 15: 117–125.

Stone, L. (1961). *The Psychoanalytic Situation.* New York: International Universities Press.

Winnicott, D. W. (1953). Transitional objects and transitional phenomena. *International Journal of Psycho-Analysis* 34: 89–97.

Zetzel, E. (1956). The concept of transference. In *The Capacity for Emotional Growth.* New York: International Universities Press, 1970.

Chapter 5

Empathy and Metaphoric Correspondences

This chapter proposes an answer to the question of how the analyst integrates the data of empathic perception, collected in his state of evenly hovering attention, into a comprehensible, valid system that corresponds to the patient. The problem is one of the perception and transmission of covert meaning from one person to another, and from one intrapsychic system to another within the same person.

I have been concerned with empathic processes as they reveal the workings of the psychoanalytic work ego—the more or less autonomously functioning aspect of the analyst at work, which is uniquely attuned to and in parallel with processes in the patient (see chapters 1-4, 6, and 7). With that model one may observe that the analyst, through his work ego, learns to know the patient, not only through the usual cognitive channels but also by a specialized attention to his own internal and internalized processes as these become mobilized and influenced in the psychoanalytic situation (see chapter 2).

A definition of empathy remains difficult to arrive at, although Fliess's (1942) discussion in terms of transitory "trial identifications" is useful. However it is defined, the basic questions remain to be answered: What does the analyst introject? What are the objective data of empathy? To what does the analyst respond, and how are the raw data made meaningful and informative? To be sure, the analyst responds to the free associations, to their form and style, to the revealed patterns of thinking and feeling. Still, it is not on verbal content alone, on the basis of the principles of contiguity, similarity, and repetition, that this process depends (Freud 1915, Kanzer 1961, Beres and Arlow 1974). In those instances of empathy that have lent themselves to study, additional factors have always been present.

Any communication operates in such a way that "acts of reference occur in the [receiver] which are similar in all relevant respects to those which are symbolized in the [sender]" (Ogden and Richards 1923). Communication plainly depends on the presence of a similar mutual universe of discourse established between the communicants. We know that the work ego is sensitive to shared organized forms of behavior that include the patient's and the analyst's vocal tones, gestures, postural tonus, and configurations of movement (see Deutsch 1952). These may be subliminal, but they are demonstrably perceptible, as determined by their effects (see Birdwhistell 1970). Microanalysis of sound films of human communication reveals that measurable units of the listener's body motion—his "configurational organizations"—are synchronous with his interlocutor's speech. It has been observed that these interactional synchronies are usually totally outside the awareness of the two persons being studied (Birdwhistell 1970, Condon and Sander 1974).

These phenomena are described and demonstrated as *patternings of movement with articulated speech*. Even the neonate is described as exhibiting "precise and sustained segments of movement that are synchronous with the articulated structure of adult speech." He is a "participant from the outset in multiple forms of interactional organization" (Condon and Sander 1974, p. 99). Condon and Sander suggest that this may provide a basis for a new approach to the study of language acquisition. Additional configurations and additional meanings accrue with further maturation and development; basic modes become expanded into hierarchies of linguistic and other behavioral patternings. That is, new acculturations and new meanings come into play while the style and form of speech, tone, gesture, and posture are developing.

The studies made by Condon and Sander lend support to what practicing analysts have intuitively known: that among the effective stimuli of their empathic processes are subliminal actions on the part of the patient. Nonverbal communication, to be sure, is not the whole source of empathy; I do not omit the importance of verbal free associations or the contributions of cognitive factors. Both empathy and nonverbal communications are, however, dependent on physical proximity, interaction, intimacy, and inwardness. When we attempt to enter into a trial identification with someone who is not physically proximate, we are relying on past empathy or on imagination and fantasy or on clairvoyance. For our further explanation and understanding we must explore the nature of these configurational organizations of speech and action and discern the relative stimulus value of each, or conclude that they represent indissoluble *Gestalten* for communicational perception.

With the Westernization of the world's populations, we are likely to overlook the fact that such interactional meanings have tended to vary from one culture to another, and even from one era of history to another within the same geographical area. It seems probable that much of the homogenizing of ways of speech and movement has been conditioned in this century by American movies and television, as well as by tourism and military occupations and invasions. We recognize, that is, that styles of communication change gradually over the years: it is necessary only to compare styles of acting in the films of forty years ago with those that are current and acceptable today. Styles of stage acting have also changed: an Elizabethan play as it was once enacted would in some respects appear outlandish to a twentieth-century urban dweller. I think it safe to conclude that we learn new as well as old idioms of interactional synchrony.

This much would suffice as a bare outline of explanation of the empathic perception and transmission of meaning if the meaning were relatively uncomplicated and uncluttered by nuances, conflicts, or dissonances. The material with which the analyst deals is, however, rarely so elementary or unitary. Except when the simplest of affects are being expressed and registered, we are constantly "reading between the lines," not only with free associations but also with other forms of communication. Can we go further in delineating the formal transmission of meaning by means of subliminal body tonus and movement? In what sense is the transmitted signal meaningful to the perceiving analyst?

Metaphor is a commonly employed literary device for assimilating the new and unfamiliar. It is an implied comparison, in which one thing is likened to another as if it were truly that other. It is imprecise and tentative, and as a vehicle of description or classification it is preliminary and even primitive. Like analogy, of which it is a special instance, it may be used as an introductory measure for collating data and for later deductive and inductive inferences. Although metaphor is a literary, rhetorical device and relies upon the stimulation of explicit imagery or the generation of allegory and fantasy, these qualities nevertheless make it a suitable model for transmission of meaning, especially when that meaning must "cross over" from one system to another—from affect to movement, for instance, or from one person's idiosyncratic experience to another's. The analogy here is to such synesthetic phenomena as the evoking of visual and kinesthetic imagery in the course of listening to music. I am suggesting that the synesthetic interface of affective and cognitive experience and of other intersystemic—intrapsychic and interpersonal— communications is in the use of metaphor and analogy. The favored vehicle of nonverbal communication, as well as of much verbal communication, is the metaphor.

I may speak now of the metaphor of subliminal or of manifest body movement, including vocalization—of action as metaphor, in fact, of a kind of enactment. Arlow, for example (1969), has written of "motor metaphor" in the context of art as communication. Just as the actor's tendentiously refined and distilled speech, movement, and context affect his audience, enabling nuances of meaning to be preconsciously discerned, or read between the lines, so too can the analysand's intonations and consciously imperceptible postural tensions and movements be perceived by the attuned work ego. Such correspondences and congruences are prominent in the psychoanalytic dyad, and it is a matter of definition whether we call them empathic when they are conscious, or when they are preconscious but have shown their effects. Although the fantasies, reveries, and associations that are generated in the analyst in the course of his evenly hovering attention are not usually isomorphic, they do correspond to the patient's processes. Meaning can thus be ascribed, subject always to subsequent clinical verification and validation. The psychoanalytic work ego is enabled to perceive metaphoric, synesthetic correspondences to the patient through observing its own parallel, internal, and internalized processes, to which it is simultaneously attuned.

One clinical vignette will perhaps serve. A patient was speaking of his feelings of deprivation at home. The analyst's attention "wandered" to thoughts of his waiting room, of the various objects of furniture that were owned jointly with his office associate and those that were owned singly. His attention returned to his patient, who was saying that he couldn't understand why he was talking about these matters. The analyst could now, in response to his own wandering out of the consulting room, clarify to the patient that, although he had been preoccupied with what he was not getting at home, he was indirectly communicating to the analyst the timorous yet demanding question, What may I claim here from you? I may add that this exchange occurred in the general context of the patient's oedipal rivalry, of his envy and ambivalent phallic love toward his father.

The analyst did not arrive at this clarification by a straightforward route of cognitive deliberation. That the patient was speaking of events outside the immediate present could have served as a cognitive clue that he was avoiding the analyst and dividing his transference. In fact, the analyst had experienced this part of the session as emotionally charged, labored, and obscure—in a word, as resistant. That the analyst had also left the room in his own reverie suggests a synchronous and corresponding set of subliminal body tensions, tending in a direction literally away from the patient, even though the reverie itself was in some respects parallel to the patient's resistance. It was this parallel removal on the part of the analyst, metaphorically corresponding to the patient's own metaphoric removal, that became the signal enabling him to recognize that the patient was avoiding facing something that he wanted from the transference imago. It would not be accurate to categorize this as a momentary counterresistance. It was a trial identification, an empathizing that involved the imagining of movement away from the patient, followed quickly by a rejoining, and finally by a verbal statement that exemplified in its content, timing, and expression what in fact could be claimed and expected of the analyst.

Freud (1900) early observed that the conditions appropriate for following the fundamental rule were analogous to those for falling asleep. Hypnagogic and hypnopompic experiences are not uncommon in analyses, and their subsequent reintegration and usefulness depend on the durability of the treatment alliance. Via metaphoric correspondence, such data move from the concreteness and ambiguity of the primary process to the synesthesia of the secondary process.[1] Freud wrote in 1925 that he "often had an impression, in the course of experiments in my private circle, that strongly emotionally

---

1. Synesthesia is an ambiguous process that suggests kinship to mechanisms of the primary process. In the present context, however, it is more related to the synthetic functions of the ego and is part of an autonomous secondary process.

coloured recollections can be transferred without much difficulty. If one has the courage to subject to an analytic examination the association of the person to whom the thoughts are supposed to be transferred, correspondences often come to light which would otherwise have remained undiscovered. On the basis of a number of experiences I am inclined to draw the conclusion that thought-transference of this kind comes about particularly easily at the moment at which an idea emerges from the unconscious, or, in theoretical terms, as it passes over from the 'primary process' to the 'secondary process'" (p. 138).[2]

Symbolization is of course one of the manifestations of primary process. In general, the symbol is a more concrete, one-to-one representation, whereas the metaphor is allusive and flexibly suited to transitions from one system to another.

Metaphor, in this sense of serving in the transition from primary to secondary process, may well constitute the analyst's principal "means to catch the drift of the patient's unconscious with his own unconscious" (Freud 1923, p. 239), in accordance with the classical recommendation as to the analyst's mode of listening. Such a vehicle — it is no more; it is not a motive force and has no intention of its own — thereby assists in the reintegration of temporary and partially regressed states of consciousness during the middle phases of analysis. These are states wherein critical judgment is relaxed, affect and cognition tend to merge, and ambiguity and a tolerance for it tend to increase. Pertinent to my references to the "patternings of movement with articulated speech" is the fact that at such times thoughts and feelings may be represented by bodily sensations (see Rubinfine 1973, p. 406). I emphasize that these states are usually transitory and brief, though of course they may be prolonged. They are also moments of separation, for the treatment alliance is mitigated or in temporary suspension, sometimes to the extent that object relations are barely retained. Greenson has pointed out that

2. In terms of the history of ideas, it is of interest that Freud's few comments about the fundamentally important subject of empathy are to be found mostly in papers dealing with "the occult" (see the *Standard Edition*, 18: 176, for a list of these writings). He dealt with these esoteric and, for those times, scientifically untouchable topics of telepathy and thought transference with characteristic tact, acumen, and startling insight. Empathy is now a respectable topic of investigation, yet is often approached in gingerly fashion.

such conditions are favorable to the development of empathic processes (1960). Empathy is thus an integrative experience, not only, by definition, involving two people, but also within one person who actively experiences it—for it brings together otherwise disparate and subliminal items of perception into a coherent organization. Its usefulness in psychoanalysis depends heavily on the synthetic functions of the analyst's (work) ego. The integration or new configuration begins with the perception of metaphoric correspondences.

Metaphoric correspondence is a function of the relationship of the persons thus engaged. It is the crystallization of a transitional process, partly self, partly not-self; but in the empathic moment such distinction is irrelevant, bringing to mind Winnicott's comments (1951) concerning transitional objects and phenomena. I suggest that these metaphoric correspondences are transitional uses of linguistic and paralinguistic processes, in Winnicott's sense of "transitional phenomena" as parts of the self relating inner and outer reality, bridging the familiar and the unfamiliar, and stemming from a period of separation-individuation from the mother (see also Greenacre 1969). In the unconscious nothing is destroyed; and reality orientation is a never-ending task. For these reasons, experiences of blurring and reintegration of self may occur during some of the deeper, but still temporary and partial states of transference regression and altered consciousness. Trial identifications or introjections also occur on the analysand's side of the dyad and may contribute to some of the mutative effects of the psychoanalytic process. But this is incidental to our main line of inquiry (see chapters 4, 6, and 7).

SUMMARY

Empathic processes in the analyst are the result of monitoring by the work ego, under the conditions of evenly hovering attention, of the configurational organizations composed of the patient's free associations and of his observable and subliminal action patterns. The analyst is selectively responsive to this interactional synchrony as it has acquired meaning in the course of individual development as well as in the development of the treatment alliance and the transference. Metaphoric correspondences furnish the synesthetic, intersystemic interfaces in the transition from primary to secondary process, and in interpersonal communication. Meaning is expressed or carried in the form of metaphoric correspondences between the interacting, configurational organizations of the two members of the psychoanalytic dyad.

REFERENCES

Arlow, J. (1969). Motor behavior as nonverbal communication. *Journal of the American Psychoanalytic Association* 17: 955–967.

Beres, D., and Arlow, J. (1974). Fantasy and identification in empathy. *Psychoanalytic Quarterly* 43: 26–50.

Birdwhistell, R. L. (1970). *Kinesics and Context.* Philadelphia: University of Pennsylvania Press.

Condon, W. S., and Sander, L. W. (1974). Neonate movement is synchronized with adult speech: interactional participation and language acquisition. *Science* 183: 99–101.

Deutsch, F. (1952). Analytic posturology. *Psychoanalytic Quarterly* 21: 196–214.

Fliess, R. (1942). The metapsychology of the analyst. *Psychoanalytic Quarterly* 11: 211–227.

Freud, S. (1900). The interpretation of dreams. *Standard Edition* 4/5.

_____(1915). Observations on transference-love (further recommendations on the technique of psycho-analysis III). *Standard Edition* 12: 157–171.

_____(1923). Two encyclopaedia articles: (A) Psychoanalysis. *Standard Edition* 18: 235–254.

_____(1925). Some additional notes on dream-interpretation as a whole. (C) The occult significance of dreams. *Standard Edition* 19: 135–138.

Greenacre, P. (1969). The fetish and the transitional object. *Emotional Growth,* vol. 1. New York: International Universities Press, 1971.

Greenson, R. (1960). Empathy and its vicissitudes. *International Journal of Psycho-Analysis* 41: 418–424.

Kanzer, M. (1961). Verbal and nonverbal aspects of free association. *Psychoanalytic Quarterly* 30: 327–350.

Ogden, C. K., and Richards, I. A. (1923). *The Meaning of Meaning.* New York: Harcourt, Brace, 1953.

Rubinfine, D. (1973). Notes toward a theory of consciousness. *International Journal of Psychoanalytic Psychotherapy* 2: 391–410.

Winnicott, D. W. (1951). Transitional objects and transitional phenomena. *Collected Papers.* New York: Basic Books, 1958.

Chapter 6

Empathy:
A Summarizing Statement

Efforts to comprehend how one understands other persons led to the concept embodied by Lipps, at about the turn of the century, in the German term, *Einfuehlung,* translated by Titchener as *empathy* and meaning, "feeling into." As the word was originally used in psychology, motor mimicry and inference by means of the subjective experience of kinesthesis were the empathic paths of understanding other personalities. The term has sprouted in meaning, so that now the distinctions, from imitation and identification, from clinical analogy, inference, and judgment, and from projective identification, countertransference, and intuition, suggest the complexities that confront rigorous definition. Precision in the use of the term *empathy* is threatened by the broadened usage of the term *counter-transference.* The latter concept, extended by many psychoanalysts to include all the feelings experienced toward the patient, is now offered as the basis for empathy and understanding. Blurred meanings have resulted for both words.

Nevertheless, the concept of empathy has great operational usefulness in clinical psychoanalysis, principally in terms of the applicability of Freud's description of "evenly suspended attention." This is the analyst's appropriate technique for listening to his patient, and Freud in 1923 was explicit in recommending that the analyst "surrender himself to his own unconscious mental activity . . . and by these means . . . catch the drift of the patient's unconscious with his own unconscious" (p. 239). The statement also tells us that, empathically, one maintains one's own individuality but shares in or resonates to the feelings of the other.

Empathy is not the sole and direct path to understanding the patient nor is it a sanction for imparting that understanding to the patient. The analyst's conscious and preconscious cognitive processes are meanwhile engaged in a continuing system of monitoring, evaluating, and reviewing; "empathic and cognitive sources of information are seen as facets of an essentially unitary experience". (Poland 1974, p. 295).

Empathy is not confined to the psychoanalytic situation, but in that situation it is a perceptual mode available to both participants. It has been studied by psychoanalysts almost solely as a means of perceiving aspects of the patient. Its understanding requires a comprehension of the psychology of the analyst, of the analyst-at-work, variously referred to as the psychoanalytic work ego, the analyzing ego, or the analyzing instrument (see chapter 7). Fliess (1942), discussing the "work ego," defined empathy as "trial identification"; Greenson (1960) relies on the formation in the analyst of a "working model of the patient," through which he listens, thus deemphasizing all that is himself.

It is part of the analyst's function of being openly receptive to the patient's psychic processes that he must experience the various affects that are induced, externalized, or projected in him. These are ways of "knowing" the patient, but they are not empathic. The subjective experience of empathy is of a more direct, seemingly nonmediated knowing, presently to be described more fully, and it requires an openness or permeability on the part of the knower that is more active than the passivity or relative inertness of being the object of a projection, externalization, or even an induced affect. Empathy involves the psychology of two persons. There must be an active object-relatedness, one that entails a caring intention to maintain and support (see chapter 2). One empathizes with the patient at hand, emotionally and physically, and not at a distance. To refer to empathizing with the patient's family members, or with the patient whom a student in supervision is describing, is to warp the concept and render it inexact. One empathizes in the presence of the supervisee or the patient and employs clinical judgment and imagination concerning the absent one.

At the same time that there is object-relatedness, there is also momentarily and alternately the regressive experience of the trial identification. By "alternately" I refer to the fact that identification is a regressive form of object-relatedness, one that in the present context is an adaptive reaction to loss. It is a substitutive reaction that represents, for the empathizer, an attempt to restore lost affective contact and communication. Empathy is connected with depressive aspects of the empathizer's response to loss. Greenson (1960) can therefore point out that the analyst resorts to empathy when "more sophisticated means of contact have failed and when one *wants* to regain contact with a lost object" (p. 423). The adaptive regression is experienced in parallel with the patient's regression, and the analyst's work ego utilizes his own regression and associated affects as a signal for returning to its function of observing and monitoring the patient's processes. Mastered regression, that is to say, is in the service of the work ego's function of empathizing (see chapter 2). The analyst through his work ego has learned to experience his own internal and internalized processes as a way of supplementing his knowledge of the patient. This does not mitigate the principles of evenly hovering attention, sympathetic detachment, and the suspension of conscious effort to remember, to cure, and to understand. These functions, as part of the autonomous functioning of the adequately trained and experienced work ego, are fundamental to the effective use of empathy.

It has been noted by some observers that the success or failure of the empathic venture depends not only on the analyst but also on the willingness or unwillingness of the patient to be understood. Probably this resistance or openness is itself empathized by the sensitive analyst, for this issue goes beyond ordinary social tactfulness. Moreover, since the empathic experience relies upon parallel regression and since regression and its associated affects may be apprehended by patient and/or analyst as either pleasurable or painful, the phenomenon may be accordingly facilitated or inhibited.

Empathic skills vary widely in the analytic as well as the general population. Miscarriages of empathy are the consequences of regression's no longer being in the service of the work ego and of the patient-member of the analytic dyad. The signal function has failed; autonomy from conflict has been superseded by regressive counter-responses.

It is of course essential that the analyst know whether his empathic perception is accurate. In this matter, the cognitive, evaluative, judgmental functions of the autonomous work ego are paramount. The analyst, that is, must preconsciously or consciously associate to his empathic perceptions in the context of his overall comprehension of the patient and of his general clinical and life experience. He may or may not intervene verbally at this time. If he sees fit to do so, the patient's response is the answer to the question of the accuracy of his empathy, as is the case with interpretations in general. If the patient, as frequently happens, anticipates his intervention and states it aloud, it is eloquent confirmation.

The empathic perception carries with it a sense of certainty that can be misleading, for it must be distinguished from a compelling but false sense of sureness that is often connected with countertransference reactions. Empathy and critical self-observation must be continually complementing each other. In any case, it is not desirable to communicate either the empathic perception or an interpretation directly arising from it without taking into account the usual cautionary principles having to do with interpretation in general.

It is true, however, that when the empathic perception is confirmed by the overall evaluation that the experienced psychoanalytic work ego carries as a kind of template, or guide to the patterning of the work, one has presumptive evidence of the accuracy of the perception. This will serve to explain the manner in which the analyst can, out of several possibilities for intervention at a given moment, select the one that is operationally valid.

The quality of mutuality accompanies the empathic experience; in view of the controlled, temporary, parallel regression in the service of work ego and patient — in order "to catch the drift of the patient's unconscious" (Freud 1923) — it seems reasonable to conceptualize this experience as one of momentary intrapsychic fusion of self-image and object-image (see chapter 1). In this connection, Freud (1925) considered that "thought-transference" of "strongly emotionally coloured recollections" could be readily accomplished. He concluded that this "comes about particularly easily at the moment at which an idea emerges from the unconscious, or, in theoretical terms, as it passes from the 'primary process' to the 'secondary process'" (p. 138).

Early acculturation is based on earliest nurturing conditions — e.g., the manner in which the infant or child experiences and learns, within the parent-child dyad, a bilateral, active, and passive influencing of each other in order to gain mutual satisfaction. In the sense of promoting the development of the other, nurturance requires that there be immersion in the needs of the other, the responses of each more or less reflecting the needs of the other. In this way an essential to survival, the more or less accurate empathic knowing of one's fellows, is learned. One is led to the assumption that this is based upon an evolutionary, biologically innate process, which becomes modified, enhanced, or inhibited in the course of individual development. For instance, there is evidence that some regressive emotional changes in pregnancy serve to prepare the mother for participation in these developments (Bibring 1959).

The primary data in the psychoanalytic situation for the functioning of empathic processes include all verbal and nonverbal activities with which analysts are accustomed to work. These include free associations and other verbalizations, vocal intonations and bodily movements, both overt and subliminal, and silences. Microanalyses of sound films of human communication reveal that measurable units of the listener's body motion are in synchrony with his interactor's speech. These interactional synchronies are usually subliminal (Birdwhistell 1970).

We may therefore legitimately speak of empathic communication; but we are left with the question as to how the transmitted signals of subliminal and overt vocal intonations and body motion, including the effects of the endocrine and autonomic nervous systems, become meaningful to the perceiving analyst. An as yet incomplete theory lies at hand, utilizing the established capacity of the human being to employ symbolization (see chapter 12). In brief, this view proposes that the synesthetic interface of affective and cognitive experience and of other intersystemic communications — intrapsychic and interpersonal — is in the use of preconscious metaphor and analogy. This refers to interactional synchronies as metaphor, as a kind of enactment, having its own syntax and idiom, to which the analyst becomes more accurately attuned in the course of his work with a patient. Such metaphoric correspondences are crystallizations of transitional processes (Winnicott 1951; see chapter 3), bridging self and not-self, and stemming from the period of individuation-separation from the mother-child dyad. This is an "intermediate area of experiencing" (Winnicott 1951) that is retained in varying degrees in imaginative living and in creative scientific and artistic work.

REFERENCES

Bibring, G. (1959). Some considerations of the psychological processes in pregnancy. *Psychoanalytic Study of the Child* 14: 113–121.

Birdwhistell, R. L. (1970). *Kinesics and Context.* Philadelphia: University of Pennsylvania Press.

Fliess, R. (1942). The metapsychology of the analyst. *Psychoanalytic Quarterly* 11: 211–227.

Freud, S. (1923). Two encyclopaedia articles. (A) Psycho-Analysis. *Standard Edition* 18: 235–254.

———(1925). Some additional notes on dream-interpretation as a whole. (C) The occult significance of dreams. *Standard Edition* 19: 135–138.

Greenson, R. (1960). Empathy and its vicissitudes. *International Journal of Psycho-Analysis* 41: 418–424.

Poland, W. S. (1974). On empathy in analytic practice. *Journal of the Philadelphia Association for Psychoanalysis* 1: 284–297.

Winnicott, D. W. (1951). Transitional objects and transitional phenomena. In *Collected Papers.* New York: Basic Books, 1958.

Chapter 7

The Psychoanalytic Work Ego

Work ego is a term proposed to denote the special attributes of the analyst-at-work—"the temporarily built-up person who [functions] under the circumstances and for the period of his work" (Fliess 1942, p. 225). The work ego, that is to say, is defined by its functions. In the experienced analyst, these have evolved into a relatively stable autonomy that varies from person to person in accordance with general stability of organization and that is responsive to the vicissitudes of the psychoanalytic situation. It is not to be confused with any aspects of role taking. It does imply a personality that manifests the special traits, talents, and motivations that enter into the optimal selection of an individual for training in psychoanalysis. The specialized training is intended to enhance and refine these qualities.

The concept offers a convenient, heuristic, and operational category for the study of the functioning analyst—his psychology, his development and motivations, his work specifications, and the facilitation or the impairment of the autonomy of his functions, that is to say, his regression into eccentric or countertransferential states. Intrapsychic and interpersonal processes are involved, and a unified model of these work ego functions has been set forth (see chapter 2). Work ego is similar to but not identical in meaning with Isakower's "analyzing instrument" (unpublished manuscript cited by Malcove 1975).

There is also considerable evidence that the analyzing functions of the patient—his own observing, analyzing ego—are structured gradually and throughout the psychoanalytic process by means of internalization of certain functions of the work ego (Olinick 1975).

The functions by which the work ego is defined will be reviewed under several overlapping and interacting categories. It must be reemphasized that these actions are relatively autonomous from drive and conflict and that an openly communicating network of functions enters into them. Consistent with current theories of psychic structuring, they are viewed as hierarchically but flexibly organized, with cognitive-affective feedbacks, and with certain functions having superordinate positions. Thus, in chapter 2 the work ego was referred to as drawing sustenance from the treatment alliance, to the degree that this dyadic function is working effectively, and especially from the analyst's own superego–ego-ideal systems, as these latter have become modified through special training and psychoanalytic working through into adaptive, scientific, therapeutic, and humanistic overviews.

The important "diatrophic function" refers to the "caring intention to maintain and support" (see chapter 2). This is a superordinate function and is part of the open network of intercommunicating functions, or feedback loops. As such, it is closely monitored by the superego–ego-ideal systems. It has often been considered to be a feminine, nurturing function and thereby associated with empathy and intuition. It has been a source of unnecessary embarrassment in some quarters because of the need to resolve the paradox of this "caring" function's coexisting with an attitude of objectivity and detachment. It frequently finds its historical roots in identification with, and rescue fantasies involving, a depressive, narcissistic mother-imago (see chapter 1). Needless to say, such a function has developed over a considerable psychological distance from its genetic roots. And in accordance with the principle of multiple function there are many motivational sources for entering into the practice of psychoanalysis.

An additional set of superordinate functions is subsumed under "tact," recently discussed extensively by Poland (1974) as a mode of activity in the psychoanalytic situation, "by virtue of its integrative nature, binding both narcissism and aggression through underlying maintenance of object relatedness and acceptance. It refers to a mode of utilization of knowledge gained both by cognitive understanding and by empathy; it is directly related to the timing and dosage of interpretations" (p. 161).

Calef and Weinshel (in press) refer to a superordinate function that they designate as the "conscience" or "keeper of the analytic process," referring to the analyst's taking the responsibility of main-taining the work and the analytic process in the face of resistances that "inevitably arise (in himself as well as in his analysand) . . ." They conceptualize three components of the analyst-at-work:

1. "an observing, listening set of functions" that operates concor-dantly with certain hypotheses and with the awareness of the effects that these hypotheses might exert;

2. an "integrative set of functions" that permits "free play be-tween primary and secondary process" without loss of control and that leads to certain conclusions or assessments; and

3. a "translating set of functions" that permits the transmission of meaning to the patient in clarifying or interpreting form.

In chapter 2 the work ego has been studied with special reference to how an interpretation or clarification arises in the psychology of the two individuals who are in transaction:

1. The analytic pact was paradigmatically described by Freud as consisting of candor from the patient and strict discretion from the analyst (1937, p. 174). The pact includes additional factors, consti-tuting the baseline functions of the work ego. The fundamental rule for the patient is matched for the analyst by observing, experiencing, and evaluating in the setting of evenly suspended attention; and fur-ther, by reliability, durability, sympathetic interest and non-possessiveness, while he is ensuring through the abstinence principle his unavailability for gratification of the patient's transference wishes.

2. The work ego within the treatment alliance momentarily and partially regresses with and observes the patient and itself, thus enabling a paralleling of processes. The availability of the analyst for such regression in the service of both work ego and patient distin-guishes psychoanalysis from other healing, service professions. The responsiveness of the work ego to the vicissitudes of the processes within the patient constitutes a paramount and essential source of the primary data of the psychoanalysis. This action permits em-pathic perception, defined as trial identification (see chapter 2). The paradox results that the analyst, through self-observation of a special kind, learns to know his patient more completely by experiencing his own internal and internalized processes.

3. The regression referred to above is partial, temporary, and controlled; it is in the service of the work ego's functions; the work ego in turn responds to its regression and the associated affects as a

signal for reintegration to the function of observing, experiencing, and evaluating. This has been preparation for interpreting or clarifying, utilizing the data that are registered during the trial regression and identification that we refer to as empathy.

4. A continuing, overlapping set of operations is involved in the scanning and collating of the primary data so obtained, as well as in the integrated cognitive-affective functions of attending to the patient's free associations, and of evaluating, coordinating, and integrating data from all sources into a comprehensive, meaningful configuration of patternings. The work ego has been prepared for these functions by special clinical and theoretical training and experience and, not least, by general life experiences and sublimated motivations. For its integrated functioning, there must be finely attuned systems of self-observation that are set into action by affect-signals and feedbacks of great complexity. While they operate with minimal or no conscious attention, a careful self-observer may retrospectively and introspectively become aware of or adduce these internal processes. The energy for all of this unusual activity can come only from the deinstinctualization of primitive rescue fantasies, urges to mastery, scopophilia, and other derivatives of oedipal and preoedipal conflicts that enter into the motivations for becoming an analyst.

5. Work ego functions must be free of conflict; also some of these functions must operate largely but not entirely in a state of altered consciousness that has been analogized with a quasi-dream state (references cited in chapter 3). Calef and Weinshel propose that during this altered state of consciousness there has been a temporary decathecting of the analyst's, or work ego's, resistances, and that the withdrawn cathexes are put into the service of observing, evaluating, judging, and critical functions.

6. While the work ego dips into regression, as described, it must be reiterated that in what is communicated to the patient and in the preparation for that communication, the work ego ultimately relies upon secondary process. The timing of interpretations and other interventions, including appropriate questioning (chapter 8) and the judgments that enter into the work ego's many decisions, involve the integration and synthesis of empathic and cognitive processes with the aim of problem solving. The verbal intervention of the analyst represents a final common pathway of the work ego in its multiple functions. In this, to repeat, the work ego is sustained by the treatment

alliance and by its own superego–ego-ideal systems. Ideally the processes and functions in both members of the analytic dyad complement and augment each other in the service of the overall analytic process. Interpretations not only enhance the alliance by initiating or reinforcing the recognition and working through of transference and resistance but also serve to reintegrate the work ego itself by means of internal and external feedback loops.

REFERENCES

Calef, V., and Weinshel, E. M. (in press). The analyst as the conscience of the analysis.

Fliess, R. (1942). The metapsychology of the analyst. *Psychoanalytic Quarterly* 211–227.

Freud, S. (1937). Analysis terminable and interminable. *Standard Edition* 23: 216–253.

Malcove, L. (1975). The analytic situation: toward a view of the supervisory experience. *Journal of the Philadelphia Association for Psychoanalysis* 2: 1–14.

Olinick, S. L. (1975). Position statement: panel on the fundamentals of psychic change in clinical practice. *The International Psycho-Analytical Association Newsletter* 7: 26–28.

Poland, W. S. (1974). On empathy in analytic practice. *Journal of the Philadelphia Association for Psychoanalysis* 1: 284–297.

_____(1975). Tact as a psychoanalytic function. *The International Journal of Psycho-Analysis* 56: 155–162.

Part II

THERAPEUTIC PARADOX

Chapter 8

The Use of Questioning

INTRODUCTION

The first of these two chapters on the psychology of the question considers the effects of a basic analytic instrument, the question, on the transference and the treatment alliance. It offers operational criteria for the use of the question and for testing the effects of that use. The question carries its dangers, both to the effective functioning of the analyst's work ego and to the autonomy of the patient and his analyzing functions, and these issues are discussed in both chapters.

Understanding the effects of questioning on the treatment alliance and the transference was greatly assisted by Eissler's publication (1953) of his "The Effect of the Structure of the Ego on Psychoanalytic Technique." In this influential paper he presented his discerning formulation of parameters, or deviations from the basic model of technique, and their applications in practice. The use of such parameters was based on the relative presence of ego modifications; this was strictly defined and discussed, and the paper moreover delineated a baseline of technique from which to evaluate the analyst's interventions and their potential effects. Misapplied this could result in the analyst's becoming obsessively concerned with his least word or gesture—a not uncommon affliction among students in training. Misunderstood it could lead to the inaccurate criticism that the analyst is a Procrustes who fits the patient to his rigid rules, stretching or truncating him to conform to the couch. Especially at the time that this chapter was first published, when psychotherapy or even "wild" analysis often passed for psychoanalysis, it was of great advantage to have these guidelines. Furthermore, it furnished a set of operational distinctions that had to be made in selecting patients for different modalities of psychotherapy and for psychoanalysis.

Eissler considered questions to be part of the basic model technique, a view from which I depart in this chapter. He had proposed that questions were an integral part of the basic model because no analysis had ever been conducted without their use. That is, in his view, individual questions and systematic inquiry are not deviations from the basic model *unless* they have been employed to such degree and/or at such junctures as to render it not possible by means of interpretation to eliminate their effects upon the transference—and, I may add, upon the development of the treatment alliance. Because I was exploring the potential pathology of the question, I came to regard this essential instrument in terms of its more drastic and undesirable results. For the question is a potent force and must be used in treatment with full awareness of its potential. I have the impression that it is more frequently and casually misused than are other forms of verbal intervention and that this is especially so in working with those patients who are most vulnerable to its less desirable effects. Nowadays we are clearer as to the countertransferential influences of many borderline, regressive patients (Kohut 1971, Kernberg 1975, 1976). These potent influences on the analyst may lead to his ill-considered misuse or overuse of a linguistic device that is intrinsically aggressive, intrusive, and uniquely defensive. I discuss this further in the following chapter and below.

Some of the case vignettes in both chapters are illustrative of the question having become a parameter, leaving open the issue as to whether the effects of this parameter on transference and treatment alliance could then be reduced or abolished. The clinical vignette offered in chapter 9 is of a patient for whom psychoanalysis was not initially suitable. In order to illustrate the usage of systematic inquiry, I presented a dramatic though not a classically psychoanalytic instance. A patient for whom the standard model technique of analysis was suitable would probably not have required so extensive an intervention as a systematic inquiry; interpretations of the resistance would probably have sufficed. On the other hand, as I hope the chapter makes clear, systematic inquiry may be required to clarify the resistance, in this way assisting the development of a treatment alliance.

I define *systematic inquiry* as a line of questioning that functions as an adjunct to the psychoanalytic process. In this the analyst is guided by an informed and understanding respect for the patient's autonomy. So far as is possible, he directs his questions so that they bear in a congruent way on what the patient himself is concerned with at that time.

Characteristically a systematic inquiry is indicated in the psychoanalytic psychotherapy of a resistant patient who has proven not amenable to the usual interventions that are intended to clarify and to interpret. Such patients usually have borderline or narcissistic personality disorders, but the situation more accurately delimits itself to the fact that the patient's orientation is passively aggressive.

Early in such work the therapist must decide whether a careful waiting game with parsimonious utterances will result only in the timeless continuance of the pathological organization, or whether it is preferable to intervene with a line of inquiry that, directed toward the resistance, explicitly refers to its current manifestations during sessions as well as in the patient's intercurrent living experiences. The aim then is to assist the patient to gain more perspective and objectivity as to his or her mode of functioning — to enhance and augment the development of that portion of the observing ego that is essential to the therapeutic work and that must be present in some degree for the patient to have been acceptable for this form of treatment. (See chapter 4; clinical vignettes will be found also in that chapter to illustrate these points.)

Care must be exercised that the inquiry not regress or deteriorate into a cross-examination of a reluctant or hostile witness. It should not be a struggle for dominance, but rather an attempt over time to demonstrate to the patient that, passively, dependently, or otherwise, he is being dominative and obstructive and that such behavior is based upon his defenses against anachronistic affects and impulses. The immediate aim is to assist in the development of a treatment alliance (see chapter 4). This is a first step toward sustaining a transference that remains within manageable limits. The patient will then be more capable of tolerating without disruption of the work the necessary transference regression and the interpretation of the transference neurosis. This entails reality testing —

making essential distinctions between fantasy and reality — so that it is gradually recognized that the abstinence rule is not directed toward inflicting pain and deprivation. Such distinctions are of course a necessary dimension of living and this necessity does not constitute an assault upon the narcissistic integrity of value systems and upon personal intactness.

A psychoanalytic article written more than two decades ago is inevitably going to show signs of age; but the old aphorism that it takes an idea about twenty years to reach meaningful acceptance seems also to apply. I find it interesting that some current pre-occupations in analysis and analytic psychotherapy are foreshadowed in this paper — as well as in others of the same period: the ideas were even then in the wings, awaiting their time. For instance, I was concerned here with the development of the so-called therapeutic relationship and the manner in which the use of questions might favorably or adversely affect this important factor in treatment. At that time what we now call treatment alliance, therapeutic alliance, or working alliance was considered to be primarily transferential, although many analysts were already expounding the reality factors that coexisted. I have more recently reviewed and explored some current issues in the matter of treatment alliance (chapter 4).

Another group of foreshadowed ideas has to do with the effects upon the analyst of the patient's regressive dynamics — effects that include his countertransference, in the strict, classic sense of that term, but also include effects that cannot legitimately be called countertransferential since they are impingements on what I may call, with apology, the normal psychology of the analyst. These are matters that have been and are currently under study (see Kohut 1971, Kernberg 1975, 1976), but it is of historical interest that these were until relatively recently "closet themes," rarely openly discussed.

The psychology of the question is not yet a finished chapter. Psycholinguistic problems of fascinating complexity are still present for study — for instance, the correlation of personality structure with the syntactic structure of the language favored by that person (see Eissler 1965). For example, hyperbole or rhetorical exaggeration for the sake of effect is commonly associated with hysterical personalities.

For a more pertinent example, there is the common use of questions by patients as veiled denials and expressions of what is being negated — the subject matter of the second of these chapters. A young woman, rather subtly and hysterically manipulative, would ask questions that her analyst recognized to be denials of what she, in a sense, knew to be the case with herself. At other times, a question from the analyst as to what she had in mind about her situation would evoke, "I don't know"—clearly intended to close off associations. It also represented the other side of the coin of her preference for the syntax of question as negation: she feared stating directly what some part of herself preferred not to know. This woman, intelligent, sensitive, married, with four children, was for long periods stubbornly resistant to talking about her mother: "It would be disloyal to her." She often raised the question as to why she kept her bedroom barely furnished, always ending with, "I don't know." Sexual relations in that bedroom were described laconically as seductions of her husband in order to terminate bitter arguments. This left her feeling more powerful than he, righteously indignant, and increasingly puzzled about this continuing motif of victimizing. She was not orgasmic at this time and was beset with guilt feelings, associated with feelings of envy. One of the first stable signs of a reliably collaborative observing ego came when she was able to recognize that changing her questions to a declarative statement resulted in an insightful self-interpretation. This both represented and contributed to constructive channelizing of her aggression, a gradual elimination of negation and denial, a mitigation of the ambivalent identification with her mother, and a moderating of her contempt, fear, and envy of men.

The correlation between negation and personality structure was adumbrated by Freud in his paper on "Negation" (1925). Eissler (1965), in his discussion of negation, points out that a sentence "may also contain a structural relation that is an outgrowth of the psychic apparatus. . . . The syntactic structure is correlated . . . with a limited area of personality structure" (p. 150). In the second of these two chapters I demonstrate that the question is a "higher" form of negation, superordinate to negation; that it serves a function of the questioner beyond the seeking of an answer; and that indeed the questioner may know and negate the answer he seeks. These are factors of basic importance to the analyst who uses the instrument of questioning. When questions are misapplied they have an adverse effect upon transference and alliance; when not due to ignorance this will occur in the service of regressive, eccentric, countertransferential actions by the analyst. The use or misuse of the question in these instances does in fact correlate with a "limited area of personality structure." I refer here to a set of factors that perhaps are potential in all who are motivated to conduct psychoanalysis or psychoanalytic psychotherapy. These are usually overlaid or subordinately organized by means of sublimatory or aim-inhibited functions that have become secondarily autonomous. For further discussion of this hypothesis and these factors, see chapter 1, chapter 2, and chapter 10 (postscript).

It is another of the numerous paradoxes that confront our work that so innocuous a matter as the structure of a sentence should have such far-reaching implications.

***

Of the technical interventions available to the psychoanalyst, perhaps none has been more taken for granted and less subjected to careful scrutiny than has questioning. It has been pointed out that nevertheless, as a therapeutic tool it is basic and indispensable, on a par with interpretation, though essentially different from interpretation (Eissler 1953).

In part, this incurious attitude may be due to the difficulties inherent in conceptualizing so commonplace a mode of communication: the commonplace blends as a figure into its own ground. In part, too, one may speculate whether there is not a general mistrust of a technique potentially so "active" as to call forth associations of cross-examination and the doctor game of children. The act of questioning is predicated on a certain reluctance or passivity on the part of the person questioned, else the information would have been volunteered. It may also, however, be predicated on the impatience and curiosity of the questioner. We should therefore expect to find in the psychology of questioning as a psychoanalytic technique much in common with the technique of managing the resistance and much that is related to the problem of countertransference.

Freud (1912, 1937) has pointed out the analyst's basic functions: to listen, to reconstruct, and to interpret. It is accepted that there are adjuncts to these functions, just as the prone position, the frequency of visits, and the exclusion of distracting stimuli are adjunctive and ancillary to the patient's efforts in the direction of free associations. The free associations are psychically determined as well as made

possible by the psychoanalytic situation; the analyst's unique function of free-floating attention is likewise psychically determined,
with the difference that its content is induced by the patient's productions. This function may be assisted by the judicious use of questions.

I refer not to those questions put to himself as a part of the synthesizing function of his own ego, but to those called forth by productions of the patient that show discrepancies, misinformation, and
omissions. These phenomena may represent resistances, but also, or
instead, they not infrequently represent the unwitting need on the
part of the patient for a guideline, for an orienting pattern. It
becomes then a matter of the utmost tact to present to the patient,
not specific directions or a blueprint of psychodynamics, but just so
much of a collaborator's nudge as will assist the patient to do the
work he requires of himself.

A simple example is the quizzically toned repeating of a word or
phrase—a slip, let us say—uttered by the patient and unnoticed
by him.

It may be objected that the same effect will be obtained by the use
of direct statement. To be sure, there are frequent indications for
employing blunt, matter-of-fact direct statements. The hazards of
the latter lie in the implications of definitiveness and autocracy; the
same content expressed as question is open ended and suggests the
possibility of joint exploratory effort. In either case, it must be
voiced with tact and consideration.

It is with the larger scope of systematic inquiry that we are chiefly
concerned in this study. Such questioning is most readily defined by
reference to the initial phases of history taking, but it surpasses—as
indeed history taking should—the matter solely of eliciting information. Any pertinent question has the effect of momentarily strength-
ening or weakening a Gestalt. Since it is voiced as a question and not
as a declarative statement, an element of uncertainty remains,
awaiting clarification by the questionee. A situation is tentatively
defined in a manner that invites a collaborative response. The ideal
response of the analysand can then be classically compared with that
"therapeutic splitting of the ego" into an observing and an experiencing part, resulting from the positive transference and transitory
identifications with the analyst (Sterba 1934). It is this division that
allows for the effectiveness of interpretations. In the instances of
questioning herein considered, it will be understood that inquiry
is frequently made in the absence or presence of only the most

ephemeral, positive transference. But the "observing ego" is nevertheless encouraged and utilized.

We may outline the early months of treatment of a young lady, uncertain as to her psychosexual role, whose efforts in analysis were at first devoted to a thoughtful exposition of her admiration and affection for her mother and her disappointment in and contempt for her father. Intellectually somewhat arrogant, though socially more than a little shy, it was necessary for her to impress the analyst, no less than herself, with her perceptivity concerning her developmental history. But it was an effort that tended inevitably toward a sense of failure in the task, because of basic misconceptions. What might have become for her a painfully interminable floundering was avoided by the analyst's initiating a directed inquiry into her own examples of the three-way relationship with her parents. As a result of specific, fact-evoking questions, she arrived at a different and more nearly valid historical orientation: she had identified herself with her aggressor-mother, who had successfully interposed herself between the child and her father. Father was inaccessible, disappointing, and contemptible only as mother made him appear so. Mother was neither admirably self-sufficient nor all-loving but was a bitterly frustrated person, seeking gratification of her ambitions through her child and against her husband.

In the course of this inquiry, the patient also learned something of the collaborative effort required in psychoanalysis, of the analyst's dedicated but detached interest, and of her own ability to face hitherto repressed anxieties. The inquiry assisted the integrative capacity of her own ego. This integration could have been accomplished in no other way than by painstakingly asking questions that were inspired by the patient day after day, as she presented her conscious and unconscious assumptions about herself, her past, and her relationships.

Such interventions by the analyst will be more frequent in the early phase of treatment; their effective use at this time assists in clarifying the task to be accomplished.

Instances of systematic inquiry are in every practitioner's experience. They may be regarded, following K. R. Eissler's useful formulation (1953), as parameters, or deviations from the basic model of technique wherein interpretation is the sole tool employed by the analyst. An example of a parameter is the analyst's advice or command to a phobic patient, at a suitable time in treatment, that he deliberately expose himself to the situation he dreads. Their use is warranted if they fulfill certain conditions:

(1) A parameter must be introduced only when it is proved that the basic model technique does not suffice;
(2) the parameter must never transgress the unavoidable minimum;
(3) a parameter is to be used only when it finally leads to its self-elimination; . . .
(4) The effect of the parameter on the transference relationship must never be such that it cannot be abolished by interpretation. [pp. 111, 113]

These conditions restate basic principles: the therapist must guard against inducing artifacts by unduly influencing the patient through his interventions.

I would stress the third and fourth propositions. A deviant technical intervention, such as a question, will not be self-eliminating when it has so complemented the transference relationship that the effect cannot be abolished by interpretation and working through. While a single question or statement may have this adverse effect, ordinarily it is easier to correct its influence on the analytic course. The more extensive form of questioning exemplified in the case cited above is more apt to be misused and may become an intrusion by the analyst into the patient's freedom of choice.[1]

This latter eventuality is most often a result of countertransference and/or unresolved anxiety in the analyst. A deviation from the basic model of technique, when it does not lead to its own self-elimination — that is, when the situation is not clarified for progressive movement — may result in enhanced transference resistance, as Ferenczi (1950) pointed out occurred with "active" techniques, but equally it may point to a scotoma in the therapist. The analyst must explore his own emotional economy *vis à vis* a patient

1. In a forthright statement of the scientific and therapeutic attitude, Freud says, "The rules of analysis are diametrically opposed to the physician's making use of his personality in [such manner as to 'play the part of prophet, saviour, and redeemer to the patient']. . . . after all, analysis does not set out to make pathological reactions impossible, but to give the patient's ego *freedom* to decide one way or the other" (Freud 1923, footnote, p. 50).

who seems to require continued resort to questioning, especially when meaningful material is not elicited (Cohen 1952).

For example, the therapist who retains a residual sadomasochistic orientation may have a tendency to employ questioning in an unconscious effort to integrate a nontherapeutic pregenital relationship with the patient. Parenthetically be it said, too, that no active technique will appeal to the passive, masochistic therapist.

It is pertinent to recall that any doctor-patient relationship is involved with regressive trends in the patient, be it a psychoanalytic, medical, or surgical procedure. Passivity is imposed on and accepted by the patient; infantile needs are remobilized, and thwarted or gratified; archaic curiosities and fears are aroused. The patient expects to be explored, verbally and physically. Probings by way of questioning may be resented, feared, and resisted with all the force of repressed anality, but present also are the passive-oral-dependent wishes. The prototype of the medical experience for the patient is the receiving of a pill or hypodermic; it is the person who has not come to terms with his passivity who scorns medication or resists psychoanalysis because of the implications of oral dependency.

Stated differently, one patient will welcome questioning as a form of active guidance, and his dependency may become a potently enhanced factor in the transference and a probable resistance to progress. Another patient, fearful of passivity, will resist questioning with his customary defenses against anxiety; still another, obsessively defensive about activity, will resist the definitive decision required in answering any question.

Ordinarily then questioning is self-eliminating once a congruent answer has been elicited. But its effect may in any case be such as to distort the transference, though not necessarily to the point where its effect cannot be abolished by interpretation and working through. This is a crucial point of differentiation between questioning employed in psychoanalysis and that employed in goal-limited adjustment therapy of the type, for example, described by Felix Deutsch (1949) as "sector therapy" and "associative anamnesis." In the latter technique, analysis of the transference is not a factor; the limited aim is the "activation of a specific psychologic process," ideally one associated with a psychosomatic symptom, by guiding the patient's associations. Questioning in psychoanalysis also makes great use of the analysand's "observing ego," with possible mitigation or aggravation of regressive-dependent potentialities. But attention to the transference forestalls any limitations to the work and dangers to the ego.

We must ask, now, in what clinical instances covered by Eissler's propositions is it therapeutically valid to depart from the basic model of technique into systematic questioning, by what rationale, and to what degree.

1. The *inarticulate borderline neurotic*, whose defenses in analysis are erected against the danger of words as carriers of feelings. Such a person not infrequently misunderstands questioning as permission to or a demand to talk; the hazards lie in the perpetuation of a pattern of conformity or in the triggering of rages or depressions. But also with these people one cannot meet silence with silence and still retain a therapeutic relationship. A prolonged period must therefore be spent in inducing the patient to become familiar with the reality of the therapist as a person who is accepting, permissive, and interested in him (Stern 1945, Fromm-Reichmann 1950). A systematic inquiry designed to elicit information useful to the therapist's understanding can equally be useful to the patient in his reality testing of the therapist. Interpretations and confrontations can best be worded as questions, prefaced by: "Is it possible that . . . ?" Against the fragile but tendentiously formidable defenses one must proceed gently, until a positive working relationship is well established. Questioning should be simply specific and should deal first with such matters as can be readily validated by the patient in his history and current relationships.

2. The patient in an *anxiety state*. The inquiry as an integrating device and, through inquiry, the evincing of interestedness on the part of the analyst, combine to offer a measure of support to a weak ego and to assuage some feelings of aloneness. It should be superfluous to note that, before inquiry is begun, the patient should be allowed latitude of expression (Sharpe 1950), no less here than in other instances of press of affect. Inquiry should be directed, to paraphrase a recommendation made by Freud (1909) concerning obsessions, to bringing the anxiety into temporal relationship with the patient's experiences, to defining the situations wherein anxiety has appeared.

3. The last statement above, as originally made by Freud applies to the inquiry into *obsessional* data.[2]

4. With the *psychotic* generally, and the *schizophrenic* particularly, the deviations from the basic model of technique involve far more than the expedient of direct questioning (Sullivan 1940, Fromm-Reichmann 1950, Eissler 1953). Those persons subject to *manic-depressive* mood swings are among the less talented participants in human relations, and their obtuseness and slowness in the type of self-scrutiny required by the psychoanalytic method make it necessary to resort to direct questioning and specific confrontations as to life experiences, as well as active intervention in other areas of technique.

5. There are many instances of the *interpretation of resistance* that require, for preinterpretive validation, an inquiry into the internal and external circumstances; for example, into the onset of a shift in attitude that made its appearance in a given hour and was not verbalized by the patient at the time, nor perhaps duly noted by the analyst.

We may synthesize our discussion by saying that questioning is to be resorted to only when the following conditions[3] are fulfilled:

1. Opportunity has been given the patient for verbal expression of his associations and affects.

2. The analyst has examined carefully his own state of psychic economy.

3. Resistance has intervened, and interpretation requires preliminary validation.

2. "The wildest and most eccentric obsessional or compulsive ideas can be cleared up if they are investigated deeply enough. The solution is effected by bringing the obsessional ideas into temporal relationship with the patient's experiences, that is to say, by enquiring when a particular obsessional idea made its first appearance and in what external circumstances it is apt to recur" (Freud 1909, p. 186).

3. A brief word may be appropriate here with reference to "rules" in psychoanalytic technique. A singularly sterile course will be run if the analyst rigidly applies rules or checks the current work in progress against any preconceived criteria of acceptability. The prerequisites of psychoanalytic treatment continue to reside in the flexibility and spontaneity of an orderly intuition. As Fenichel (1941) puts it, "What is meant is that, after we have reflected upon it, we should always be able to explain what we are doing, why we interpret, and what we expect each time from our activity" (p. 52).

4. Anxiety has intervened, and the patient requires support and orientation.

5. The character defenses or the ego structure are such that a preparatory period of familiarization, ego support, and reality testing, is necessary.

With these conditions fulfilled, the questioning should result in or lead to an integrative experience that will, allow the analytic work to proceed. We referred earlier to the anticipated similarities between questioning as a psychoanalytic technique and the management of the resistance. We see from the preceding discussion that questioning is used as a mode of assisting the patient to confront himself with facts of which he has until then been unaware. This should not be taken to mean that the questioning is intended to circumvent the resistance; analysis of the resistance proceeds concurrently.

When a question or a systematic inquiry has been effective, it has succeeded in restructuring the field of operations: the patient emerges with a new perspective. This is not necessarily insight in the sense that a conflict has been resolved. Rather, the questioning is preparatory to insight. In so far as this is true, questioning is also preliminary and preparatory to interpretation and subsequent working through.

The last statement must be tempered with the recognition that it refers to polarities that approach each other centrally. Systematic inquiry and interpretation both release potential energy for the reconfiguration of experience and action; both furnish the ego with an added increment of autonomy over instinct components. It seems to me that any distinction must be a quantitative one, and that the exact point at which systematic inquiry leads into the translation of the system Ucs into Pcs and Cs must probably await final definition until a coherent psychology of insight and creative experience is available.

The systematic inquiry of the psychoanalytic patient is intended to lead to a readiness for insight; it is not intended as an intrusion by the analyst into the patient's autonomy. On the contrary, it furnishes the patient with the wherewithal to pursue his self-exploration collaboratively and with that integrity of self-esteem that is a sine qua non of psychoanalysis. Where this does not occur, it must be that the therapist has exploited the regressive authoritarian-dependent axis of the relationship. The outcome then depends upon quantitative factors, as to whether the patient rebels and leaves treatment the worse for his experience or whether an interminable course as timeless as the unconscious ensues.

REFERENCES

Cohen, M. B. (1952). Countertransference and anxiety. *Psychiatry* 15: 231–243.

Deutsch, F. (1949). *Applied Psychoanalysis.* New York: Grune and Stratton.

Eissler, K. R. (1953). The effect of the structure of the ego on psycho-analytic technique. *Journal of the American Psychoanalytic Association* 1: 104–143.

———(1965). *Medical Orthodoxy and the Future of Psychoanalysis.* New York: International Universities Press.

Fenichel, O. (1941). *Problems of Psychoanalytic Technique.* New York: Psychoanalytic Quarterly.

Ferenczi, S. (1950). Contraindications to the 'active' psycho-analytical technique. In *Further Contributions to the Theory and Technique of Psycho-Analysis.* London: Hogarth Press.

Freud, S. (1909). Notes upon a case of obsessional neurosis. *Standard Edition* 10: 153–318.

———(1912). Recommendations to physicians practising psycho-analysis. *Standard Edition* 12: 109–120.

———(1923). The ego and the id. *Standard Edition* 19: 3–68.

———(1937). Constructions in analysis. *Standard Edition* 23: 255–269.

Fromm-Reichmann, F. (1950). *Principles of Intensive Psychotherapy.* Chicago: University of Chicago Press.

Kernberg, O. (1975). *Borderline Conditions and Pathological Narcissism.* New York: Jason Aronson.

———(1976). *Object Relations Theory and Clinical Psychoanalysis.* New York: Jason Aronson.

Kohut, H. (1971). *The Analysis of the Self.* New York: International Universities Press.

Sharpe, E. F. (1950). Anxiety: outbreak and resolution. In *Collected Papers on Psycho-Analysis,* chapter 2. London: Hogarth Press.

———(1950). The analysand. In *Collected Papers on Psycho-Analysis,* chapter 2. London: Hogarth Press.

Sterba, R. (1934). The fate of the ego in analytic therapy. *International Journal of Psycho-Analysis* 15: 117–126.

Stern, A. (1945). Psychoanalytic therapy in the borderline neuroses. *Psychoanalytic Quarterly* 14: 190–198.

Sullivan, H. S. (1940). Conceptions of modern psychiatry. *Psychiatry* 3.

Chapter 9

Questioning and Pain, Truth and Negation

THESIS

I examined the use of questioning as it pertains to psychoanalytic technique in chapter 8, which may be regarded as preamble and pragmatic survey. Further exploration of the psychology of the question, including its applicability to problems of technique, is attempted in the present chapter. The view will be taken that the question is a relatively unique phenomenon in the interrelationship of thought and language, of language and metapsychology. My thesis is that any act of questioning is an instance of the general "interrogation of nature" that has come to be the special prerogative of science and philosophy; that, in whatever context, questioning is an aggressive and often violent act inextricably linked with a seeking out of knowledge and truth, variously defined; that the discerning of this "truth" with the aid of the question is a painful process, against which the human organism has erected quite efficient defenses; and that paradoxically the question not infrequently is utilized to bar access to what might become known. In this connection, the relationship of questioning and the defense mechanism of negation will be examined.[1]

The phrase "psychology of the question" is of course elliptic: what is intended is "the psychology of the person while he is in the act of questioning." I hold that there are certain common denominators to be discerned in the "psychologies of persons while they are

1. I am most grateful to Dr. K. R. Eissler for drawing my attention to this link between the question and negation, and for stimulating my interest in these problems.

in the act of questioning," and refer to these generically as "the psychology of the question," or simply, "the question." It will be evident that much of what is to be said applies to the psychology of curiosity; but the "psychology of the question" deals with more discrete items of personality, language, and action than does that more central and general concept. We shall be concerned, in other words, with "establishing the factors which make it possible that an ego can raise a question" (Eissler, personal communication).

MASTERY AND AGGRESSION

The act of questioning involves an exploratory, investigative function. In general it is directed to eliciting progressive approximations to the factual truth—at best, as both parties come mutually to validate it, but often, as the questioner alone sees it. If the potential questioner has no hypothesis concerning facts to be elicited, he will of necessity remain silent. At least the most barely recognizable of hunches that information is at hand is essential as the impetus to the question. The question may then be regarded as a searching, acquisitive, prehensile organ of the questioner; but it seeks, acquires, and attaches only that for which the questioner is set. "The eye sees what the mind desires."

These observations about the question are written with a background of Western culture in mind, and specifically of the predominantly English-speaking areas. It seems to me that they apply with special force, but not exclusively, to those peoples who live under conditions deriving from the English common law, for it is they who have developed the most vigorous, coherent, and defined philosophy of the inviolability of the individual person. It is this inviolability that the question intrudes upon or attacks, for, clearly, the questioner wants something from the questionee that the latter is unwilling or unable to volunteer.

This inviolability may be understood as a generally utilized defense against masochistic surrender, biologically rooted and socioculturally facilitated. For example, I may cite a reconstruction arrived at with a young man, bisexually and sadomasochistically oriented, who sought analysis because of impotence and work inhibitions. On particular occasions as a child he became curious about some items of genitourinary physiology; the adults whom he interrogated were closemouthed and apprehensive. The child reacted with suppressed anger: "When I asked them, they wouldn't tell me, or they put me off, or got mad; but when they wanted to know something from me, I had to tell them the truth!" The intrusive questioning against which he reacted with stubborn, covert rebelliousness was manifested on still another level by the patient's mother, who subjected him throughout childhood to repeated enemas and rectal thermometer readings.

Ostensibly it is some type of knowlege that is the questioner's goal. But one quality of a question is that it is active and assertive, if not indeed aggressive, however tempered it may be with tact and graciousness. The questioner seeks power or mastery. It is clinically demonstrable that scoptophilia is the main component of the child's sexual curiosity. The observation of sexual facts may give way as an aim to the knowing of sexual facts as an aim of its own. Its further vicissitudes (see Fenichel 1945) involve the possibilities of the child's endless questioning, of the adult's scientific, philosophic, or journalistic curiosity, or, for that matter, of blocked and repressed intellectual interests. The linkage of curiosity and orality also should be mentioned as indicative of the origins of an acquisitive, consuming curiosity in oral-sadistic incorporation fantasies. Thus, a ten-year-old girl with a penetrating curiosity about the affairs of the adults in her world would follow up the answers to her questions with, "It isn't so!" or "How do you know?" The effect was to disconcert and annoy her elders. Although denied by the mother she had probably witnessed primal scenes; her generally anxious mother was prone to handle all unpleasantnesses by means of denial as a defense. "It isn't so!" was an overdetermined effort actively to reverse the expected denial, at the same time that she mimicked her mother. "How do you know?" was the expression of doubt and challenge. Earlier this child had eaten poorly and vomited on school-day mornings but eaten amply and retentively on holiday mornings. In either case, questioning or eating, her aim was to acquire power — power to master her anxiety as well as the external stimuli of that anxiety.

We see here the question employed as a device for the expression of aggression and active mastery. This child sought to master anxiety by means of an incipiently intellectual, linguistic, vastly overdetermined maneuver, professedly intended to elicit information. It is pertinent to a theme to be further developed later in this chapter that the child simultaneously rejected this information; and that also on an even more primitive oral level, she had previously been rejecting of introjected material.

Two additional case vignettes may be illustrative. A male patient referred during his associations to "some things I want to know from you." The analyst interrupted later to inquire what they were. The patient hesitated, looked embarrassed, and replied that he doubted that he would get an answer if he asked. The analyst responded with a reference to the fundamental rule and then, with the patient still hesitating, asked if it might be that questioning the analyst seemed too assertive or aggressive. The patient agreed with feeling and went on to describe an incident of his early twenties that typified his inhibitions. Briefly, he had been too shy to put his arm around a woman whom he knew liked him. Hungry for sexual experience, which he had never had, he nevertheless could not "ask" for it. He could master his own drives sooner than he could assert himself to the receptive and flirtatious woman.

Another patient, a passive-aggressive, depressed housewife had referred to her disgust for sexual intercourse. The analyst questioned her about this. She haltingly said that the sexual act threatened her with "losing some part of myself." To avoid the violation, "I block before the loss." She went on to mumble that it was like being questioned.

In the latter instance the analyst had questioned for content, against resistance; in the first case, the questioning had been directed toward clarifying the resistance. In each instance the associations affirmed a linkage between questioning and sexual mastery. I am not prepared to say that the mastery to which I refer is always of so immediate a sexual derivation as in these two instances. I follow Fenichel (1945) in conceiving of a principle of mastery as a general organismic tendency, directed to the integrative satisfaction of perfected responses.

Curiosity and the question, then, serve the mastery principle as well as the various sources of the need to have knowledge or information. Stated broadly, the question so regarded is paradigmatic of the practice of any of the branches of learning, all of which require an active curiosity. More concretely, the question is an expressed, actuated, more or less disguised wish, genetically related to the needs to know and to master. Whether the wish be egocentric or altruistic, motivated by greediness or a resultant of reaction formation or sublimation, its frustration or gratification will set in operation certain consequences. It is then a matter of quantification, of psychoeconomics, as to how efficient are the defensive adjustments of the questioner against shifts in his internal balance of tensions; that is, as to how he will respond to success or failure in his efforts.

For example, a narcissistic-aggressive psychotherapist conceivably would experience as more or less traumatic a failure in pursuing a line of inquiry. Possibly he would then attempt to recoup his narcissistic losses by various improvisations of technique of an increasingly active and correspondingly rationalized nature. Such maneuvers may entail an exploitation of the authoritarian-dependent axis of the doctor-patient relationship, to which I referred in chapter 8. We understand such authoritarianism as an unbridled expression of those drives to know and to master that are at the roots of the original choice of profession and in some part remain active in the practice of the profession. The drive to mastery could be evinced first in the commitment to accept the patient for treatment. Then, consecutively and with mounting frustration at each step, in an effort to know and understand in order to master the patient (ostensibly, the neurosis), our hypothetical therapist would question actively and in due course exasperatedly. It is well known that therapeutic ambition is frequently a mask for narcissism; here would be an example of a therapist so led astray by his ambitions as to invest unduly in or, stated differently, to demand heavily of the patient and the therapy. As the patient fails to respond in the manner desired by the therapist, the latter traces a series of regressive steps in the expression of his drive to mastery. Questioning lends itself readily to hypocritical maneuvers that are superficially professional and ethical but may be basically contemptuous and exploitative. Thus our frustrated therapist, through questioning, enters into an embarkation of no return, wherein the treatment aims and goals are stripped away to reveal a pregenital attempt at domination.

The example is perhaps exaggerated; it is by no means nonexistent in its *formes frustes*. Not a few courses of treatment bog down into such power struggles, to terminate in boredom and discouragement, or petulance and querulousness. To be sure, the act of questioning is not per se the source of such difficulties; but by its nature intrusive, it may serve a function of the total personality of the user that we can variously refer to, depending upon the emotional context of meanings and values, as mastering, dominating, assertive, aggressive, or sadistic.[2]

It may appear that some questioning is an expression of dependent clinging and helplessness rather than of domination. The apparent contradiction is quickly resolved when we recall that helplessness and dependency in any but the very young and the infirm are very active techniques for influencing the environment. And even the young and the infirm, besides being actually dependent, may also employ a pseudodependency as a means of managing their sources of supply.

These remarks apply equally to the therapist, who, uncertain of himself, uses questioning not in order to assist the patient but rather to enlist aid for himself, and so to strengthen his position.

THE QUESTION, PAIN,
SUFFERING, AND REVELATION

From another quarter we arrive at a confirmation and extension of these views. The Second Edition of Webster's *New International Dictionary* gives the derivation of the word *question* under the listing for "query": "L. *quaere,* imper. sing. of *quaerere, quaesitum,* to seek, or search for, to ask, inquire, of unknown origin." Harper's *Latin Dictionary* (1907) gives *quaeso,* the old form of *quaero,* as the root, to seek, and derives it from the Sanscrit *cish-,* to hunt out. The fifth definition of *quaeso* is pertinent, for it is given as "to question by torture, put to the rack." From *quaero* comes *quaestio,* its second listed definition being, "A public judicial investigation, examination by torture, a criminal inquiry, inquisition . . . *a questionibus,* an attendant in examinations, a torturer, inquisitor. . . ."

Further, the *quaestors* were a class of Roman magistrate, some of whom were in charge of pecuniary affairs of the State, while others conducted certain criminal trials as delegates or commissioners of the people. To document additionally their association with physical

---

2. For analogy, two other forms of linguistic behavior that may be employed neutrally, malevolently, or ambiguously, are gossip and words referable to elemental bodily processes. In this connection, see Ferenczi (1911) and Baker (1950).

violence, they were obliged to provide the populace with gladiatorial combats.

The third listed definition of *question* in Webster reads as follows: "Examination with reference to a decisive result; investigation; specif., a judicial or official investigation; also, examination under torture." We may also recall in this connection the phrase "to put to the question"—i.e., to put to torture.

Finally, "The law of the later [Roman] empire, relating to torture, is set forth at length in the titles *De Questionibus* of the *Digest* and the *Code*. . . . Torture was used both in civil and criminal trials. . . . The Romans believed that this was the most efficacious means of obtaining the truth. . . . Through the *leges barbarorum,* Roman doctrines relating to torture were transferred, with modifications, to mediaeval Europe" (*Encyclopaedia Britannica* 1953, article: Torture).

The word *question* could have come to be associated by contiguity with the act of investigation and torture, and then by metonymy as one of the instrumentalities it came to stand for the whole process. But this particular instrumentality would not have been selected out unless its qualities lent themselves specifically to represent the entire process; e.g., as the sword symbolically represents war.

A complete review of the historical and etymological connections between torture, judicial investigation, and the question is beyond our scope, but some further limited remarks are pertinent to the theme of the common psychological denominators and may throw more light on some aspects of the psychology of the question. A long tradition exists in Western culture, accepting the association of pain and suffering with the acquisition of truthful information and with the regard of one's fellows. Its historical roots lie in Judeo-Christian origins and also in the North via the early Germanic and Nordic invaders. From these, we have our traditions of hermetical mysticism — of unitive knowledge through self-mortification — as well as the customs of ordeal by fire, water, and combat to determine innocence or guilt, right or wrong. Inflicted pain as the condition of truth seeking is evinced in such disparate phenomena as mysticism, the investigative and judicial processes as formerly known and persisting in the practice of "the third degree," the Inquisition, and the *Malleus Maleficarum,* the poet starving in a garret and presumed to be purifying his creativity, down to the masochistic protagonist of the modern-day detective story who attains the truth by being beaten about the head for several hundred pages.

The general theme of this interconnection between pain and a quest for truthful information is illustrated in the custom of the ordeal, which—attesting by the way to its great antiquity—is epitomized in an assertion of the Hindu code of Manu: "He whom the flame does not burn, whom the water does not cast up, or whom no harm soon befalls, is to be taken as truthful in his oath" (*Encyclopaedia Britannica* 1953, article: Ordeal). What is referred to, of course, is a precursor of the medieval Judgment of God, a divine, miraculous or magical decision as to the truth of an accusation or claim.[3] Truth was revelation. "Indeed, at the level of rudimentary law the distinction between trial and punishment is imperfectly drawn. A judicial process is normally conceived as a mode of bringing a conditional curse into operation, so that a man is automatically declared guilty by the very fact that he suffers" (*Encyclopaedia Britannica* 1953, article: Law). In other words, by the fact that he suffers the truth becomes known.

The pain and death were superhuman attestations to the subject's guilt and untruthfulness. Thereby they indirectly pointed the way to the truth. The question, either verbally or as a physical assault, was here tacit in the demand for the oath and for the act of the ordeal. Exemplifying basic identity in ancient and modern justice is the old oath to the effect of, "May the gods strike me down!" and the question in a modern court of law, "Do you solemnly swear to tell the truth . . . so help you God?"

The development of torture in medieval judicial process is traced to the decline of the ordeals (*Encyclopaedia Britannica* 1953, article: Ordeal; Lea 1892), although as we have seen, a tradition and precedent were in any case carried down from Roman times. Apologists for the use of torture invoked the law of God as a rationale, thus forming a direct link with the rationale of the ordeals. Truth could still be defined as revelation. However, divine judgment was no longer invoked to decide guilt or innocence, and accordingly a

---

3. Not always did the ordeal directly involve pain or suffering: for instance, the medieval notion that the murdered corpse's wounds would bleed in the presence of the murderer. In contrast, the ordeals of poison, combat, fire, and water were directly dangerous to life and limb.

confession or deposition from the accused or the witness was deemed necessary. The question was put, and the answer—and often the punishment—was simultaneously given.

"In looking back over the martyrdom of man, we are appalled by the thought that any rational search after the truth in courts of law is a luxury of modern civilization. . . . In mediaeval England the first step in that direction was taken by Henry II, when he laid the foundation of the jury system in place of these antiquated procedures" (Trevelyan 1953). The extraction of a confession of guilt thus became unnecessary in the English common law—an important chapter in the history of the inviolability of the person. On the Continent, however, confession was still considered the best evidence, and torture—the *quaestio*—was one of the methods organized by the law to obtain it, until as recently as the nineteenth century (*Encyclopaedia Britannica* 1953, article: Torture). In Canon Law torture was potentially applicable in heresy cases until the promulgation of the Codex Juris Canonicus in 1917 (Coulton 1938).

These data have been cited as additional documentation of the question as an agent associated with dominance, with intrusion into the other person's privacy, and with cruelty. We see that in world history and in individual development this intrusiveness has frequently been associated with pain and suffering in the service of a judicial or other search for truthful information and justice.

We must see also that the question is two edged, applicable to others and to oneself, as evidenced in self-imposed ordeal and in torture, in soul-searching and in judicial examination. Just as the question served ancient and medieval men in their ruthless and irrational quests for truth and rightness, so may the question today serve as the instrument of an implacable superego. In our society the collective superego is manifested, *inter alia,* as Justice, personified, interestingly enough, as a blindfolded woman bearing scales and a sword. The scoptophilia in which curiosity originates has been repressed and fused with other elements, or it may be sublimated. In the otherwise more subtle and concealed matriarchy of our time, a female figure inevitably represents the setting aright process; it is the mother who questions, who searches out the truth, and who punishes or assuages. Inflicted pain as the condition of truth seeking and the question as the agent of these activities are functions of the superego—that often unpredictable blend of violence and the sense of justice.

QUESTION, PAIN, TRUTH, AND DEFENSE

To epitomize the discussion thus far: the question is intrusive, searching, and acquisitive; it is at the service of the mastery principle. It may be directed to the control or mastery of one's own anxieties by means of its seizure of dominance in the interpersonal field—a field that may be real or imagined, objectively or subjectively structured. That is, the effectiveness of a question as an antidote to the pain of anxiety will depend on its capacity for turning passivity into activity. Conceivably, the questioner may be induced to sadistic lengths in order to attain success. The origins of the question are those of curiosity generally and lie notably in partial instinctual drives such as scoptophilia and orality, modified and altered by the exigencies of anxiety. Etymologically, historically, and psychologically, linkages are demonstrable between questioning, the search for knowledge and truth, the pain of torture and ordeal, guilt and anxiety, and the sense of justice.

I shall explore further the psychology of the question relevant to the triad of question, pain, and truth, opening the way to a theory of the question as defense.

The prototype of later activities of judgment, discrimination, and discernment, and thereby the earliest test of the congruence and validity of knowledge and of truth subjectively defined, is the infant's action, elementally judging of good or bad in terms of the pleasure principle when he takes into his mouth, tastes, and retains or spits out (Freud 1925). This action is also a basic model of the question, as the expression of drives to know and to master. Through his senses, the infant scans, tests and screens, and then introjects or rejects his environment; the question is similarly employed by the adult.

Inevitably associated with the infant's acts will be some degree of pain or discomfort. Relevant to the adult's psychic pain it is useful to recall that the information sought is characteristically hidden within the questioner, if not in actual content then certainly in terms of the operations required to attain it and most assuredly in terms of the unconscious values assigned the information and the methodology. An appropriate answer leans upon the question asked; in turn, the framework chosen for the question is not arrived at by happenstance but is strictly and psychically determined. An explanation of the association of question and pain must be sought in the balance of drives and defenses motivating the question. The veil hiding truth and knowledge is composed primarily of repression and denial, and the pain of lifting that veil is the pain of anxiety and guilt. A question is directed against a barrier; but what at first appears to be an external barrier resolves into an inner, subjective one, the breaching of which constitutes a psychic danger.

The actual attainment of truth, knowledge, and mastery may be accompanied, however, not by pain but by a sense of relief, of lightened burden concomitant with heightened insight. The phenomenology of insight frequently includes the experience of felt anxiety *just prior to* the opening of insight.[4] But in the actual solution of a problem, or the fulfillment of a search, in the closure of any Gestalt, there is often an experience more akin to elatedness than to pain. One is reminded, for instance, of the sense of well-being that follows the successful work of mourning, itself a problem solving, wherein the mourner is confronted with the necessity of reevaluating his relationship with the lost object, wherein the superego questions and punishes, and new objects are sought. In this connection there is the often difficult clinical distinction to be made between the heightened self-esteem that comes with successful mastery of a problem and the appearance of the affect of elation, the function of which is to ward off anxiety by denying it (Lewin 1950). Truth, question, and

4. The impromptu remarks of the nuclear physicist, J. Robert Oppenheimer (1955), are applicable to this phenomenon as it applies to both objective and subjective data. Asked whether he ever became frightened at what he is "finding out here in this area that can't be measured in either time or space," he answered: ". . . I only get frightened when — and it happens very rarely I think — I have an idea. That is, what people find isn't frightening but the understanding of it sometimes has this quality. I remember a man who was my teacher in Gottingen, who is in Chicago now, James Franck. He said, 'The only way I can tell whether my thoughts are — really have some weight to them is the sense of terror when I think of something new.'" The special appositeness of these remarks lies in the fact that no one thinks of something new without first asking some question.

pain are still associated, only there are instances when pain is mastered, and other instances when the question is repressed.[5]

It is not conceivable that persons with largely repressed curiosity (the drives to know and to master) could survive for long: the successful mastering of environmental and inner tensions is directly proportional to the flexibility of defenses and the availability of free energy expressed as active, disciplined curiosity. The drives to know and to master, for instance, have ever been manifested in the face of the inescapable realities—birth, death, suffering, chance, guilt, and others. Jaspers (1951) calls these "ultimate situations"—"situations which remain essentially the same even if their momentary aspect changes and their shattering force is obscured . . . ." In the face of these existential problems, the drives are made known as questions: Where do babies come from? Where do we go when we die? What is life? Why hast thou forsaken me? From such questions may arise philosophy, science, and the arts. Ironically such questions are often included in the phenomenology of incipient schizophrenic states; this is related to the rejuvenescence and recasting of earlier conflicts during adolescence and the upsurge of such questions at that time.

It is a paradox that curiosity and, *pari passu*, the question, are stimulated into being by anxiety but also inhibited by anxiety. The development of the intellect or its suppression are decided by a delicate balance. To dissolve a repression or, on the group level, to break a taboo requires among other factors a certain assertiveness and tenacity of drive, accompanied by a capacity to tolerate and come to terms with pain. Freud (1908) early referred to the "dire necessity" of curiosity:

> The child's desire for knowledge does not awaken sponta-
> neously . . . but arises under the goad of a self-seeking impulse
> which dominates him when he is confronted by the arrival of a
> new child—perchance at the end of the second year. . . .

5. It is appropriate here to recall the origin of the word "pain": ". . . fr. L. *poena*, penalty, punishment, torment, pain, from Gr. *poinē*, penalty; akin to Av. *Kaēnā*, OSlav. *cěna*, honor, reward, price, Gr. *timē*, Skr. *cayate*, he revenges" (Webster's *New International Dictionary*, Second Edition). The retaliatory principle is well marked. One recalls the painful consequences of eating of the tree of knowledge, as reported in Genesis.

Under the stimulus of these feelings and anxieties the child thus comes to consider the first of the great problems of life, and asks itself the question where children come from. . . . The afterecho of this first riddle seems to be observable in the innumerable riddles of myths and sagas. The question itself, like all inquiry, is a product of dire necessity, as if to thought were entrusted the task of preventing the repetition of an event so greatly feared. At the same time, we may assume the child's thinking becomes independent of the stimulus, and continues its activity as a separate impulse towards investigation.

There are fortunately always those who are able to explore some facet of the "great problems of life," invested as these problems are with values that are an extension of or an extraction from the forbidden areas of infantile curiosity. Their explorations are need serving and vicariously satisfying to the majority or the dominant minority. Thus, the shaman, mystic, philosopher, scientist, physician, and others who question the mysteries of life and death, may be sanctioned by the group's collective needs. At the same time, they may expect censure for their violations.

Whatever the area of interrogation, in the search for knowledge and truth a certain prototypal sequence may be observed: dire necessity and/or ultimate situation — pain — curiosity (the expression of the drive to know and master: the question) — pain — truth, knowledge — pain and/or relief.

Sophocles' account of Oedipus illustrates this sequence by means of its universally appealing dramatization of certain ultimate human situations. The riddling Sphinx who plagued Thebes and slew those who could not answer her question is surely symbolic of punitive conscience and of some of its constituents — thwarted impulses to know and to master, in the face of a mystery representing an "ultimate situation" and setting up an internal "dire necessity." It is significant also that the Sphinx appeared at Thebes either soon after Oedipus had unknowingly killed his father, or concurrently with that act. Oedipus correctly answered her riddle, thus leading to the self-destruction of the Sphinx and the fulfillment of the second part of the prophecy made before his birth: he marries the Queen, his mother. Already Oedipus bore the mark of his infantile suffering, as commemorated in his descriptive name ("Swellfoot").

The hero then ruled successfully with the wife-mother until again the suffering of his people and his curiosity about his own origin and destiny forced him to learn from the blind Tiresias of his parricidal and incestuous guilt. It will be recalled that Tiresias, "in whom alone of all men the truth lives," responded to Oedipus's angrily persistent questioning by deploring the knowledge that would bring misfortune and suffering in its wake.

Oedipus nevertheless learned his origins and thereafter wandered, a tortured and tragic exile, accompanied by his daughter, Antigone. In *Oedipus at Colonus* we find a protagonist who has come to terms with his guilt and virtually completed the task of mourning. He finds peace at last, fulfilling the whole of the original prophecy, although not until he has cursed the sons who deserted him and the city that exiled him. He dies, accepted and sanctified by the Eumenides.

In living out the oracular prophecies, Oedipus is Everyman seeking his destiny and searching for a meaning of his predetermined existence. The quest includes the linguistic device of the question, suffering, the attainment of truth by revelation, more pain, and eventually, peace and self-knowledge among the tamed Furies. The two plays thus illustrate the universal experiences of the human being in his struggles with dire necessity, narcissistic losses, repressive forces, and curiosity, from birth to death.

Numerous examples exist in world literature of the theme of the dangers of knowledge and the ascetic, painfully self-renunciatory search for the truth. Besides the Oedipus of Sophocles and the Garden of Eden story briefly alluded to, the Faust legend, which in its pre-Lessing and pre-Goethe form depicts the evils of secular learning, reflecting its sixteenth-century context, may be cited. In the larger context of all of human history, there have always been repressive forces exerted against now this and now that form of learning. Antiintellectualism has always been with us, using the same technical device in its search for truth as do advocates of the liberty of thought: the question may variously be employed in the service of the collective, rigidly self-righteous superegos or of the collective, free-ranging egos.

THE QUESTION
A HIGHER FORM OF NEGATION

Earlier in this chapter many of the factors involved in the act of questioning were elicited, utilizing information from a variety of sources. An essential conceptualization is lacking, however. This has to do with a problem verging on the origins and interrelations of thought and language — a problem of the adaptation of the internal and external realities. It is significant, for instance, that in individual development the period of most intensive questioning by the child coincides with a period of intensive reality testing and signs of incipient intellectual development.

"At *four years* [the child] asks innumerable questions, perceives analogies, displays an active tendency to conceptualize and generalize. He is nearly self-dependent in routines of home life" (Gesell and Ilg 1943). This is also a period of intensified oedipal conflicts, during which "dire necessity" plays a prepotent role.

This is apparent again in adolescence, during "the first recapitulation of the infantile sexual period" (A. Freud 1946), when the attempt is made yet again to master the upsurge of instinctual processes by bringing them under the secondary process into the systems Pcs and Cs (Freud 1900, 1915a, b; A. Freud 1946; Kris 1950), when they can be dealt with verbally and by means of thought.

> . . . This intellectualization of instinctual life, the attempt to lay hold on the instinctual processes by connecting them with ideas which can be dealt with in consciousness, is one of the most general, earliest and most necessary acquirements of the human ego. We regard it not as an activity of the ego but as one of its indispensable components.
>
> . . . We have the impression that the phenomena here comprised in the notion of "intellectualization at puberty" simply represent the exaggeration, under the peculiar conditions of a sudden accession of libido, of a general ego-attitude . . . a function of the ego performed by it at other times . . . silently. . . .
> If this is so, it means that the intensification of intellectuality during adolescence — and perhaps, too, the very marked advance in intellectual understanding of psychic processes which is always characteristic of an access of psychotic disease — is simply

part of the ego's customary endeavour to master the instincts by means of thought. [A. Freud 1946]

To be sure, questioning as such need not be prominent at this time; my point is that the same processes are at work in the psychology of the question as in other manifestations of the ego function of intellectualization. We have already traced the investment of the question, as one example of intellectualization, with the capacity for violence and linked it with the concept of superego, an organization capable of the utmost refinements of civilized violence. These manifestations, together with data from cases of obsessive doubting and questioning as well as other clinical instances to be cited below, suggest a relationship between the question and the transition from primary to secondary process. The ego is most prone to employ questioning at a time when cathexis is moving from the system Ucs to the Pcs and Cs; that is to say, when material is crowding into awareness and forcing an evaluation of internal stimuli by the psychic apparatus.

As indicated earlier, no question conceives of the completely unknown. On the contrary, the question denotes knowledge, or at any rate the availability of knowledge. We may take a hint from lay opinion, for whom the ability to ask many questions implies great knowledge, or in the case of a child, the capacity for great knowledge. Many questions contain—in the double sense of comprehend and restrain—their own answers. The questioner, in a certain sense, knows the answer to his question, as did the riddling Sphinx and as did the medieval inquisitors and torturers who sought in their victims a heresy they "knew" to be in themselves. The small child's questions about the origins of babies, even where factual information is forthcoming, will result nevertheless in endogenously derived fantasy productions. The question in all instances arises out of an inner need, a "dire necessity," and the self-derived answer also responds to the inner need. Where the answers are so tendentious, we may assume that the answers are primary and the questions secondary; that is, that the questions serve some purpose having to do with the answers. These answers have to do with unconscious or preconscious material. The questioner "knows" the answer well enough to evade it by expelling or projecting it or by looking elsewhere than where it may be found. The ego becomes extraordinarily skilled in its ability to expel, deny, and attribute to outside agencies any unwanted events; the acquisition of language is immeasurably important in these defensive efforts to master the anxiety-threatening situation.

It may be said that all mastery is vicarious, projective, and at bottom self-mastery. In the time-worn joke concerning two analysts, one of whom greets the other with "You're all right; how am I?" the inverted greeting reveals a mutual and presumably hitherto secret insecurity, projected and vicariously mastered. This is not a joke on analysts alone, but on all of us who observe the social custom of inquiring, "How are you?" Rarely does this question convey genuine altruistic interest. Rather it attests to the guardedness of social encounters and the setting oneself at ease by mastering a potential source of anxiety in the interpersonal field. The question, *qua* mastery, intrusiveness, or aggressiveness, has the function of externalizing or of utilizing an externalization in order to master anxiety. "How are you?" means "I am insecure, but hope you are no threat and that I can strengthen myself." Castration anxiety motivates this question.

In one sense, the question is intended to serve the maintenance of repression; in another, it aids the return of the repressed. This is of course inevitable, in so far as a dynamism associated with the repressed becomes cathected with, and reveals some aspect of, "the true psychical reality" (Freud 1908). Thus, the questions of children and, though less frequently, of adults will reveal their unconscious preoccupations and will also become the more regressive, intrusive, and aggressive, the greater the unconscious pressure. Thus again we have the inquisitors and torturers, whether ancient, medieval, or modern.

The intention of the question is to master actively, in the service of defense. That it does so ambiguously, utilizing a kind of assertion as a way of denial, is not without precedent: this is the mode of function of the defense mechanism of negation: "The result is a kind of intellectual acceptance of what is repressed . . ." (Freud 1925). "Negation is, at a high level, a substitute for repression" (Freud 1915c).

In the paper on "Negation," Freud (1925) suggests the possibility of eliciting a suspected piece of unconscious material by asking the patient what he thinks would be the "most unlikely thing in the world in this situation?" Rapaport (1951) comments that the aim of this question is "to create the same psychological situation as the one which prevails when a 'negation' spontaneously arises.'' It is the drive representation that is to be negated, thus obviating the danger of its being acted on, that in turn is the reason for repressing it; ''the question permits a loosening of repression by preparing the ground for negation'' (Rapaport 1951).

One is reminded of those patients who ask questions at the end of an analytic hour, in an effort to prolong the hour and thus to fulfill dependent needs—that they will deny—and also in order to negate what has been arrived at previously, thus safeguarding the repression. The resistance here employs negation, and the patient wishes the analyst to say in his response what the patient is himself unwilling to acknowledge.

An example is available from a patient who, after considerable though not sufficient working through of his sadomasochistic provocations of the analyst, asked, ''Do I provoke you in order to avoid any homosexual feelings for you?'' The analyst responded with, ''Do you ask that as a way of acknowledging what you can't as yet express?''

The question as a form convenient for the expression of negation may be further illustrated with the following example. Let us postulate a scoptophilic impulse, expressed demandingly as, ''Let me see!'' Let us compare this with the question, ''Let me see?'' or ''May I see?'' Clearly the question includes the primary demand, but it masks the demand; and accomplishes this as would a negation— by repressing the affect while releasing the idea of seeing. Interestingly, in this example repression of an affect-quality of demand results in an affect-quality of pleading, which for some people is even more overpowering than is a demand. Through the medium of a question, the repressed is allowed to return.

A final, general example has to do with those patients who, following a comment by the analyst, parry with the question, ''Do you mean . . .,'' and proceed to repeat some implication of the comment. I suggest that such a response is, in its intended effect, a negation, the purpose of which is to mask the sought-after content and to master the external threat and the internal imbalance by means of an attempted projection as well as by temporizing. It is a trick familiar to every schoolchild, who hopes in this way actively to master what he passively fears.

As these examples show, negation and the question each protect repression by discriminating between and dissociating the intellectual and the affective processes. That is, the effect of negation ''is a kind of intellectual acceptance of what is repressed, though in all essentials the repression persists" (Freud 1925). We may contrast the results of negation and the question with another kind of "becoming conscious" — feelings of uncanniness (Freud 1919b), wherein the person *feels* helpless, even overwhelmed, and without appropriate ideational content. With negation or questioning, on the other hand, there is a specious sense of control of the situation.

In the course of analysis, questioning may result in mere intellectual awareness on the part of the patient: resistance has been circumvented, but only in part. This is comparable to negation that allows an idea to be derepressed, but without its affect.[6]

It must be emphasized that the question, as communication, is necessarily a function of a relatively highly developed ego, in the sense of one that is at least beginning to deal effectively with the inner and outer realities. Both questioning and negation are *inter*personal events that attempt to resolve *intra*personal tensions by means of multiple mechanisms — projection, denial, isolation, intellectual substitution and displacement, and rationalization (Rapaport 1951).[7] I would regard the question in this context, as an adjunct to negation, lending its reality-testing and mastering functions to the acceptance side of the conflict between denial and acceptance of the repressed content. Just as negation is, at a higher level of integration, a substitute for repression, so is the question an altered and higher form of negation. "The achievement of the function of judgment only becomes feasible . . . after the creation of the symbol of negation has endowed thought with a first degree of independence from the results of repression and at the same time from the sway of the pleasure principle" (Freud 1925).

Negation, then, is a precursor not only of intellectual functions and judgment but through the latter of the question itself. The question, as a linguistic item, serves those judgmental and intellectual functions whose existence depends upon negation.

The question, that is, relies on a judgmental awareness of the relativity of qualities and values. On this basis it is tempting to

6. Freud (1927), in a later paper than the ones previously cited, suggested that "repression" relate to the affect, and "denial" to the idea.

7. Freud (1925) attributed negation, the derivative of expulsion, to the instinct of destruction. Negativism, or "universal negation," he considered to be probably a sign of defusion of instincts.

speculate that the question was a relatively late development in the history of human speech, as it is ontogenetically (Gesell and Ilg 1943). Perhaps also we may regard the question as a kind of halfway house between internal and external perception. As such, it might under suitable circumstances be taken as a sign of attempted perception by one system Ucs of another.

To recapitulate, both negation and the question serve actively to master a feared repetition: they safeguard repression. At the same time both require some acceptance of external reality in order effectively to function. Also, both reveal in their functioning some aspects of inner reality. Each asserts as a way of denying. Each is a linguistic form, whether of inner or external speech, and each is intended to attain interpersonally an intrapersonal goal. Finally, bearing in mind that a negation is to be interpreted in the affirmative, there being no negatives in the unconscious and ''No!'' being a function of the conscious and preconscious ego and superego, ''every question can be transformed into a negative statement by preceding it with 'I do not know that' or 'I don't know whether''' (Eissler, personal communication), thus reverting it to a negation.

SUMMARY

The following generalizations have been reached:

1. A question denotes an intent on the part of the questioner to master a situation of ''dire necessity,'' wherein passivity and anxiety threaten.

2. Against such painful situations, a question is directed as an intellectual instrument for the mastery and shaping of reality. (Reality is here conceptualized as the changing configurations of an internal state and external milieu, variously impinging upon and affecting each other.) As an agent of intellectuality, the question is primarily, but not exclusively, concerned with the unconscious as ''the true psychical reality'' (Freud 1900). Mastery presupposes knowledge, understanding, awareness: therefore, the effective question ''knows'' its answer; the effective questioner ''knows'' the answer he seeks.

3. A question may operate as a form of negation of reality.

4. The association of the question with pain, truth, and negation has been demonstrated as part of a regular sequence in individual human experience.

5. The possibilities are not vitiated of a well-developed ego employing a question in a valid, realistic endeavor, in the best tradition of science, philosophy, and self-knowledge.

6. Any single act of questioning, chosen at random, will not necessarily demonstrate all these generalizations. I can offer no classification of questions, except as the above generalizations may serve.

REFERENCES

Allport, G. W. (1937). The functional autonomy of motives. In *The Nature of Personality: Selected Papers*. Cambridge: Addison-Wesley Press 1950.

_____(1937). *Personality*. New York: Henry Holt.

Baker, S. J. (1950). Language and dreams. *International Journal of Psycho-Analysis* 31: 171–178.

Coulton, G. G. (1938). *Inquisition and Liberty*. London: William Heinemann.

Eissler, K. R. (1953). The effect of the structure of the ego on psychoanalytic technique. *Journal of the American Psychoanalytic Association* 1: 104–143.

Encyclopaedia Britannica. (1953). Article: Law (primitive). Chicago: Encyclopaedia Britannica.

Encyclopaedia Britannica. (1953). Article: Ordeal. Chicago: Encyclopaedia Britannica.

Encyclopaedia Britannica. (1953). Article: Torture. Chicago: Encyclopaedia Britannica.

Fenichel, O. (1941). *Problems of Psychoanalytic Technique*. New York: Psychoanalytic Quarterly.

_____(1945). *The Psychoanalytic Theory of Neurosis*. New York: W. W. Norton.

Ferenczi, S. (1911). In *Sex in Psychoanalysis*. New York: Basic Books.

Freud, A. (1946). *The Ego and the Mechanisms of Defense*. New York: International Universities Press.

Freud, S. (1900). The interpretation of dreams. *Standard Edition* 4/5.

_____(1905). Three essays on sexuality. *Standard Edition* 7: 135–243.

_____(1908). On the sexual theories of children. *Standard Edition* 9: 207–226.

_____(1915b). Repression. *Standard Edition* 14: 143–158.

_____(1915a). Observations on transference-love. *Standard Edition* 12: 159–171.

_____(1915c). The unconscious. *Standard Edition* 14: 161–215.

_____(1919a). Lines of advance in psycho-analytical therapy. *Standard Edition* 17: 159–168.

_____(1919b). The uncanny. *Standard Edition* 17: 219–256.

_____(1925). Negation. *Standard Edition* 19: 235–239.

_____(1927). Fetishism. *Standard Edition* 21: 149–157.

Gesell, A., and Ilg, F. L. (1943). *Infant and Child in the Culture of Today.* New York: Harper.

Harper's *Latin Dictionary.* (1907). New York: American Book Co.

Hartmann, H. (1939). Ego psychology and the problem of adaptation. In *Organization and Pathology of Thought,* ed. D. Rapaport, pp. 362–396. New York: Columbia University Press.

Jaspers, K. (1951). *Way to Wisdom.* New Haven: Yale University Press.

Kris, E. (1950). On preconscious mental processes. *Psychoanalytic Quarterly* 19: 540–560.

Lea, H. C. (1892). *Superstition and Force.* Philadelphia: Lea Brothers.

Lewin, B. D. (1950). *The Psychoanalysis of Elation.* New York: W. W. Norton.

_____(1954). Sleep, narcissistic neurosis, and the analytic situation. *Psychoanalytic Quarterly* 23: 487–510.

_____(1955). Dream psychology and the analytic situation. *Psychoanalytic Quarterly* 24: 169–199.

Oppenheimer, J. R. (1955). In transcript of television interview by Edward R. Murrow. Columbia Broadcasting System.

Rapaport, D. (1951). *Organization and Pathology of Thought.* New York: Columbia University Press.

Sophocles. Oedipus Rex, Oedipus at Colonus. In *Greek Plays in Modern Translation,* ed. D. Fitts. New York: Dial Press, 1947.

Sterba, R. (1934). The fate of the ego in analytic therapy. *International Journal of Psycho-Analysis* 15: 117–126.

Trevelyan, G. M. (1953). *History of England,* vol. 1. New York: Doubleday.

Chapter 10

The Negative
Therapeutic Reaction

INTRODUCTION

Not infrequently the analyst is confronted with reactions in his patients that are alarmingly the opposite of what would ordinarily be expected, reactions that seem counter to biological sense. For example, the organism tends to maximize its gains in its search for satisfaction, security, and efficient functioning. With certain patients it is otherwise: a correctly timed and accurate interpretation or other event that should lead to amelioration of the patient's distress has just the opposite effect and produces an exacerbation. These persons have an intolerance for success or enjoyment: they tend to pay as they go in psychic and physical suffering for any success that fate or their often considerable talents may bring about. They are negative therapeutic reactors, and they are sore trials to themselves, their families and friends, and their analysts.

A paradox in itself and in its name, the syndrome has a special interest and fascination for practitioners and laymen. It represents a highly organized combination of unconscious guilt or need for punishment, sadomasochism, injured narcissism, and negativism, in a setting of the vicissitudes of aggression, often with depression, and together with a partial change of function from externally directed aggression to inner conflict. Loewald (1972) has aptly said of these patients that "They show, in distortion, something of the glory and the misery of the human condition" (p. 239). They are often individuals of superior intelligence and potential creativity or talent. I have sometimes thought that their ability to survive at all in instances of severe negativism must draw on an extra degree of autonomous intellectual ability — an extra sharpening of the wits or a special talent. The origins in negation of the skills of judgment and evaluation, as delineated by Freud (1925) and Spitz (1957), suggest that there are specific developmental bases, not only for this syndrome but also for its association with special intelligence.

In this chapter I have emphasized the negativism of the reaction as originating in an adaptive organization that makes a characteristic appearance in the toddler's development. In persons who develop the negative therapeutic reaction this becomes chronically defensive and develops further into a central, organizing factor in the preoedipal development with a depressive, narcissistically injured maternal imago. This is structured into a correspondingly skewed and incompletely resolved oedipal situation.

The accumulated man-years of psychoanalytic practice since Freud's formulation (1923) of the negative therapeutic reaction have produced only a few attempted contradictions or additions. Most psychoanalytic writers now deal with the syndrome as a component of masochism; appropriate technique in treatment has involved attention primarily to the masochism and other prevailing pathology. But there is an aspect of the syndrome that has been deemphasized since Freud's description and discussion of it in *The Ego and the Id* (1923) and which had been prominent in his earlier, less well-known description (Freud 1918). This is the negativism that is a *sine qua non* of the reaction. In the patient's own idiom of expression and communication, the presenting fact of the negative therapeutic reaction is negativism — a fact that is still compatible with the usual considerations of sense of guilt, need for punishment, and moral masochism.

I propose here to reexamine the ego psychology of the negative therapeutic reaction as a special case of negativism. This point of view facilitates the understanding and therefore the management of the syndrome by permitting us to view from a new vantage point certain technical and theoretical problems concerning the concomitance of negativism, sadomasochism, and depression.

The syndrome itself represents the nucleus of the patient's defenses; its appearance is analogous to the recapitulation of the neurosis that is evinced in the terminal phase of analysis. These defenses are highly cathected, narcissistic devices, originally evoked in the face of dire necessity during infancy and childhood and now reevoked in the genetic and dynamic regression of transference. In their negativistic rejections of the psychic and external realities of their situations, the patients may repudiate success and fulfillment, sometimes endangering their lives with exacerbated symptoms and actions. It is my view that the negative therapeutic reaction is often unrecognized as such, or otherwise becomes unmanageable, when the analyst has become infected with the patient's negativistic rejection. He identifies with the negativism, mistrusting his own valid interpretation and failing to give due attention and credence to the sequence of events in the patient's life leading up to the reaction. However, even in the absence of such undue involvement, these patients present complicated problems in treatment.

HISTORICAL DEVELOPMENT

In 1918 Freud wrote of the patient who has since become known as the Wolf Man:

> In fact he never gave way to fresh ideas without making one last attempt at clinging to what had lost its value for him. . . . He still behaved in just the same way during the analytic treatment, for he showed a habit of producing transitory "negative reactions"; every time something had been conclusively cleared up, he attempted to contradict the effect for a short while by an aggravation of the symptom which had been cleared up. It is quite the rule, as we know, for children to treat prohibitions in the same kind of way. When they have been rebuked for something . . . they repeat it once more after the prohibition before stopping it. In this way they gain the point of apparently stopping of their own accord and of disobeying the prohibition.

The syndrome so described was given further definition and refinement in *The Ego and the Id* (1923) and assigned the aptly paradoxical designation of "negative therapeutic reaction." Significant changes were made in the formulation:

> Every partial solution that ought to result, and in other people does result, in an improvement or a temporary suspension of

symptoms produces in them for the time being an exacerbation of their illness . . . .

There is no doubt that there is something in these people that sets itself against their recovery and dreads its approach as though it were a danger. We are accustomed to say that the need for illness has got the upper hand in them over the desire for health. If we analyse this resistance in the usual way—then, even after we have subtracted from it the defiant attitude towards the physician and the fixation on the various kinds of advantage which the patient derives from the illness, the greater part of it is still left over; and this reveals itself as the most powerful of all obstacles to recovery, more powerful even than such familiar ones as narcissistic inaccessibility, the assumption of a negative attitude towards the physician or a clinging to the advantages of the illness.

In the end we come to see that we are dealing with what may be called a "moral" factor, a sense of guilt, which is finding atonement in the illness and is refusing to give up the penalty of suffering.

The formulation of "superego resistance" in 1925 (Freud 1926) further clarified the dimensions of guilt and need for punishment. Since then, negative therapeutic reactions have come to be subsumed under this heading or even identified with it (Glover 1955).

Abraham (1919) gave an account of "A Particular Form of Resistance Against the Psycho-Analytic Method." He described markedly narcissistic patients who, while overtly compliant with the methods of psychoanalysis, resisted genuine free associations and produced only ego-syntonic material. They were "particularly sensitive to anything which injures their self-love. They are inclined to feel 'humiliated' by every fact that is established . . . and they are continually on their guard against suffering such humiliations." He characterized them as anal-sadistic-omnipotent. Toward the analyst their attitudes were antagonistic, begrudging, negativistic, demanding, and exacting. Abraham did not explicitly refer to "negative therapeutic reaction," but there is no doubt that he was referring to the same type of patient.

In 1935 Joan Riviere (1936) presented before the British Psycho-Analytical Society "A Contribution to the Analysis of the Negative

Therapeutic Reaction," a paper that drew upon Melanie Klein's theoretical views. She stressed the crucial roles of hypomanic denial and infantile omnipotence as defenses against depression. Horney (1936) analyzed various forms of the negative therapeutic reaction in terms of conflicts of rivalry and affection and the fear of success. Gero (1936), with later confirmation by Lewin (1950, 1961), noted that negative therapeutic reactions characterized the analyses of patients with depression. Eidelberg (1948) referred the reaction to the masochist's intolerance of success: the patient's megalomania requires that defeats be self-imposed. Sullivan (1953) drew attention to the "malevolent transformation of personality," referring to the sadomasochistically developed person who, under the stress of severe and chronic anxiety when needing tenderness, acts in a defensively malevolent way, thereby bringing his malevolence back on to himself. Fenichel (1941, 1945) and W. Reich (1933) have also written on the subject and will be referred to below.

Glover (1955) maintained that superego resistance, "sometimes called the 'negative therapeutic reaction,'" is operative throughout therapy; that on the one hand it prevents a full expansion of transference and on the other hinders a resolution of transference; and that these resistances cannot be effectively uncovered apart from the transference.

Melanie Klein saw the negative therapeutic reaction as formed in part by the splitting off of envy and hate from "the original wish to please the mother, the longing to be loved, as well as the urgent need to be protected from the consequences of their own destructive impulses . . ." (1957).

MISCONCEPTIONS

Notwithstanding the work already done, there continue to be misconceptions as to the nature of the reaction, failure to recognize its presence, and lack of clarity as to its significance for ego psychology and therapeutic technique. These misconceptions may be grouped as follows:

1. The concept is outmoded, as being descriptive only of symptoms. It is said to stem from a period in the history of psychoanalysis when symptom interpretation was the sole method of treatment, as

compared with what later came to be known as resistance analysis or character analysis. It is evident from the quotations cited that Freud, far from dealing only with symptoms, sought and elicited the meta-psychology of the reaction and discussed it as character defense. He did, however, leave the negativism on a relatively descriptive and meagerly developmental level of understanding.

2. It would be more accurate and useful to consider the reaction as a therapeutic impasse, resulting from some mismanagement by the physician of the analyst-patient relationship. This view, that the reaction is no more than a consequence of an incompetently man-aged negative transference, was first expressed by Wilhelm Reich (1933). He claimed, on the basis of the experience of the Vienna Seminar for Psychoanalytic Therapy between 1923 and 1930, that the negative therapeutic reaction did not occur if one followed two rules: first, to make conscious the "secret negative attitude" of the patient, while liberating and securing discharge for all aggression and treating any masochistic tendency as a "masked aggression" outward; second, to leave positive manifestations of love alone until they either "turn into hatred" ("disappointment reactions") or concentrate in ideas of genital incest.

It must be emphasized that even if adherence to Reich's two rules were followed with successful results, it does not prove that they were successful because, as Reich (1933) claimed, negative thera-peutic reactions are results of "inadequate technique for dealing with the latent negative transference." Also there is evidence that the reaction is prone to occur in the presence of latent *positive* transference. Clinical experience disposes of the proposition that the phenomenon is solely an artifact of poor technique, while acknowl-edging that it may in fact be exacerbated by poor technique.

3. One occasionally still hears the term employed as a designation for any and all worsenings of the patient's condition during treat-ment. This gratuitously nullifies the meticulous clinical observations of previous writers.

4. Fenichel (1945) held that not all negative therapeutic reactions resulted from moral masochism and referred to those exacerbations that occur when an interpretation is given from the id side before complete analysis of the defense. This I should prefer to call a counterfeit negative therapeutic reaction: it is limited to this one occasion, its origin can readily be traced, and it does not have the

immediately self-damaging, character-rooted quality of the true reaction. That is, it is likely, assuming the analyst does not make the same mistake again, that it will neither endure for long nor again recur, as the masochistically rooted reactions tend to do. Fenichel referred also to the adverse reaction of some patients to a change for the better in their neurotic equilibrium. This also, as he pointed out, is not necessarily due to masochism but to an investment in the neurotic state as the lesser of two evils.

REFORMULATION AS SPECIAL CASE OF NEGATIVISM

To a valid and properly timed interpretation of defense that contains the tacit promise of understanding and eventual autonomy, or to any situation holding forth the hope or possibility of emancipation from the old, crippling form of living, certain persons react not with clinical improvement but with worsening of their condition. This exacerbation occurs in the affective context of an often resoundingly dramatized "No!," utilizing a combination of defenses of which denial by action or acting out, negation, and negativism are prominent. I stress *dramatized* in order both to emphasize the power of their behavior to stir the emotions of the other person and to indicate that the negativism may be totally or partly nonverbal. The behavior need not be theatrical or melodramatic. "Acting out" in the classical sense (Freud 1914) is frequently an important part of the reaction.

This dramatic enactment of the negative, with its effect on the other person, is a reformulation that extends the concept of symptom- and illness-exacerbation to include also patterns of living—i.e. the fluctuations of character defenses. The people who are prone to negative therapeutic reactions are in fact special instances of the "neuroses of destiny" (Fenichel 1945).

1. For examples, we turn first to one of Freud's instances (1916)[1] of "Those Wrecked by Success": the spirited young woman who ran away from home in search of adventure. After many changes of

---

1. It is a curious and noteworthy fact that a culling of the literature, while producing an abundance of references to the negative therapeutic reaction, elicits only a handful of clinical descriptions; e.g. Freud (1916) and Lewin (1950).

fortune she came to live with an artist who appreciated her finer qualities and to whom she became a faithful companion. There followed years of rehabilitation, during which he reconciled his family to her and prepared to make her his legal wife. From that time she began to neglect the house, imagined herself persecuted by the lover's family, hindered her lover in his work and social life, and finally succumbed to an incurable mental illness. The paradoxical behavior of this woman resulted from the imminent fulfillment of wishes that were felt to be dangerous (Freud 1916, 1936), and it is to be seen as a negativistic rejection of that which was wished for but forbidden.

2. Another illustration of this paradoxical, negativistic quality: an obsessional patient boasts that he has not had his habitual headache for weeks; soon he proceeds to suffer from one (Freud 1925).

3. A young man entered treatment with principal complaints of sexual impotence, an angry attitude towards friends and colleagues, and generally over-compensated reactions to passivity, submission, and dependency. His voice was loud and booming, his gestures emphatic, and his opinions categorical and unyielding. He reviewed his history with reproachful indignation that life had not dealt more kindly with him.

Questioning by the analyst, intended to clarify or inform, led to angry rejections, although in subsequent sessions the patient might bring up these matters himself. In minor ways the patient picked up some of the analyst's traits of speech. Concurrent with these signs of a covert identification and reflecting a conflicted father-transference, he complained bitterly that the psychoanalytic work was not producing the desired effects of improvement in his work and marriage and in his general well-being. Business contacts that were vital to his career he also dealt with ambivalently at best and often destructively. His behavior during analytic sessions gradually produced in the analyst feelings of dissatisfaction and doubts about his own ability to continue to work with a patient who was so completely negativistic to all that was said to him.

One could discern, behind his vigorous and bombastic complaints and his imperious commands that he be treated as he saw fit, a frightened little boy pleading for father's affection and assistance and for mother's nurturing; but the reaction formations to dependent needs were violent in the extreme, and the positive transference remained latent.

Enuretic as a child, he had been subjected to painful and repeated urethral dilatations. He and his younger sister had received enemas from the compulsive, depressive mother. Always sickly, the sister had early succcumbed to a chronic illness and became moribund and died of carcinoma of the bowel while he was still early in treatment.

The patient's defenses were so heavily invested with the drive derivatives against which he was defended, he was in such turmoil of manifest contradictions, and the transference was so quickly developed in terms of impossible demands and expected disappointment and humiliation, that only the most tentative and tactfully expressed interventions could be attempted. Even these were rejected, usually with eruptions of negativistic, reproachful attacks on the analyst. The sister's marriage, final illness, and death, during his first year of treatment also increased his anxieties. His grief was masked by an increase of sadomasochistic behavior, which led to the termination of this analysis. His analyst was at the time inexperienced in the management of negative therapeutic reactions and fell prey to the sadomasochistic provocations. A longer period of work with a second analyst also ended in failure.

4. A muted version of the same theme presented itself in another young man. To him the interpretation was offered that his feelings and behavior were comprehensible as a duplication of his father's depression and work disability. The characteristic sequence developed of quick denial, evasions of the subject, and in the following hour bitterness and reproaches toward the analyst with worsened symptoms. Over a period of time the interpretation came to be accepted.

It is the greater tribute to the dissembling ability of these people that it is so often accepted at face value that they are dogged by ill fortune. This effect on the observer is unconsciously intended. No one must suspect the presence of forbidden wishes; consequently, the wish is repressed and the prohibiting agency attributed to the fates. Success or, for that matter, sympathy over failure will induce shame, guilt, depression, and resentment, for both threaten his narcissistic sense of perfection and seductively confront him with his forbidden id derivatives. Therefore he must suffer the strictures of his superego or again reconstitute his defenses. The projection on to the fates having failed, it is once more projected, but perhaps this time on to a "persecuting" sympathizer.

Supposing now that these events occurred in the course of treatment, as they do following confrontation or interpretation, wherein is this a negative therapeutic reaction rather than the effect of an economically and structurally wrong interpretation?

a. The reaction is paradoxically negativistic in that it refuses, repudiates, and renounces inappropriately to the external situation. The negativism is directed not so much at the issue raised by the confrontation or interpretation as at the person of the confronter or interpreter in an intensification of transference.

b. This transference is overtly negative and hostile, but it is latently or unconsciously positive. It is the pressure of the drives and affects encompassed by the positive transference that arouses the sequence of defensive rejection, self-punishment by symptom exacerbation, and alloplastic attack upon the therapist.

c. The general orientation is sadomasochistic, and resistance arises from the superego.

d. Out of this matrix there develops the dramatic, alloplastic intent. It is not only that the patient projects on to the analyst but he also vigorously attempts to mold the analyst into the very prototype of the hated yet beloved introject. The transferred impulses and affects are ambivalent, pregenital, and intense.

e. There is, finally, an uncanniness about these reactions (Kris 1951), which I believe to be related to the resonant affects and impulses in the analyst induced by the patient's profound narcissistic conviction that his very existence depends on his ability to transform reality in accord with his infantile omnipotence.

CHARACTER DEVELOPMENT AND NEGATIVISM

What René Spitz (1957) calls "the ideational concept of the negative" he finds to be first expressed between the fifteenth and eighteenth months in the head-shaking gesture of no. He demonstrates that normally "the phylogenetically preformed pattern of . . . rooting behaviour becomes the matrix of the semantic gesture of negative head-shaking." Negativism was stressed by Freud (1925) as essential in the subsequent development of critical judgment and discrimination and Spitz sees it as also essential in the replacement of action by communication and in the eventual humanization of the individual.

Interruptions of the child's activity, as for instance with prohibitions, invite or enforce a return to passivity, a regressive step toward the narcissistic organization of the ego. Impelled, as Spitz says, by the biological urge to progress from passivity to activity and further motivated by the aggressive cathexis provoked by the frustration experience, the child "at the end of the first year of life and throughout the second year" conspicuously employs "in practically every situation requiring mastery or defense" the adaptive mechanism of identification and in particular identification with the aggressor or frustrator. In this, "The No (gesture or word) is the identificatory link with the libidinal object . . . [and] the suitable vehicle to express aggression . . ." (Spitz 1957).

As with other of the ego's synthetic functions and defenses, the line between the adaptational and the regressively pathological is thin and fluctuating. Consider for instance a possible development of a child's "no," first as the aggressive warding off of excessive stimulation. At this point the anxiety signal leading to the "No" might be conceptualized as "Too much to be safe"—that is, too much excitation to be assimilated. Later, when additional external forces are introjected as part of the superego system, ordinarily gratifying experiences will evoke negativistic responses, as being "Too good to be true" or as one patient quoted her envious mother, "More than the law allows." Moreover, as Anna Freud and others (A. Freud 1952; Bychowski 1958; Sterba 1957) have shown, the now self-abnegating negativism, although inappropriate to many of the processes of living, may come to be defensively employed in the face of the subjective feeling of threatened emotional surrender or enslavement in a regressed, submissive, helpless, dependent position. The automatic obedience and "waxy flexibility" of some catatonics, for example, represents a degree of regressive compliance that ambiguously says both yes and no.

Many years ago Rank (1929) commented that the first manifestation of what he called "Will," or "dynamic organization of the impulse life," was to be found in the very young child's negativism. Observation of any two-year-old in this phase of development confirms that there is indeed self-affirmation and assertiveness in this behavior. Frequently this expresses an urge to master lest one be mastered. Albert Camus (1951) stated it boldly as, "I rebel, therefore I am." The small child struggles in the necessary distinguishing of self from nonself, and such a struggle for autonomous identity is pursued through all of life (Erikson 1956).

NEGATIVE THERAPEUTIC REACTION

From reconstructions it is my impression that those people who display the negative therapeutic reaction were endowed from birth with greater than average funds of aggressive orality and anality. This in turn made the mothering relationship stressful (as it may later the analytic) by investing it with realistic anxieties about filling an assigned role with these masterful infants and children. One is reminded of the earlier observations of Riviere (1936) and of Horney (1936), who separately pointed out the prevalence of defenses entailing tyrannical control of self and of others. Inevitably the mother's resentful helplessness and overcompensating, possessive demands and the infant's or child's impotent aggressiveness will reinforce each other, with the result that the child grows up to be a welter of contradictions: demanding, but so fearful of disappointment as to be spuriously independent and rejecting; apprehensive of intrusion, yet fearful of isolation; wanting love, but able only to command or buy its counterfeit, dependence on and from the partner.

At the same time, the father has become unavailable, either psychologically or through divorce, death, or desertion. Whether his abdication is the result primarily of his own renunciation of the paternal role, or whether he is pushed aside by the joint efforts of mother and child, or both, I am not prepared to say. In any case, mother and child form an alliance wherein are intermeshed their defenses against dependency and fear of abandonment. Needless to say, no true oedipal triumph has ensued. The child's superego consists of preoedipal, ambivalent introjects, and he is therefore constantly guarded against the fulfillment of his id wishes. From the superego a generally negative attitude is erected against temptation and wish. Phobic, obsessional, and counterphobic defenses are seen. Should all fail, there is released a sadomasochistic rage and/or depression.

Frequently the history of these patients contains references to the severe illness or death of a sibling or friend. Gastrointestinal disturbances are prominent in their own medical histories. These findings are relevant to the importance of passive-active and oral-anal conflicts (see chapter 11).

Freud (1923) observed that the patients we are considering do not feel guilty but ill, although harried by a punitive superego. Their discomfort is largely that of "social anxiety," with hypersensitivity to neglect and the possibility of aloneness and the expectation of humiliation and mortification. Consequently they resort to an irritable guardedness. That is, their character defenses take the form of a rude querulousness, of the kind sometimes seen in the over-indulged child who has also been subjected to importuning and nagging by an insecure and possessive parent. Their early passive experiences of frustrated, guilt-imbued needs have led to the development of defenses that, as one patient put it, are intended to "boycott" life. The usual "If you can't lick them, join them" (identification with the aggressor) evolves into "If you can't lick them or join them, destroy them."

This failure of the defense of identification follows a disturbance in the delicate internal balance of activity-passivity, increases the imbalance, and results in the threat of guilt and annihilation. The patient, in other words, in his impotent efforts toward self-aggrandizement, rages destructively at his introjects. Meanwhile he rejects those external temptations that conspire to fulfill his fantasies and thus precipitate his crisis. Alternatively he may project his guilt and find a scapegoat who will accept the guilty role.

DEPRESSION, SADOMASOCHISM, AND NEGATIVISM

Riviere (1936) stated that it is an underlying depression against which these patients direct their complicated defenses. The depression is dreaded as death or destruction: the world will be empty, and they will be abandoned, drained, and alone. To this should be added the proposition that the dread is of regression, and specifically regression to what Anna Freud (1952) has referred to as "primary identification with the love object," a forerunner of object-love proper. This is feared as a loss of intactness or annihilation of self and is defended against by negativism. I would further propose that this dreaded helplessness and emotional surrender is inherent in the *ambivalent identification with a depressed, preoedipal maternal* love object.

Lest this dread circumstance develop and endure, the patient offers himself as a reciprocating partner in the dialectic of sado-masochism, as though preferring a relationship in which some control remains to one in which he is helplessly engulfed (Eidelberg 1948). In the sadomasochistic relationship the patient experiences his partner variously as the introjected or projected bad object — the depressed, devouring, but positively needed maternal imago. Lewin's concept (1950) of the oral triad is useful here in comprehending the vacillations between hypomanic denial and depression.

The frequently observed, overdetermined coincidence of depression and masochism may be due in part to the masochism — itself a negative attitude toward the processes of living — functioning as a defense against depression. That is, on the basis of the regular effect of the masochistic behavior on the other person — the dramatic quality of the negative therapeutic reaction — it would be legitimate to refer to the mechanism of this defense as the projection of depression and its induction by provocation in the other person. For in raging against himself the masochist dramatically and effectively evokes the experience of helplessness, guilt, and rage in the other person: not he is depressed, but the other one. The more usual forms of this response in the analyst may include the defenses of boredom, irritability, and dozing (see chapter 11). Stated differently, in the course of the life or death struggles with his hated and hating introject, his sadomasochistic techniques of relatedness may result in his finding an actual partner who is himself prone to dependency, depression, and sadomasochism, and to whom he is at the same time acceptable as an introject. In such a relationship it is now necessary to defend by negativism against that which was induced in and projected into the partner. The no-saying, then, is defensive against that same dependent depression and masochism as it is now perceived in the other person. Sadomasochism "projects" depression, and negativism "rejects" depression.

When the negativism is thus admixed with sadomasochistic components, with rage and destructiveness from and against the introjects, and not least, also admixed with a flair for the dramatic or alloplastic in behavior, we then have the negative therapeutic reaction. I may now denote this reaction as a depressive, sadomasochistic rage, which is projected and induced in the other person in a desperate effort at defense against the expectation of inner loss and helpless regression. Negativism is the linkage between the various parts of the picture, the common denominator among the varied elements.

THERAPEUTIC MANAGEMENT

The technical problem of the negative therapeutic reaction is the management in the patient of an acute, recurrent, negativistic emotional crisis in a sadomasochistic person who is prone to depression. The reaction occurs during a latent positive transference, and it is the press of the forbidden positive feelings and impulses that triggers the automatic "No." The matrix in which the reaction develops is one that requires the presence of others with whom the patient can attempt to enact his intrapsychic conflicts of omnipotence versus dependent gratification. At the same time, he is likely to deny their importance, except as intrusive agents of frustration and pain.

The conditions of the psychoanalytic situation, inviting and enforcing the dynamic and genetic regression of transference, establish once again in a susceptible patient the requirements of reinforcing the infantile, defensive "No." The dominant-submissive axis of the therapeutic relationship is enhanced (see chapter 11), the patient experiencing as dangerous the requirement of voluntary receptivity and submission to the subjective experiences of the couch and to the interventions of the analyst. The physician is encountered as a frustrating and untrustworthy figure who must be resisted lest utter passivity and helplessness be exacted. The crisis is precipitated when he is perceived as tempting opposition to the patient's superego mandates and restrictions. The resulting negativistic rejection may be in the form of a "simple" repudiation of success on the one hand or a violent, sadomasochistic storm at the opposite extreme. The more regressed the patient, the more violent will be this superego crisis.

It is only when the patient has recognized the importance of the other person as a vehicle for his own projections and provocations that the sadomasochism, having become ego-dystonic, can begin to yield to psychoanalysis. Until then one has been able only to point out systematically and consistently and with infinite patience and tact that the patient's negativism is obstructing further understanding. Until then, also, the patient uses the analyst as he uses his other partners, as an adversary who may divest him of his magic cloak of secret, megalomanic wishes, evoke superego reproaches, and so expose him to defeat and helplessness. In the face of these expected dangers, it is not surprising that the patient "chooses" the lesser threat of maintaining the status quo by frustrating his own wishes for recovery.

It is usual in the literature on the subject (e.g. Brenner 1959, Eidelberg 1948) to emphasize that the principles of treatment of these patients are not different from those in other character analyses. With this I am in full agreement. However, the often repeated statement that the analyst must and can remain calm, observant, and understanding in the face of the patient's skillful provocations and discouraging negative therapeutic reactions says too much in too few words. To the neophyte analyst these words are heard as an exhortation, perhaps to emulate his idealized seniors; to the more experienced but not yet fully seasoned analyst they may not evoke the guilt of failing to measure up to the ideal, but instead a puzzled *pro forma* acquiescence that may inadvertently touch off his own defenses and dissociate him from the patient.

Needless to say, by reason of the conditions of his work the analyst is in a peculiarly vulnerable position. His "freely hovering attention," empathic identification, and the usual motivations that enter into his choice of profession tend to open his ego boundaries to the operations of the patient. This is necessary and useful, but under certain regressive conditions, it may overcarry. The dominant-submissive axis of the therapeutic relationship is then reversed, with the patient dominant, although only in the temporary sense of a child in a tantrum.

For example, in the course of one negative therapeutic reaction the patient worked himself into a cold, articulate attack upon the analyst as incompetent and malicious. In so doing, he was guarding himself from feeling guilty and helpless. Yet such was the intensity of effort, the subtlety of the twisted logic, and the distortion of facts, as to produce in the analyst the apprehension that perhaps the patient was right. Momentarily the analyst felt guilty and helpless. Recognizing that he had introjected "something bad," he could extricate himself from the role he was being forced into and await his opportunity to interpret the defense.

In such instances distinction must be made between humane consideration for the patient's anguished defense and undesirable acquiescence in the dramatically alloplastic transference. In fact, the analyst's angry assertiveness against such manipulation is at times indicated, if it is tactfully motivated and timed and clearly intended as the setting of limits. Not so, however, in the instance cited above. Here it was indicated to wait out the period of time until the patient could hear it said that his repudiation was one of a long chain of automatic no-saying. With much working through, it was then possible to take up the second part of the defense having to do with the attack on the analyst. This was the more difficult, as it dealt with a projection, and considerable time elapsed before the occasion was right and more time for working through. The sadomasochistic induction and projection of guilt and helplessness was a measure employed to protect from depression, and therefore it was particularly important that the defense not be reinforced nor the depression abruptly precipitated.

The analytic *pas de deux* must always be conducted with special, tactful attention to the patient's pace, rhythm, and capacity of expression, and here is one of those many areas in psychoanalytic practice where science and art have to be delicately combined. The analyst must sustain himself against the patient's ambivalent need to destroy, always recognizing the presence of the other side of the ambivalence but interpreting only when the patient is, as one perceptive woman put it, "almost not saying 'No.'" By not yielding to the projections of guilt and depression, the analyst becomes available as a guilt-free introject, and this strengthens the patient's nonmalevolent and accepting potentialities.

In order to be utilized as a good object, the analyst must know that the uncanny threat of destruction that he feels from the patient during the negative therapeutic reaction is only secondarily if at all the result of disappointment of therapeutic zeal. Primarily this threat is felt to be aimed at his own sense of psychological integrity and identity and is the counterpart of the patient's fear of annihilation. In fact, the patient's continuing negativism and projections must sooner or later impinge upon the most wholesomely developed analyst, however lightly and temporarily, or it is a sign that the instrument of empathic identification has given way to defenses.

For work with these patients, it is essential that the analyst has a capacity for empathic identification in a context of having worked through his own projective distortions and sadomasochistic defenses and has developed his own realistic sense of the relativity of values. There is now a realistic appraisal and appreciation of the irony of a critical situation when confronted with these people. The approach is throughout intended to establish within the patient a new set of intro-jects that are less hateful and hated than those already present. With less stringent superego and ego ideal demands, the freed psycho-analytic process may be expected to work through the mourning and depressive constellations. The final therapeutic task is the analysis of the "primary identification" with the depressed, preoedipal mother. None of this should imply, however, that the analytic course is one of successive removal of layer upon layer of defense. The intricate net-work of defense and impulse is a formidable challenge to the fortitude and perceptivity of both analyst and patient.

CONCLUSIONS

1. Misconceptions about the syndrome of the negative therapeutic reaction are reviewed and discussed. A selective review of the historical development of the concept of the reaction is presented.

2. The ego psychology of the negative therapeutic reaction is reviewed and discussed as a special case of negativism—that is, as an acute, recurrent, negativistic emotional crisis in a sadomasochistic person who is prone to depression. The syndrome represents a cate-gory of superego resistance.

3. The recurrent pattern of living of those prone to the negative therapeutic reaction is of intolerance of gratification. At its height, the depressive, sadomasochistic rage is projected and often induced in the other person. Defenses are directed against expected inner loss and helpless regression to the primary identification with the depressed mother. Schematically, sadomasochism "projects" depression, and negativism "rejects" depression.

4. The therapeutic management is presented with particular emphasis on the frequent transference-countertransference tensions. Schematically, interpretation proceeds from the side of nega-tivism through the alloplastic, projective defenses, to the task of analysis of depression.

POSTSCRIPT 1979

When "The Negative Therapeutic Reaction" was first published in 1964, there had been few studies of the phenomenon since Freud's descriptions and brief sketches of the psychodynamics in 1918 and 1923. Papers by Horney and by Riviere had appeared in 1936, and there were scattered references in the psychoanalytic literature. Freud, it will be recalled, had introduced the concept in *The Ego and the Id* to indicate the workings of an "unconscious sense of guilt" and the functions of the superego. As I have said, it was and is a fascinatingly paradoxical concept, and it presents disturbingly difficult technical problems in the course of analysis. It also presents, as we shall see, complex questions that deal with the scope of psychoanalysis as a therapeutic modality.

There have been many more publications and seminars on the subject since 1964, including numerous passing references in the psychoanalytic literature; this has been especially noticeable since the 1970 panel discussion that was held under the auspices of the American Psychoanalytic Association (Panel Report 1970). Certainly the new data and formulations concerning preoedipal development (e.g., Spitz 1957, 1965, Mahler and Furer 1968, Mahler, Pine and Bergman 1975) gave impetus to this activity, for new and expanded explanatory concepts now lay at hand. In addition, however, the question of the accessibility of the syndrome to psychoanalytic intervention hinges upon a vexing issue—whether in fact our methodology can gain access to reactions that stem from infantile distortions of instinctual and ego development. Insofar as psychoanalytic methodology depends upon interpretation, how can it deal with disorders that are rooted in preverbal experience? Can the patient learn to organize verbally that which was impressed preverbally? Wise and cautious adjudication is desirable in adducing clinical examples on either side of this ledger. I should like to offer here not a clinical example, but one from a study of psycholinguistics, to be included among the numerous observations that will ultimately help analysts to decide this issue. A book review in *Science* (Goldin-Meadow 1978) of *Genie: A Psycholinguistic Study of a Modern-Day "Wild Child"* reports that Genie "was discovered at the age of 13 years, 7 months. . . . From the age of 20 months, she had been confined to a small room and allowed no freedom of

movement, no perceptual stimulation, and no human companion-
ship. . . . It is hardly surprising that Genie did not develop
language" (p. 649). The reviewer later states that

> Genie's speech also contains references to events that occurred
> before she possessed language. For example, she described the
> fact that her father had beaten her during her years of confine-
> ment: "Father hit arm. Big wood. Genie cry." . . . This is a
> striking example of a human's ability to encode and recall
> events experienced before the acquisition of language. (p. 651)

To be sure, psychoanalytic methodology rests on more than interpretation alone. And in recent years there has been a considerable
clarification of such factors as the treatment alliance (or
"therapeutic" or "working" alliance) and of the special transference
and countertransference vicissitudes encountered in working with the
narcissistic and borderline syndromes. But these clarifications have
brought in their wake further problems and a vast increase in the
debate: I mention without bibliographic references the extensive
literature associated with the names of Kernberg and Kohut.

At one time, to profess to treat these conditions, these complexities that derive from developments earlier than the oedipus complex, was to risk the suspicion that one was not doing psychoanalysis
at all. It was the legitimate concern of psychoanalysts to maintain
the integrity of their work and to prevent its dilution if possible with
maneuvers derived from other therapeutic modalities. The wisdom
of this self-discipline may, with hindsight, be questioned, but these
differences in points of view are not captious or merely semantic;
they are of profound importance to an understanding of the
borderlands of psychoanalytic treatment and the limitations and
extensions of our techniques. I shall be returning to this topic in
subsequent discussion.

Continued clarification of the negative therapeutic reaction cannot but increase our understanding of otherwise cryptic behavior in
other branches of medicine and in the general experience of living.
When I first presented this paper at a university hospital, one of the
members of the audience rose to describe what had been until then a
puzzling finding in his investigative work with psychopharmacological
agents and which he now paraphrased "the negative placebo reaction."

Internists and other medical colleagues must see the counterparts of the negative therapeutic reaction in their daily work, and certainly any astute observer can recognize them.

It is nowadays considered respectable and acceptable to discuss openly the fact that these patients are uncannily able to arouse both eccentric and countertransference reactions in the analyst. Most recent writers on the subject refer to this. It is hard now to recall the atmosphere that prevailed when a distinguished analyst, taking issue with my views, wrote that he did not agree that a patient's continuing negativism and projections will eventually have an impact on the well-integrated and well-trained analyst. The implication was that for such an effect to take place the analyst would surely have been beyond the turning point. There was, at this time in the history of psychoanalysis, something tacitly disgraceful about the experience of countertransference and perhaps even about affectively experiencing the patient.

We are now, I believe, explicitly agreed that every analyst has his threshold for countertransference reaction. Perhaps we are not yet in full agreement that the analyst must in fact experience the patient affectively; yet, when this does not happen, it may be a sign that empathic identification has given way to defense. Countertransference reactions will occur, but these and other eccentric or idiosyncratic reactions can be mastered, not always by their deletion but by the experience being changed to that of signal function.

By "eccentric or idiosyncratic reactions," I refer to an important distinction—to *non*countertransference responses that represent inappropriate *or* appropriate reactions to the patient. For instance, to feel irritable in the continuing presence of certain passively aggressive, chronically withholding patients is not unusual. To experience compassion at times is to be expected (see chapter 12). Often enough, these feeling states and our associations to them in the context of our inner model of the patient may be of great value in furthering our understanding of that patient. These then are reactions that, in the course of the development of the analyst's work ego, have come to assume the invaluable functions of "signals" as to the nature of the transactions between and within the two members of the analytic dyad.

There have been some notable additions to the literature (Loewald 1972, Sandler et al 1973, Valenstein 1973, Asch 1976, Langs 1976) that warrant discussion here. I shall be selective in what follows: more comprehensive discussion.of the recent literature may be found in the works of Sandler et al (1973) and Langs (1976).

Loewald's 1972 paper was an extension of his presentation in the panel discussion (1970), and it admirably illustrates for those who are skeptical or uninformed the congruence and mutual enrichment of metapsychology and clinical experience. He emphasizes, and I agree, that the negative therapeutic reaction is not primarily an interpersonal phenomenon directed against the analyst, although its clinical appearance sometimes leads to this misunderstanding. It is appropriately to be distinguished clinically and metapsychologically from what Langs (1976) aptly denotes as forms of "interactional resistance." These I would signify as "counterfeit" or pseudo-reactions, including among them those "Misconceptions" to which I have referred in 1964. Langs's terms are appropriate for referring to the contributions by the analyst to the patient's negative reaction, some of which are inevitably due to the special form of the psycho-analytic situation and dyad; but they are not rooted in the patient's character in the sense that I have described. What I may call the pure form of the negative therapeutic reaction occurs when the patient says no to his own wishes — when his wishes are interdicted by primitive superego forces, which in turn are projected, externalized, and even induced in the other person.

This is an important issue, and I should like to ensure its clarification. The negative therapeutic reaction is the expression of a need for punishment, as most writers have agreed. It expresses superego resistance, negativism, sadomasochism, injured narcissism, and envy-induced splitting. These are the basic elements of the intra-psychic organization of defenses and adaptations, necessary for the syndrome to make its appearance. Many of the elements are non-specific, but it is their patterning and context as part of the characterology that are essential to delineation of the syndrome. The intrapsychic process of transference focuses these patterns and seeks an external source of nutriment; transference, that is to say, actualizes the syndrome through its reviewing of selected aspects of past interactions, but now with a current and often plural cast of characters. The negative therapeutic reactor, in other words, seeks an aggressor, one who will punish, a sadomasochistic partner who will confirm, complement, fulfill, and reciprocate, in the regressive, no-win alternatives of "It's this or nothing."

Loewald (1972) reformulates instinctual drives "as relational phenomena from the beginning, and not as autochthonous forces seeking discharge . . ." (p. 242). These interactional forces are present from the beginning of the mother-child matrix, and the infantile psyche gradually matures and develops as an increasingly autonomous center of psychic activity. He views the syndrome as arising out of an imbalance of libidinal and aggressive drives, and he proposes that the superego is a structured representative of the death instinct.

Loewald further points out that in its more intractable forms the negative therapeutic reaction is "rooted in preoedipal, primitive distortions of instinctual and ego development," and it is therefore "hardly amenable to interpretations in terms of guilt, conscience, and need for punishment" (p. 244). I would comment that the effectiveness of an interpretation depends, among other factors, on *some degree of* intactness of hierarchical ego structures, including superego and ego ideal, and this development has required the taming, fusing, transforming, and otherwise containing of the instinctual drives and the affects. The patients with whom we are concerned here, to be sure, experience guilt and remorse in the precursory forms of social anxiety, shame, and dread of separation and loss. With mitigation of the structured negativism, however, there can ensue a much belated and relatively limited individuation and separation and a restructuring of the destructive forces into a form more accessible to psychoanalysis. The negativism and primitivism of the negative therapeutic reaction are closely linked with the preoedipal, narcissistic and depressive maternal imago. Therefore a tardy and perhaps limited separation-individuation process (see Mahler et al 1975) is an essential part of treatment with these patients. This in turn relies upon carefully measured and evaluated interventions by the analyst, and in more severe cases a prolonged and careful holding operation (see chapter 4).

Sandler and his coworkers (1973) in a carefully evaluative review also emphasized the importance of careful delineation of the syndrome, following Freud's initial definition. While negativism is of clinical importance, they are concerned that it is not a "useful extension of Freud's concept, and may diminish its utility" (p. 93). To this I must point out that Freud's initial description of the syndrome was of a *"negative* reaction" and that his subsequent references retained the designation of negativism. Clinically the negativism is apparent and the syndrome is, as I have said, a special case of negativism. On the other hand, I would agree with Sandler and his colleagues that to refer to a character reaction of contrariness or oppositionalism as negative therapeutic reaction, without the presence of the other factors discussed in my paper, would be inaccurate and to no purpose.

Valenstein (1973) also sees the nuclear determinant of the negative therapeutic reaction as located developmentally "earlier than definitive superego development." He describes a group of patients whose attachment to painful feelings "signifies an original attachment to painfully perceived objects and inconstant objects at that" in the very early setting of the primary object tie before differentiation of self and object. He offers a useful discussion of the development of affects in relation to objects, an illustrative case report, and discussion of the technical problems. He concludes that despite the fact that psychoanalytic interpretations cannot reach the earliest verbal and preverbal developmental defects, the therapeutic outcome can still be significant by means of "corrective experiential reeducation supplemented by cognitive understanding."

Where Valenstein was guided by Spitz's findings (1965) and formulations of infantile development, Asch (1976) follows Mahler's elucidations (1968) of the early mother-child dyad. He elaborates on two main topics:

1. three varieties of intrapsychic, developmental conflicts giving rise to negative therapeutic reaction: (a) the masochistic ego, a response to a special pathology of the ego ideal; (b) "unconscious guilt," or Freud's category of the need for punishment, expanded to include "crimes" antedating the oedipal period; and (c) the negativism of anal and oral conflicts, serving as a "special characterological defense against the regressive pull to symbiotic fusion" (p. 385)—i.e., the negativism is developed against an ambivalent identification with a depressed, preoedipal maternal love object (I would add that the defense is against the conflicted fear and wish concerning this merging—a merging that portends depressive affects and the phenomenology of the oral triad noted in Lewin 1950).

2. problems of technique with emphasis on the special countertransference difficulties: Asch sees these conflicts as being established

preoedipally and having effects on ego, superego, and especially ego-ideal development, the latter throwing considerable light on the problems of narcissism that are inherent in the reaction.

Langs (1976) recalls to us Freud's description of the negative therapeutic reaction in making the important suggestion that "a true negative therapeutic reaction would have as one of its basic features a response to an interpretation that initially validates on some level the analyst's intervention, . . . followed by an intensification of symptoms and by other major resistances" (vol. II, p. 139). Validation, he adds, should include careful attention to the analyst's subjective assessment and self-analysis. These matters are essential to clear clinical observation and thinking. Frequently such validation is present; but often in a sudden access of negativism, the patient denies to the analyst any confirmatory evidence by means of a hiatus in the free associations. Confirmation must then depend entirely on the analyst's clinical experience and subjective assessment. These issues were discussed in the aforementioned panel discussion (1970); also discussed was an illustrative example of differences of opinion as to whether a given clinical vignette was indeed a valid negative therapeutic reaction. In the Report of that meeting, I adduced the reasons for the range of clinical definitions and disagreements:

"(1) the difficulty of describing in adequate detail the context of the patient's situation pertinent to the specific confrontation or interpretation made by the analyst. Often too the patient's response is delayed, coming as it sometimes does in the hour subsequent to the interpretation; (2) it is easier to discern pathology in more severe or dramatic forms; but many negative therapeutic reactors are relatively silent and passive, as Tower pointed out in her paper, or undramatic, as Brenner indicated in his discussion; (3) there are semantic differences among analysts that require careful elucidation. These do not necessarily indicate theoretical and clinical differences and distinctions but may reflect personal style or the variable usages of psychoanalytic terms, from Freud to the present day; (4) countertransferences occur in all analysts and may be particularly liable to occur in response to the prevalent characterology of the negative therapeutic reactor. The necessary openness and permeability of the analyst's work ego may result in temporary misperceptions; (5) many of the elements in any clinical syndrome are nonspecific, although still essential to the delineation of the syndrome." [1970, p. 661]

Concerning the delineation of the syndrome, there now seems to be general agreement among writers on the subject, with some differences of emphasis. I tend to believe that, given the complex interdigitation of elements contributing to the negative therapeutic reaction, there are variants within the general reaction, and that this accounts for the differences in clinical emphasis among recent writers.

There are issues raised by the negative therapeutic reaction that correlate importantly with some aspects of the psychology of the analyst. I deal with this topic more extensively in the chapters on empathy, but I shall outline the salient points here.

In chapter 1, I discussed what I consider to be a powerful set of motives for being drawn to the practice of the healing arts and specifically to psychoanalysis. This motivation finds its developmental origins in the child's rescue fantasies. I refer to a complex defensive and adaptive system that is resorted to in order to shore up injured narcissism resulting from the mother's psychological or physical disability. The depressive mother in particular has an unwitting but remarkable ability to evoke and induce such fantasies and, in fact, to generate mothering behavior in her child; and this is of course integrated with the child's own developing needs. It is inherent in a relationship founded on mutual dependence, even when one partner is more dominant and the other submissive, that each will expect fulfillment through the other and that what is not actualized externally will be fantasized internally. Thus, the child's developing autonomous ego functions will be pressed into the service of the mothering one. The child will be pressed into becoming the idealized mothering one and into additionally becoming one day the rescuing champion of the distressed woman or man, for the sexualizing and gendering of the rescue motif may cut across and interpenetrate the usual male-female lines. The youth's subjective justification for existence in the course of further growth and development will be in the direction of service as an imperative ideal or standard of living.

all times unconflictedly clear as to who he is and who is the patient. A cognitive understanding is by comparison easy to attain but no less desirable.

I close with a minor question arising out of a major issue. In this chapter I say: " . . . distinction must be made between humane consideration for the patient's anguished defense and undesirable acquiescence in the dramatically alloplastic transference. In fact, the *analyst's angry assertiveness against such manipulation is at times indicated, if it is tactfully motivated and timed and clearly intended as the setting of limits*" (italics added). By the "best" patients, those eminently suited for psychoanalysis, such an intervention could indeed be accepted, not as hostile and rejecting but as a loving emphasis. But when a patient has reached this level of the development of object constancy and capacity for treatment alliance, he is already close to definitive analysis of the oedipal conflicts, of separation and loss, and therewith of termination. The quoted words are well-intended but are insufficiently operational. Should they therefore be deleted? I think not; I think they may be retained as a cautionary statement, with the recognition that, in Freud's words, "What is given to the patient should indeed never be a spontaneous affect, but always consciously alloted [sic], and then more or less of it as the need may arise. . . . To give someone too little because one loves him too much is being unjust to the patient and a technical error" (Binswanger 1957, p. 50). On this subject, volumes have been written and undoubtedly will continue to be written.

REFERENCES

Abraham, K. (1919). A particular form of neurotic resistance against the psycho-analytic method. In *Selected Papers,* pp. 303–311. London: Hogarth Press.

Asch, S. S. (1976). Varieties of negative therapeutic reaction and problems of technique. *Journal of the American Psychoanalytic Association* 24: 383–407.

Binswanger, L. (1957). *Sigmund Freud: Reminiscences of a Friendship.* New York: Grune and Stratton.

Brenner, C. (1959). The masochistic character: genesis and treatment. *Journal of the American Psychoanalytic Association* 7: 197–226.

I regret that I can offer no clinical vignettes of this d
Most of the case material is necessarily drawn fr
analyses, and for reasons of confidentiality and recog
sources cannot be breached.

The applicability of these themes to the present subje
therapeutic ambition, or zeal to cure, against which Fre
psychoanalytic writers have warned, is a clear and pre
among therapists motivated as I have described. T
prescribed and established way of working with his pat
him additionally available and permeable to their aff
and defenses as these are expressed through their transf
controlled, adaptive regression is essential to his use of e
is a defining condition of his work. It is ironic that this
and mode of working on the part of the analyst should,
rarily fails or falters in its sublimatory and adaptive fun
the very form against which the negatively reacting
strongly and ambivalently defended. Therapeutic am
totally regress to its motivational origins in identifying w
cuing the depressive, hungering, narcissistically de
possessive, preoedipal maternal imago. It need, howeve
tially regress in order to be experienced by the negative
reactor as a dangerous situation. It need only be present
of striving to succeed or in the sense of the etymological o
word *ambition* as "soliciting the favor of." Therapeutic
other words, doomed to fail with those patients who are
prone to fail by reason of their fears of invasive influe
being devoured (see Lewis [1950] on the oral triad) shoul
to their ambivalently dependent, oral wishes. This, it see
the principal transference-countertransference impasse
source of failure with this group of patients.

Indeed, I think it is this fact that has made me least
with that part of this chapter dealing with "Therapeuti
ment." It is not that I disagree with that section, but th
with any guide to therapeutics an inadequacy in the face
tean forms of patients' resistances, not least, of the sup
tance of which we are taking note. It is superfluous to sta
implicit in all psychoanalytic teachings—but the bes
technique and management is a thorough understand
patient. An empathic understanding requires that the ar

Bychowski, G. (1958). The struggle against the introjects. *International Journal of Psycho-Analysis* 39: 182–187.

Camus, A. (1951). *The Rebel.* New York: Knopf 1954.

Eidelberg, L. (1948). A contribution to the study of masochism. In *Studies in Psychoanalysis.* New York: International Universities Press.

Erikson, E. (1956). The problem of ego identity. *Journal of the American Psychoanalytic Association* 4: 56–121.

Fenichel, O. (1941). *Problems of Psychoanalytic Technique.* New York: Psychoanalytic Quarterly.

_____(1945). *The Psychoanalytic Theory of Neurosis.* New York: Norton.

Freud, A. (1952). A connection between the states of negativism and of emotional surrender (abstract). *International Journal of Psycho-Analysis* 33: 265.

Freud, S. (1914). Remembering, repeating, and working-through (further recommendations on the technique of psycho-analysis II). *Standard Edition* 12: 145–156.

_____(1916). Some character-types met with in psycho-analytic work. *Standard Edition* 14: 309–333.

_____(1918). From the history of an infantile neurosis. *Standard Edition* 17: 1–122.

_____(1923). The ego and the id. *Standard Edition* 19: 1–66.

_____(1925). Negation. *Standard Edition* 19: 233–239.

_____(1926). Inhibitions, symptoms, and anxiety. *Standard Edition* 20: 75–175.

_____(1936). A disturbance of memory on the acropolis. *Standard Edition* 22: 237–248.

Gero, G. (1936). The construction of depression. *International Journal of Psycho-Analysis* 17: 423–461.

Glover, E. (1955). *The Technique of Psycho-Analysis.* New York: International Universities Press; London: Baillière.

Goldin-Meadow, S. (1978). Book review: Genie. A psycholinguistic study of a modern-day "wild child," by Susan Curtiss. *Science* 200: 649–651.

Horney, K. (1936). The problem of the negative therapeutic reaction. *Psychoanalytic Quarterly* 5: 29–44.

Kernberg, O. (1975). *Borderline Conditions and Pathological Narcissism.* New York: Jason Aronson.

_____(1976). *Object Relations Theory and Clinical Psychoanalysis.* New York: Jason Aronson.

Klein, M. (1957). *Envy and Gratitude.* New York: Basic Books; London: Tavistock.

Kohut, H. (1971). *The Analysis of the Self.* New York: International Universities Press.

Kris, E. (1951). The development of ego psychology. *Samiksa* 5.

Langs, R. (1976). *The Therapeutic Interaction.* 2 vols. New York: Jason Aronson.

Lewin, B. (1950). *Psychoanalysis of Elation.* New York: Norton.

_____(1961). Reflections on depression. *Psychoanalytic Study of the Child* 16: 321–331.

Loewald, H. W. (1972). Freud's conception of the negative therapeutic reaction, with comments on instinct theory. *Journal of the American Psychoanalytic Association* 20: 235–245.

Mahler, M., in collaboration with Furer, M. (1968). *On Human Symbiosis and the Vicissitudes of Individuation.* New York: International Universities Press.

Mahler, M., Pine, F., and Bergman, A. (1975). *The Psychological Birth of the Human Infant.* New York: Basic Books.

Olinick, S. L. (1970). Panel report: the negative therapeutic reaction. American Psychoanalytic Association. *Journal of the American Psychoanalytic Association* 18: 655–672.

Rank, O. (1929). *Will Therapy and Truth and Reality.* New York: Knopf, 1945.

Reich, W. (1933). *Character Analysis.* New York: Orgone Institute Press, 1945.

Riviere, J. (1936). A contribution to the analysis of the negative therapeutic reaction. *International Journal of Psycho-Analysis* 17: 304–320.

Sandler, J., Dare, C., and Holder, A. (1973). *The Patient and the Analyst.* New York: International Universities Press.

Spitz, R. (1957). *No and Yes.* New York: International Universities Press.

_____(1965). *The First Year of Life.* New York: International Universities Press.

Sterba, R. (1957). Oral invasion and self-defence. *International Journal of Psycho-Analysis* 38: 204–208.

Sullivan, H. S. (1953). *The Interpersonal Theory of Psychiatry.* New York: Norton.

Valenstein, A. (1973). On attachment to painful feelings and the negative therapeutic reaction. *Psychoanalytic Study of the Child* 28: 365–392.

Chapter 11

The Analytic Paradox

INTRODUCTION

This chapter is an overview of some major issues that present themselves in psychoanalytic practice. The beginner in psychoanalytic or related training will find information pertinent to the primary principles or rudiments of his work as a therapist. The more seasoned analyst may find ideas to ponder relevant to the general nature of his work.

I have dealt here with several subjects, each of which warrants lengthier exposition. These are the paradox, the polarities of relatedness, the rule or principle of abstinence, and the necessity for the analyst and, eventually, the patient to have developed his own sense of tolerance, of sensibly composed acceptance of the many dimensions of the experience of living. For the patient this is also part of the postanalytic work in which he must engage.

The paradox to which the title refers is of course also a paradox of living, of growth and development—that, to become mature, "independent," and self-directing, one must first trace a way through the twisting and turnings of dependence and submission. This paradox of analysis—that the analyst as the advocate of autonomy is also the agent and initiator of a process of regressive dependence—is one that, for the therapist, has become resolved through familiarity and comprehension. Not so for the patient, for whom this is often a thicket of problems and resistances. The relative presence of the two polarities of the dyadic analytic process, the axis of dominance-dependence and that of mutuality-separability, may serve as criteria of the therapeutic movement and point the way to actual, practical resolution of the paradox. Although central and pivotal, this paradox is of course only one among many in psychoanalysis (see chapter 12).

The chapter was written before Spitz's (1957, 1965) and Mahler's (1968, 1975) remarkable investigations and observations of infantile development were fully reported. Mahler's work in particular is apposite to the theme of the two polarities. The halting, progressive-regressive movements along the two axes during the treatment process are at time cognate with the progressive-regressive shifts that reflect the innate thrust within the mother-child unit toward separation and individuation.

The analyst, although he stands as the advocate of individual integrity, inviolability, and spontaneity, is at the same time the initiator and agent of a process that for painfully long periods of time must be traced through a maze of submissiveness and intrusiveness. The necessity to assist the patient to the point of his "ego's freedom to choose" (Freud 1923) along a route of dependence, via the psychoanalytic processes of dynamic and genetic regression, constitutes a paradox, upon the solution of which depends the outcome of the therapy. There is no lessening of its stress from the fact that this paradox confronts every parent and indeed every authority figure in a society where the privileges and obligations of the individual are traditionally honored.

The limitations of therapeutic psychoanalysis, as formulated by Ferenczi (1927) and Freud (1937), were set by the woman's wish for the penis and the man's fear of passivity, the factor in common being the attitude to the castration complex. As the scope of psychoanalysis increases, less reference is made to this general formulation of limitations and more to individual explanations in terms of the clashings and interdigitations of specific needs of the two participants. It is nowadays customary to say that certain analyses have foundered on inadequately managed transference-countertransference tensions; but it would be heuristically useful to be able to state more precisely the nature of these tensions in order to arrive at encompassing generalizations that would in turn permit accurate predictions.

For instance, the "matchmaking," or tacit prediction as to outcome that is involved in the initial bringing together of prospective analyst and analysand is based on grounds that are largely unconscious and irrational and rarely carefully formulated. At the same time, the degree of success or failure of an analysis is not infrequently settled in these earliest interviews or even during the first telephone contacts. Even so early, a subthreshold intertwining of needs may be initiated, taxing all subsequent efforts at their resolution. This paper, then, presents approximations toward the goal of a principle or model that will enable one to recognize, predict, and resolve these entanglements.

THE POLARITY OF MUTUALITY AND SEPARABILITY

A closer examination of the fundamental paradox I have stated as it relates to treatment processes will be possible with attention to the requirements for *mutuality* and for *separability* or *inviolability*.

The human being requires the recurrent experience of being at one with his fellows. This may take different forms, variously admixed with combined and permuted metapsychological factors. Random examples would include the emotional and physical closeness of lovers, the transcultural communication of some scientists, and the shared participation of individuals in group activities, whether sandlot ball games, associations advocating world citizenship, or religious organizations. The infant-mother symbiosis is paradigmatic of this group of observations.

The human being also requires the recurrent experience of being separate or separable from his fellows. Examples would include the processes of individuation whereby the developing and maturing person gradually differentiates himself from mother and father, to become, more or less uniquely, the *Gestalt* of himself. The requirement for separability may appear as a striving for, or a groping toward, autonomy and identity. It is clearly expressed in the person's felt need to be alone; but in his apprehension of the world as being too much with him, it is often experienced as the need to feel inviolable. It may miscarry into pseudoindependence and isolation, with a rigidly defensive character armoring, and, in admixed or impure forms, it may include much rebellion and negativism.

It will be clear that these two propositions are reciprocal and complementary. They are two poles of relatedness; human experience consists in, among other things, a continual oscillation between them (see Little 1951, Milner 1956, Reich 1951). The experienced analyst, in the laboratory of his own consulting room, is possessed of considerable expertise in the detection and evaluation of this oscillation. The raw data consists of the verbal and nonverbal communication between patient and analyst; the operational tests are numerous and require no little apprenticed experience for their valid application (Freud 1925, 1937). The skill and tact of interpretations and the sensitivity of the analyst's use of free-floating attention, controlled regression, and identification are among the hallmarks of a rational therapeutic instrument. The point for discussion here is that the analyst's use of such techniques contributes to the initiation and development of steady but flexible relatedness; and these techniques, as they appear in the therapy, are also to be viewed as *indices* of that relatedness as a matrix, in which the patient may find possible his own idiomatic expression of the psychoanalytic process, leading to "new beginnings" (Balint 1953).

For example, successful interpretation is one of the pieces of operational evidence of the movement of the patient on the mutuality-separability continuum. That is, the analyst can interpret successfully, at the right time and directed to the right point of defense, only if there is between him and the patient a relatedness that can be described in terms of its optimum—a mutuality without loss of self-identity or autonomy and a separability without loss of the other person. The desirability of such a matrix should not obscure the fact that it connotes a diversity of affects and drives in the participants.

In other words, I do not imply the uncomplicated state of contented and mutual love that is to be found for certain vegetatively induced intervals in the mother-infant symbiosis and between lovers. On the contrary, many tensions and affects will be active, including sundry aspects of hate, all furnishing the impetus to continued and constructive change. I am referring to a collaborative coequality, in which one may know and feel a segment of the other person with something like the certainty one may have in regard to oneself, with no loss of the knowledge of discreteness or separateness. This, if you will, is empathic identification. What one then says to the patient cannot fail to be congruent: the patient himself is almost ready to know or say it without the analyst's explicit intervention. The analyst, on the basis of his own introjective-projective mechanisms, utilizing largely subliminal clues that the science and art of psychoanalysis have hardly begun to describe and classify, is enabled to state that which is preconscious and pressing for expression in the patient. At these fleeting moments of mutuality, a process of individuation or separation has already begun, and a step toward completion of the analytic work has been taken.

THE POLARITY OF DOMINANCE
AND DEPENDENCE

Full, collaborative coequality, or the experience of mutuality, is a goal that may be eventually approximated to a greater or lesser degree. But except for intervals of varying duration, the treatment relationship is largely constructed along an axis that may be named after its most frequent manifestation: dominance-dependence. This is a built-in tenet of the work, as it is of all human relations. It is a polarity that is enhanced by the processes of dynamic and genetic regression. Descriptively it is recognizable in antitheses, variously permuted, of activity-passivity, ascendance-submission, and sadism-masochism. These sets of opposites have been studied far more intensively than has the polarity of mutuality-separability, probably because the functioning of the latter is so much more sensitively fluctuant and readily screened or obscured by the participant's vigorous movements on the active-passive axis.

To some degree I am conceptualizing sets of vectors from different fields of discourse. Mutuality-separability is a psychological construct, while activity-passivity is traditionally biopsychic. Theoretically and empirically there is basis for considering the axis of mutuality-separability to be a relatively late emergent in the development of the human being. This is clear in Erikson's similar formulation (1950) of a stage of ego-development that he calls "intimacy" and antithesizes to "isolation." He relates intimacy to genitality, but rightly states that it is not a "purely sexual matter." At any rate, in the treatment situation it is often not clearly apparent until considerable working through along the other axis has been accomplished.

The woman's wish for the penis and the man's fear of passivity are the biopsychic models for these two axes of treatment. The models are interchangeable to the extent that the wish on the one hand or the fear on the other may partake more of the quality of one or the other set of polarities. An example is provided by the following:

A woman patient gave a history of a succession of relationships with men, each ending predictably in frustration, not only in her failure to attain sexual climaxes but also in her ultimate failure to possess and retain the man. In the transference she spoke of her great need to look at and to touch the analyst. At times she could not herself bear to be looked at.

The patient had had a protracted homosexual relationship with an older woman, which, as time went on, had become physically violent. This had terminated with the insidious development of the other woman's florid paranoid psychosis, which was concurrent with the patient's beginning rebellion from her former dependence and submission. The patient's father had been distant, aloof, and dependently demanding; her mother had also been inaccessible to the daughter, but in an Olympian, dominating way. The patient's only experience of mutuality had been in her earliest childhood with a beloved nursemaid; she had never again been able to attain such an experience, in large measure because of her ambivalence about being sadistically dominated and violated.

In the psychoanalytic situation the patient's relationship needs were met with a permissive, nondirective, but active participation. Her silences, emotional distances, and fretfulness gradually lessened in the face of the analyst's steady, benevolent commitment and his interpretations of her defenses against her oral dependency; this included pointing out to her the transactional[1] nature of the effects upon him of her behavior, as this appeared in the transference. This firm and dedicated responsiveness was most unexpected to her, to the exact degree that she unconsciously desired it, initially on an infantile level. In short, her verbal and nonverbal affectively negative defenses were consistently and systematically met with specifically affirmative responses, primarily in terms of an actively modulated mutuality.

The patient's passively aggressive, manipulative efforts to induce the analyst to dominate her and thereby paradoxically to protect her from her own feelings and impulses were met with the standard analytic

---

1. I use this term in the sense employed by J. P. Spiegel (1954): "Transaction . . . describes the inter-penetration and mutual, reverberating, and reciprocal effects of processes which can no longer be referred to organized, detachable entities. It is . . . system in process with system."

procedure of nondirectiveness and steady, inquiring interest. Her oral dependence was conflicted because of the unfinished mourning over her childhood losses; clarifications and interpretations were therefore directed to this, and especially toward the provocative and dominative nature of the intended effect of her behavior on the analyst and on others. These interventions, in the setting of a firm and benevolently interested "systematic inquiry" (chapter 9), resulted in the easing of her frantic feelings and behavior. Her separation anxiety and grief were lessened, and her polarized involvements in a dominant-dependent axis were largely replaced with a commitment to greater mutuality and openness of relatedness. She married after termination of treatment, continuing in her professional work. Her husband later entered treatment with another analyst, and the marital relationship seemed to prosper.

It is important to note that, as difficult a patient as she was, the analyst found her a likeable person whom he could respect and about whose future he could feel reasonably optimistic. He sympathized with her in her experiences of deprivation and loss, with the fact, for example, that she married too late to have the children she now wished for and that so much of her past life had been an unhappy interlude. The treatment alliance, that is, was emphatically and empathically marked with warmth and increasing mutual respect. With termination of the work there was mutual sadness over the separation.

There has been a tendency to look askance at references to the relationship between analyst and analysand as being approvingly and prescriptively mutual, warm, and therapeutically motivated. There is in fact indication for concern when the analyst is overly zealous in his efforts to treat and to cure, lest he thereby dominate and compromise the patient's autonomy. His appropriate stance is rather to understand and to impart that understanding to the patient. It is therefore not surprising that there should be cynical mistrust of warmth and mutuality, for in such a context they do suggest seductiveness and thereby another form of domination. When I first explored this area twenty years ago, these were greater concerns than they are now; but even now the mode of application of human caring in psychoanalysis is a matter of great importance lest it adversely affect the development of transference and treatment alliance. In these matters, the two polarities of the analyst-analysand relatedness must be examined in the setting of judicious, comprehending application of the abstinence principle (Freud 1919). The interpretation and working through of elements of the dominant-dependent polarity prior to or concurrent with establishing mutuality-separability may serve as a primary guide. It is when a quasi– or pseudo–mutuality-separability is established early in treatment that critical eyebrows are with justification raised, especially when this is combined—as it so often is—with neglect or abolition of the abstinence rule and of the basic principle that transference gratification is inimical to the analytic goals.

In the clinical vignette cited above, the patient's narcissistic pressures for transference gratifications were toward impossible fulfillment of conflicted defenses entailing an assertive, Atalantalike separatism and dependence. She desired and feared a penis because, among other factors, she respectively feared and desired passivity. She was defensively and irritably dominating because she feared and wished for phallic assault. She denied dependent needs lest the condition of their gratification leave her more helpless and humiliated than their disavowal. Clarifications and interpretations, often demanded by her, were as often experienced by her as seductive, challenging, or affronting. It was therefore taxing to the analyst's empathy and tact to know when it was feasible to speak. She had invested the analyst's comments and voice with a regressively erotized transference and with qualities of oral, narcissistic supplies, perhaps of transitional phenomena (see chapter 12). The analyst's silence was felt to be depriving and starving of the dependently regressed or arrested child. Her transference strivings were intended to dominate the analyst into acceding to her conflicted needs, and the axis of treatment was one of dominance-submission. The mutuality-separability axis was latent and unformed, and separability was experienced only in the mode of the anxiety, anger, or grief of the isolated, hungering, humiliated child.

The usual application and rationale of the abstinence principle, as I have said, is to renounce transference gratification, thereby reevoking in the supportive setting of a treatment alliance the traumatic conditions that determined the onset of illness. One must acknowledge here that all analyses contain some gratification for the analysand, even at times of masochistic or dependent needs. These matters have been extensively discussed by Stone (1961). Freud referred to the encroachments of the countertransference in this area of gratification of the patient as one of the most difficult technical problems. In a letter to Binswanger (1957) in 1913, he wrote:

> I regard [the problem of countertransference] as more easily solvable on the theoretical level. What is given to the patient should indeed never be a spontaneous affect, but always consciously alloted [sic], and then more or less of it as the need may arise. Occasionally a great deal, but never from one's own Ucs. This I should regard as the formula. In other words, one must always recognize one's counter-transference and rise above it, only then is one free oneself. To give someone too little because one loves him too much is being unjust to the patient and a technical error. All this is not easy, and perhaps possible only if one is older. [p. 50]

Patients such as the one described here have a stormy time in the presence of any imposition of abstinence, yet premature relief from unconscious conflict through transference gratification will vitiate the full effects of the analysis. If the intolerance for frustration is insuperable, it will be necessary to modify the analytic principles and engage in a psychotherapy that is less exacting in its aims and results. But whatever the limitations it must be said, following Freud and with Stone's exegesis in mind, that necessary gratifications include sympathy, respect, intellectual interest, and those factors that derive naturally from the doctor-patient relationship (Stone 1961, p. 23). These principles are in fact more readily and automatically in evidence in the application of standard methodology to a psychoneurosis than with the stormy borderline patients so often met with nowadays. With this patient it was appropriate to apply the abstinence rule not only to forestall transference gratification but also, when possible, to offer the demanded and feared verbal interventions or gratifications at the point of her "almost not saying, 'No!'" (see chapter 10)—i.e., when the transference was balanced in the conflict between wanting and disavowing the want, with the balance swinging from the negativistic side toward the side of accepting gratification. The efficacy of this strategy depends upon accurate, empathically based timing. Such a psychoanalytic situation is not rare, and the central problem is to interpret the developing impasse in terms of the dominant-dependent polarization of conflict. It is this conflict as an internal phenomenon that is projected and externalized as an obstruction to progress and change—as a resistance.

In view of the motivations and motivational hierarchies that enter into the practice of psychoanalysis—the reaction formations and sublimations, some attaining a functional autonomy, some still reversible—it is not surprising that the prolonged integration with a relatively helpless, supine analysand should wander for longer or shorter periods into detours and dead ends. If the deepest analysis is still only, as Hanns Sachs once observed, the scratching of the surface of an unknown continent, then it is understandable that analysts will themselves at certain periods and under certain stresses be confronted with residual conflicts and unresolved instinct components. In the context of the analytic paradox and the two polarities of treatment, the consequent encumbering of the transactional processes between patient and analyst may be observed with particular clarity.

IRRITABLE ASSERTIVENESS, BOREDOM, AND DROWSINESS IN THE ANALYST

Common examples of these miscarriages are irritable assertiveness, boredom, and drowsiness in the analyst—none of which appears when he and the analysand are meeting in collaborative mutuality. The stubborn and persistent use of dominative, irritable self-assertiveness is particularly likely to appear in certain aggressive-narcissistic therapists, in the confusion and frustration attendant upon the analytic paradox (see chapter 9). Therapy then becomes an exploitative, subjugating indoctrination of the patient into a more-or-less systematized set of attitudes toward himself and the world. The patient may rebelliously break loose, or an indefinite stalemate may ensue. Like other relationships that do not dissolve in the face of the overt dissatisfactions of the partners—indicating that prepotent, hidden mutual needs are being satisfied—so may some analyses deteriorate into mutual *folies à deux*, wherein all is systematized and dominated, if not understood, by at least one of the participants at a time. The arrangement is not without some benefit as a security device to one or both participants: the alternatives, they may unconsciously and mistakenly assume, would be the loneliness and panic of separation or of masochistic surrender or a mutually sadistic, debasing alloy involving loss of autonomy and individuality.

In other instances the paradox will be solved in an opposite but equally erroneous way: the analyst becomes bored and even drowsy. Boredom appears only in the more submissive and dependent of any pair or larger group. In the analytic pair it is a consequence of a deadlocked power struggle along the axis of dominance-submission with a reversed field of force, so the analyst now becomes disappointedly dependent on the patient for gratification. The patient, out of the necessities of his own transference-resistance, and possibly also the complementary necessities of the analyst, comes to dominate a relationship which he earlier experienced as too threatening. These "necessities" I would conceptualize as the ultimate biopsychic anxieties of passivity, helplessness, and masochistic surrender; and the defenses against them are their opposites—activity, dominance, and sadism.

The therapist, frustrated in his therapeutic ambitions and inhibited in his capacity for empathy, evades the patient's demands and his own guilty rage by sulkily yielding to a deprived, weary, and often sleepy mood. This is an orally regressed position of evenly balanced conflictual vectors, entailing a "defense in depth," a withdrawal to revery. Like anxiety these states of boredom, irritability, and drowsiness are useful affect-signals of untoward tensions between therapist and patient. The analyst need not and should not rely so passively upon his filtered listening as to await the patient's stimulation and initiative in disencumbering the psychoanalytic process.

One can hardly think of these matters without reference to Lewin's oral triad (1950)—to eat, to be eaten, to sleep. This active-passive dialectic, the law of the jungle and of the infant, continues to be a regression or fixation point for human nature (see Fries 1958). With the aid of Lewin's formulations, one can see that the analyst's drowsiness, and *pari passu* his boredom, may be in the active or passive mode. Sleep may be passively responsive to satiation, as in the well-suckled infant, or it may be an active withdrawal, a reaction to frustration, as in the stuporous infants studied by Spitz (1945). Infrequently an analyst may identify with his patient so protectively and wishfully that he expresses the hoped-for satisfaction and security by himself drowsing. The prototype is the mother who sleeps while her infant suckles and is satiated.

CONCLUSIONS

Before anyone can attain autonomy—responsibility for himself— he is dependent; accordingly, he invites a complementary domina- tion. But with autonomy attained, he can recognize himself and be recognizable as individual and separable, yet in need of recurrent experiences of mutuality and interdependence. The preeminence of the dominant-submissive axis comes to be tempered by the increas- ing importance and availability in his relationships of the qualities of mutuality and separability. The ability of a person to distinguish clearly in himself the functioning of one or another of the aspects of these two polarities I would submit as being among the criteria of emotional maturity. In the course of observing psychoanalytic pro- cesses, I have been struck by the frequency with which intercurrent difficulties and threats of foundering can be usefully conceptualized in terms of the confusion by one or both participants as to which polarity of life-experience is to be dealt with. Now one and now the other polarity is employed as a makeshift defense. For instance, the rebel's efforts at domination are in large measure resultants of his own needs to be nurtured. Again some patients will desire mutual- ity, yet shun it as threatening dominance and annihilation; others will avidly seek a pseudomutuality, which turns out to be the fool's gold of dependence.

The unencumbered psychoanalytic process leads to an acceptance of one's actual and potential condition, with an increased scope of awareness and movement within the limits of that condition. The familiar gibes at psychoanalytic therapy, such as, "If van Gogh had been analyzed, he would still have cut off his ear, but he'd have known why he did it," contain a mocking truth, but a truth about the irony of life and man's position, rather than about the theory and practice of psychoanalysis. Psychoanalysis can offer the patient's ego "freedom to choose" between morbidity and health, but freedom, as someone has said, requires the knowledge of necessity. This freedom to choose, within the necessities of man's condi- tion and optimally within the framework of a benevolently disciplined knowledge of oneself and others, is a distinguishing fac- tor between psychoanalytic therapy and other forms of treatment. In psychoanalysis, other things being equal, it makes for the distinction between successful outcome and stalemated, interminable, or interrupted processes. The analytic paradox is largely responsible for these latter. The paradox is enhanced, but not caused, by such unresolved vectors as adversely affect the analyst's as well as the patient's freedom to move experimentally along the two dimensions of mutuality-separability and dominance-dependence (Balint 1953, Nacht 1957). The unique psychoanalytic collaborative process requires that both analyst and patient participate in it as a learning experience. Frustration, intransigence, and despair are otherwise the consequences.

REFERENCES

Balint, M. (1953). *Primary Love and Psychoanalytic Technique.* New York: Liveright.

Binswanger, L. (1957). *Sigmund Freud: Reminiscences of a Friendship.* New York: Grune and Stratton.

Erikson, E. (1950). *Childhood and Society.* New York: Norton.

Ferenczi, S. (1927). The problem of the termination of the analysis. In *Problems and Methods of Psycho-Analysis,* vol. 3 of *Selected Papers.* New York: Basic Books.

Freud, S. (1919). Lines of advance in psycho-analytic therapy. *Standard Edition* 17: 159–168.

———(1923). The ego and the id. *Standard Edition* 19: 3–68.

———(1925). Negation. *Standard Edition* 19: 233–239.

———(1937). Analysis terminable and interminable. *Standard Edition* 23: 216–253.

———(1937). Constructions in analysis. *Standard Edition* 23: 255–269.

Fries, M. E. (1958). Review of the literature on the latency period. *Journal of the Hillside Hospital* 7: 3–16.

Lewin, B. D. (1950). *The Psychoanalysis of Elation.* New York: Norton.

Little, M. (1951). Countertransference and the patient's response to it. *International Journal of Psycho-Analysis* 32: 32–40.

Mahler, M., in collaboration with Furer, M. (1968). *On Human Symbiosis and the Vicissitudes of Individuation.* New York: International Universities Press.

Mahler, M., Pine, F., and Bergman, A. (1975). *The Psychological Birth of the Human Infant.* New York: Basic Books.

Milner, M. (1956). The communication of primary sensual experience. *International Journal of Psycho-Analysis* 37: 278–281.

Nacht, S. (1957). Technical remarks on the handling of the transference neurosis. *International Journal of Psycho-Analysis* 38: 196–203.

Reich, A. (1951). On countertransference. *International Journal of Psycho-Analysis* 32: 25–31.

Spiegel, J. P. (1954). Integration and conflict in family behavior. Report no. 27 of the Group for the Advancement of Psychiatry.

Spitz, R. A. (1945). Hospitalism. *Psychoanalytic Study of the Child* 1: 53–74.

———(1957). *No and Yes.* New York: International Universities Press.

———(1965). *The First Year of Life.* New York: International Universities Press.

Stone, L. (1961). *The Psychoanalytic Situation.* New York: International Universities Press.

Chapter 12

Paradox and Metaphor: Transitional Phenomena and the Work Ego

INTRODUCTION

In this chapter I examine transitional phenomenon, paradox, metaphor, and empathic process with emphasis on discerning what impels the work ego, or autonomous analyzing functions of the analyst, to move alternatively between evenly hovering attention and verbal intervention. The study is based on the premise that there are interfaces, which I attempt to clarify and broaden, between aspects of the psychoanalytic and literary perceptions of human experience, as these latter have been traditionally epitomized and structured in paradox and metaphor. Paradox and metaphor are seen as forms adapted from literature and rhetoric which represent, indicate, and focus on dilemmas, predicaments, and conflicts of living. Provisionally, I conclude that they are adaptive and defensive processes, directed against primitive affects deriving from the separation-individuation period of child development, that they are closely linked with and expressive of adult forms of transitional phenomena and processes associated with the stresses and conflicts of the same period, and that they constitute an important segment of the data from which the ego work draws its stimuli and information. I offer clinical vignettes and literary instances illustrating these connections.

While this book was in press there appeared a study by Kumin (1978) which parallels in many details the findings of this chapter. It too draws upon Winnicott's concept of transitional phenomena and processes and Mahler's developmental findings. He concludes that the dualism, or opposites, of reality are due to our inherent way of perceiving reality, that the sources of paradox are to be found in infantile experience, modified by later psychosexual development, that failure in the adult to perceive and respond to paradox is a defensive ego operation, and that ego maturity includes the capacity to tolerate ambiguity and paradox. He does not apply these findings, as I have, to the operations of the analyst's work ego.

What factors impel the analyst to move from his position of evenly suspended attention to one of verbal intervention in the form of clarifying, questioning, and interpreting? If we leave aside the imponderable of free will in the cognitive, conscious decisions that the analyst makes, what stimulates the autonomously functioning work ego of the analyst to move alternatively from one mode of action to the other? In this study, I single out paradox and metaphor as the secondary-process forms taken by some of the adult transitional phenomena and processes that must be dealt with in the analyst's work. I propose that the experiencing of these forms are *among the factors* serving to alert and to stimulate the analyst to exercise his unique analyzing functions, his autonomous work ego (Fliess 1942, see also chapters 2 and 4).

I shall first discuss transitional phenomena (Winnicott 1953, 1965, Greenacre 1971, Mahler, Pine and Bergman 1975) and indicate some of the ways in which paradox and metaphor are their carriers, and I shall try to locate and test the bridges and points of contact between the analyzing functions of the analyst and the concepts of paradox and metaphor. The development of infantile into adult transitional experiences is such that the phenomena are not always readily discernible or describable; they are often fleeting and possess the qualities of illusion. We must recall that Winnicott's own statements about them are often presented in an allusive form that is interestingly consonant with the phenomenon itself. I shall explore the conceptual interfaces and commonalities in paradox and metaphor as they are employed by both literature and psychoanalysis in the study and depiction of human experience. Clinical illustrations will be used, but for the reasons cited they cannot be expected to be fully self-explanatory (see chapter 3).

In attempting to throw light on the manner in which the analyst works, I hope to offer some ideas infused from other humanistic fields that will in a modest way broaden and deepen our appreciation of our own theory and practice. There should be no doubt in the reader's mind that, as is true of many aspects of psychic functioning, there is much in these topics that is obscure and difficult to define or delimit. This study does not offer final answers; it is a preliminary effort to broaden a field of inquiry.

TRANSITIONAL PHENOMENA

Transitional phenomena were described, named, and placed in developmental perspective by Winnicott (1953, 1965). In the infant and small child these are manifestations of what he termed an "intermediate area of experience, between the thumb and the teddy bear" (1953, p. 230). Commonly, of course, the transitional object appears as some variant of the well-known security blanket—an object cherished, preserved, used, and abused beyond all reality attributes.

I shall summarize some salient points about transitional phenomena to be discussed in this paper:

1. Transitional phenomena and objects make their appearance initially in a setting of separation-individuation from the mother-child unit (Mahler, Pine, and Bergman 1975). In the course of development to adult life, analogies to, and virtual identities with, this initial situation continue to be or to become manifest. This is especially true within the psychoanalytic dyad. They may be expected to appear in combination with regressive preoedipal dependency conflicts and/or developmental arrests.

2. The transitional object and phenomenon serve to soothe and palliate separation anxiety and the affects associated with object loss. Their function is both adaptive and defensive.

3. The transitional object or phenomenon is part of an "intermediate area of experience" (Winnicott 1953), neither self nor nonself, neither inner nor outer. Its later epigenetic development and vicissitudes involve the "transmuting internalization" of its functions (Tolpin 1971, discussed further below). Manifestations of transitionalism are part of the social and cultural life of the individual.

Both inner reality and external life contribute to this third, or intermediate, area of experience; it is a perpetual human task, as Winnicott says, to keep inner and outer reality "separate yet interrelated" (1953, p. 230). Winnicott's findings and suggestions on transitionalism have been confirmed by Greenacre (1971), by

Mahler and her coworkers (1975), and by many others. Greenacre refers to the transitional object as "a monument to the need for . . . contact with the mother's body" (1971, p. 208), and in this connection she discusses the importance of the sensory modalities, vision in particular, in establishing body image, body ego, and the discrimination of self from non-self—factors of ultimate importance to transitionalism.

It is of special interest to the study of the analyst's functions that, with the limitations placed on visualizing the patient and the emphasis on evenly suspended attentiveness, he must resort to more inward forms of vision in perceiving and organizing his experience of the patient (see chapter 3). In a similar vein, Greenacre, in the introduction to her 1971 compilation of her papers, drew attention to the close comparison between the analyst in his work and the artist, "whose perceptions are determined by a subtle pervasive interaction between himself (including his bodily reactions) and that which he is experiencing from the outer world" (p. xxii).

Further extending the concept of the transitional from object to process, Mahler, Pine, and Bergman (1975, p. 100) refer to the reading of stories to the child, as well as to the storybooks themselves, as transitional activities and objects. I shall return to this particular extension of the concept of the transitional in later outlining some of Holland's findings (1973) from his studies of readers' responses to their reading. Here I emphasize that the persistence of transitional phenomena and processes into adult life need not be entirely a pathological development (see Greenacre 1971, Volkan 1976, 1978). As Winnicott (1967) pointed out, this persistence can also be a source of inspiration, imagination, and creativity. The difficulties and incompletion of the toddler's developmental task of separation and individuation from the mother-child unit are subject to the integrative and synthetic functions of his developing ego. Milner (1957), in an unusual account of her postanalytic freeing of herself from an inhibition in painting, has given a wealth of subjective data that bears out this thesis. In effect, I touch here on a more explicitly defined set of influences on later secondary-process development—influences that the older psychoanalytic writers explained in global terms as the effect of good mothering on later imaginative and creative living. Even deficient mothering may have a positively motivating effect upon the form and goal of a person's development. Mahler and her colleagues (1975) indicate very clearly that the infant's move toward individuation is an innate process and that the adaptive capacity of some infants permits them to derive the necessary narcissistic supplies from a less than suitable environment, while others may founder in what appears to be a more favorable setting.

As Winnicott pointed out, any object, thought, memory, or concept can be experienced in terms of "an intermediate area of experience." Recognizable adult forms of this middle area occur in hypnagogic or hypnopompic states: the Isakower phenomenon (1938) would be an example of such experience. Human experience is seldom in purely secondary process, and we may expect that transitionalism will make its appearance, however fleetingly and obscurely, during a variety of waking states.

Tolpin (1971) has focused on an aspect of the transitional object as a "soother"; she differs with Winnicott, who conceived of the transitional object and phenomenon as becoming "diffused" through the intermediate area between inner reality and external world (1953, p. 233). She proposes rather that the "soothing functions" of the transitional object become internalized as mental structure. The security blanket in whatever form it exists "functions as a psychic 'preserve' analogous to the realm of fantasy in later development (Freud 1911); . . . the blanket eases the stress of transition to object constancy," a point also made by Greenacre (1971). Tolpin emphasizes that it is the "cathexis, optimal loss, and internalization of supporting maternal functions which build the ego during infancy" (p. 331). "The *special case* of the blanket as a transitional self-object imago thus illustrates the *general psychic tendency* to preserve the lost psychic effects and functions of an imago needed for inner regulation" (p. 330, emphasis in original). In other words, the soothing functions of the mother and the transitional object are transmutingly internalized "as soothing psychic structure" (p. 333).

Clinical observation and reconstruction confirm the connections between the security blanket and adult equivalents or elaborations. In Western culture the activities of listening to and playing music, of reading, and of watching television would involve instances of what Tolpin formulates as "an auxiliary soother which ultimately becomes part of an inner regulatory structure" (1971, p. 332).

A famous example from another sphere is the "Leonardesque smile," a probable sublimation of a transitional phenomenon that is represented in da Vinci's paintings (see Freud 1910). I acknowledge that Mona Lisa's smile is many psychological steps removed from the magically endowed, talismanlike "subjective object" (Winnicott 1965, p. 57). In depicting the smile, the artist's creativity has extended the transitionalism into an attribute that produces a celebrated, uncanny esthetic effect on the viewer (Freud 1919). Freud's discussion of da Vinci (1910) points to the fact that the smile in question had its origins in the artist's presumed unconscious wish to participate in a "secret of love . . . in this blissful union of the male and female natures" (1910, p. 117). This evokes a resonating, parallel wish and/or fear in the viewer.

I find Tolpin's formulations satisfyingly precise in supplementing the allusiveness and impressionism, as well as the brilliant clinical acumen, of Winnicott. The necessities in the analyst's work for regressions in the service of the work ego enable us to recognize that the "intermediate area of experience" is still potentially extant and available to the analyst, as is also true in other fields of endeavor. What has been internally structured may still partially and temporarily regress in the course of the work ego's necessary operations, in ways that I have reviewed (see chapters 1, 2, and 3).

Some of Winnicott's formulations, though descriptive and metaphoric, are useful and important on the level of clinical theory because the descriptions are so close to the actual subjective experience. For example, the *experience* of either play, fantasy, or transference is indeed in an intermediate space, although not all individuals are able to locate it; nor are they interested in such arcane matters. Yet these experiences have themes in common (for play and transference see chapter 1), not the least of which is that of empathic perception and integration (see chapters 3 and 4).

Transitionalism, the Work Ego, and Empathy

The special technique of evenly suspended attention used by the analyst (Freud 1912, pp. 111–112) is one of the *sine qua nons* of the practice of psychoanalysis. This form of attention is receptive to the patient in every part of his multifaceted appearance and simultaneously to the analyst's own inner processes. The work ego is both inner- and outer-oriented, attentive to that which proceeds between and within the two participants in the analytic processes (see chapter 1, Langs 1976).

The analyst knows his patient cognitively, observationally, and also through the contextual meanings (in terms of the patient) of inner and internalized psychic events within the analyst himself. In this latter sphere, that which transpires within the patient is known by what occurs within the work ego. I paraphrase Winnicott (1953, p. 239f.) that it is a matter of tacit agreement that the analyst need not ask himself *until after the clinical fact* whether the data were presented from without or conceived within. This is the way empathy works, based on a transitional phenomenon of adult life — a phenomenon of the third area of experiencing, with origins in the remote mother-child unit.

These processes in the work ego meet Winnicott's criteria as I have previously summarized them. They are introjective and projective (Loewald 1960). They are amalgams of objectively clinical and introspective perceptions or observations, and their integration is part of the operation of the autonomous work ego (see chapters 4 and 5). Their configurations are greater than the sum of their parts, a factor of great importance that contributes to their illusory substance and their elusiveness to clear description. For the psychoanalyst the perception and integration of the data of his specially receptive attention result in a curiously satisfying quality; this is not always evident, but when evident it bears a kinship to the "soothing" quality of the transitional object. This is an aim inhibited, sublimated, or transmuted narcissistic satisfaction. Needless to say, the data must be clinically validated to justify and enable the use of an appropriate verbal intervention.

I anticipate my later discussion by asserting that we are in the field of paradox in discerning and denoting these matters. I suggest that the psychoanalyst's need to recognize and solve these paradoxes must serve in a measure (and among other factors) to draw him to his particular work and career. The analyst is drawn to human situations of apparent dissonance and ambiguity between the real and the illusional. Paradoxes of living, called by that name or by another, delight, puzzle, and disquiet the person who is motivated to be a psychoanalyst, and he is ineluctably pressed to understand these disequilibria and to transform them into mastered secondary process.

Operations of the Work Ego in the Transitional Sphere

1. The work ego, for its optimal functioning, requires a sound treatment alliance (see chapters 2 and 4). It will operate in the absence of alliance, but in such an event it is more subject to deviation into eccentric or countertransference reactions—that is, into reactions that arise out of the work ego's insufficient stimulus nutriment, its relative absence of confirming or invalidating, positive or negative, feedback loops of information from the patient. Emotional reactions of irritation, boredom, discouragement, and other manifestations of frustration can ensue as inevitable outcomes of the affective isolation in which the analyst must work over long periods of time in the face of narcissistic barriers and other resistances erected by the patient. The reactions in the analyst may also at times be appropriate positive sentiments toward the patient (Stone 1961). These are natural and inevitable, but they are, like the negative reactions, *eccentric* to the optimal detached functioning of the work ego, which must repeatedly reconstitute or reintegrate itself (see chapters 1 through 5). Alternatively, arising out of these reactions, the analyst may regress to countertransference in anxious and/or other affective response to the unavailability of the patient.

2. Such responses can take on signal functions (chapter 1) and thereby alert the analyst to return to his appropriate stance. It is this temporary loss, or interactional distance, of the patient that leads to the trial identification of empathy in the regression in service of the work ego (Fliess 1942, Greenson 1960, chapter 1). The regression enables and facilitates empathic perceptions and integrations.

3. When successful, the whole experience is encouraging, invigorating, even "soothing" to the self-esteem of the analyst. The effect may be compared to that of solving or beginning to solve a problem, but with the additional element that an affective separation from or temporary interactional loss of the patient has been obviated. Stated otherwise, the combined cognitive-affective integration results in a calm sense of well-being that is conducive to the continuing analytic processes. Triggered into action by the various modes of separation, the work ego has drawn upon inner resources of hope and trust. It also draws importantly on its capacity to use the combined defensive-adaptive operation of trial identification, or empathy, in dealing with loss and separation. These resources can be traced

backward in time to the configurations of interrelatedness that gave the necessary impetus to aid growth and development—that is, to progress and regress in the usual forms of adequate psychic development. This responsiveness to loss with its attendant cognitive and affective concomitants is a feature that renders the work ego susceptible to paradox. The experience of paradox is unsettling, as we shall see. While I do not imply that paradox *per se* indicates loss, I am suggesting that, confronted with paradox, the work ego is momentarily taken aback, nonplussed, or "at a loss"; it is thereby separated from the patient.

4. The adaptive regression and other combined operations resulting in successful empathic perception and integration draw upon preconscious fantasy and upon such inward actions as review of and associations to fantasies, images, and thoughts; these are brought into play for the purposes of the problem solving.

5. An essential part of the analyzing functions takes its data from a regressive state analogous to, *but not identical with,* presleep in both patient and analyst (see Freud 1900, Lewin 1954, chapters 3 and 4, Malcove 1975). The "element essential to all analytic work," Malcove writes, citing Isakower's unpublished views, is "the state of consciousness that activates the affect or mood which is associated with the content of the experience" (1975, p. 9). Whether in fact the state of consciousness activates the affect or vice versa need not concern us here. These are states that are peculiarly suited to and cultivated for the experience of transitional phenomena; they represent the "intermediate area of experiencing, to which inner reality and external life both contribute" (Winnicott 1953, p. 230). In the course of the work ego's forays into regression in service of the psychoanalytic process and of the patient, reality orientation and secondary process are temporarily and partially suspended (see chapter 1). This area of the work ego's experience and functioning can be "located" topographically in the preconscious or in the organized unconscious. I prefer the additional concept of transitionalism as having the advantage that it connotes the rapprochement subphase of separation-individuation (Mahler, Pine, and Bergman 1975) and, especially, a quality or classification of experience between inner and outer reality. This is a developmental process involving separation and loss, individuation, and restitution that may be in varying degrees arrested, completed, or compromised

in its end products. Transitionalism takes note of the fact that the work ego at times perceives the analysand as a combined external object and "subjective object" (Winnicott 1965, p. 57). The nature of the analyst-analysand relationship at these times is indicated in Stone's terms as "separation in intimacy" (1961), a quality referable to the mother-child unit and strongly suggestive of transitionalism.

Critique of an Expanded Concept of Transitionalism

It is beyond the scope of this chapter to give the issue the full discussion it warrants, but having come this far in my exposition I must call attention to the fact that the concept of transitionalism is undergoing a considerable expansion. In the course of psycho-analytic writers' exploring later developments of this "intermediate area" into adult cultural, as well as into pathological, experience, it appears that the adult phenomenon is often only remotely connected with the child's transitional objects. Such thinking may be open to the genetic fallacy of assuming the adult developmental outcome to be identical with the genetic origins. One also comes to be skeptical of the usefulness and validity of an explanation when so many psychological facts are allegedly explicable by a single factor.

Tolpin's formulations (1971), outlined above, offer some explanation and understanding. Also, in the sense that psychic structure is never destroyed, but only superseded and may return to tangible function, one is justified in referring to matters such as reading (Mahler, Pine, and Bergman 1975, Holland 1973), fantasies (Volkan 1976), art (Freud 1910, Coppolillo 1976), humor and play (Loewald 1976), and bodily imagery (Greenacre 1971) as having their common reference points in regressive similarities to transitional phenomena of the separation-individuation process. Winnicott and others have also referred to the analyst's being used by the patient as a transitional object, a not infrequent clinical fact that can be confirmed by most practitioners.

Nevertheless, perhaps it would make for clearer delimiting and defining of the elements entering into the work ego's processing of information if we were to refer instead to the area of experience, to the altered states of consciousness, and to the regressive experiences and pressures, thereby avoiding the pitfalls of the genetic fallacy. In this, however, as in so much of the semantics of psychoanalysis and of other fields, we must defer to common, current usage. I shall therefore continue to refer to transitional phenomena in the present study and trust that the varied states of consciousness and associated affects, of regressive shifts and contents, will be implicitly understood.

Reading Process and Psychoanalytic Process

Holland, a professor of literature, has brought a psychoanalytically trained imagination and discipline to the study of the reading process (1968, 1973, 1975). In Coleridge's phrase, the reader's willing suspension of disbelief—his temporary suspension of defenses against affective, empathic, regressive experiences— permits him "to compose from the elements of the work a match to his own characteristic style" (1973, p. 145); this takes into consideration patterns of defense and adaptation, fantasies, and the reader's own moral, intellectual, and esthetic requirements. In this way, each reader transforms what he reads in accordance with his own theme of identity. Nevertheless, the individual differences among readers do not preclude the similarities, so that the same work of fiction, for example, may appeal to a large audience who possess a variety of both shared and dissimilar induced reactions to the reading.

This is an aspect of what Winnicott called the "location of cultural experience" (1967). It is in this sense that Holland draws on Winnicott's contributions and proposes that the reader, absorbed in his reading and engaged in the synthesizing and regressive functions that are integral to it, will "blend and merge in a potential space between perceiver and perceived, where distinctions between inside and outside, self and other, found object and created object, objective reality and created symbol, have ceased to matter" (1973, p. 146). This statement about the reader and how he experiences his reading may be objected to as descriptive and metaphorical, but it should be evaluated in the context of what Winnicott, Greenacre, and Mahler have said about transitional objects and phenomena, and especially about their later vicissitudes. Holland's statement is germane to the experience of the analyst with his patient at certain empathic moments (see chapters 1 and 3). The analyst, like Holland's reader and Winnicott's acculturated person, has empathic experiences which take place in a "potential space" that both joins and separates him and his patient and which corresponds in structure and origin to the genetically earlier psychic space of the mother-child unit. The work ego is aware of and responsive to the transitional phenomena that constitute much of the raw data from which he so frequently must draw his understanding of the patient.

When I speak of raw data, it is with considerable license. It is doubtful that many of the analyst's perceptions are thus unorganized. This is not to say that he comes to his patient with preconceptions; rather, as his information about and comprehension of his patient grow and develop over time there also grows and develops an increasingly coherent, organized working model of the patient (see Greenson 1960, see chapter 4) in terms of which all perceptions come to be tested and assimilated.

The work ego, as we have seen, operates in an intermediate, transitional mode of experience in the course of its recurrent, controlled regressions in the service of the work ego and of the patient (see chapters 1, 3, and 4). I have described this more fully in the writings just cited; it is also, I believe, implicit in Isakower's unpublished views of the "analyzing instrument" (Malcove 1975). To apply Winnicott's words, this mode of experience is "between the oral erotism and true object relationship, between primary *and later* creative *and analytic problem solving* activity and projection of what has already been introjected, between primary unawareness of indebtedness and the acknowledgement of indebtedness" (1953, p. 230, italicized words added).

The analyst, to be sure, does not always work in this manner. I have the further impression that some analysts operate very little if at all in this way, though this impression is derived largely from the fact that in their descriptions of their work they seem to rely excessively on efforts to fit all experience into secondary process and cognitive modes.

There is a density to the work of the analyst: it is embedded in a matrix of dyadic complexities of affective detail and form, and it can be described only arduously and often ambiguously (see chapter 3). The work of the preconscious and the unconscious can only be discerned after the fact; and Fenichel's words on how the analyst arrives at an intervention continue to be relevant almost four decades later: "I do not mean to say that we should replace intuition and freely floating attention with exertion of the intellect." Nor, may I interject, should the opposite be the case. "What is meant," Fenichel continues, "is that, after we have reflected upon it, we should always be able to explain what we are doing, why we interpret, and what we expect each time from our activity" (1941, p. 52).

In the interest of expanding this understanding of the analyzing functions, of enhancing and facilitating appropriate activity, I emphasize the necessity of studying the forms taken by the work ego's controlled regression in response to the patient. The work ego's data include a variety of phenomena that are within the third or intermediate area of experiencing. It is the analyst's unique talent, augmented by his training, that he is enabled, perhaps during and surely after the fact, to verbalize his own inner and internalized processes as the residue or product of his interaction with the patient's inner processes. From these data he can then free associate, analogize, collate, scan, and otherwise cognitively "compute" in his continuing problem-solving efforts in the service of the patient.

We may now turn to investigate the manner in which paradox and metaphor enter into the work ego's functions.

PARADOX

Paradox, according to the dictionary, is an "assertion or sentiment seemingly contradictory, or opposed to common sense, but that yet may be true in fact." Equally, paradox refers to what seems true, but that is not true in fact. In psychoanalysis the many forms of opposition between illusion and reality constitute paradoxes. The distinction of paradox from irony, which may also deal with the discrepancy between appearance and actuality, need not concern us. Irony deliberately evokes humor or dramatic potential from the discrepancy, incongruity, or contrast, and for our purposes I suggest that irony is a complexly subjective, affective experience, while paradox, though also complex, is more objectively intellectualized.

The general theme of the paradoxical opposition and fusion between the illusional and the real has been announced and exploited by countless novelists, dramatists, and others; it is perhaps a major theme of all literature in depicting the universal dilemmas, conflicts, and affects inherent in human situations and psychic events (see Empson 1930, Brooks 1939). Man has been referred to as an embodied paradox, a bundle of contradictions, and, by Empson, as searching for a way to maintain himself "between contradictions" (Empson 1935). Browning wrote of "a paradox/ Which comforts while it mocks,/ . . . What I aspired to be,/ And was not, comforts me." Herrick wrote that: "A sweet disorder in the dress/ Kindles in clothes a wantonness" and, having detailed the delights in disorder, he concludes that such, "Do more bewitch me than when art/ Is too precise in every part." John Donne addresses Death admonishingly to be not proud: 'One short sleep past, we wake eternally,/ And Death shall be no more: Death, thou shalt die!"

In these representative examples of paradox the writers have depicted and resolved the disparities and contradictions by means of the language, form, and content of the poetry. These are manifestations of the principle of multiple function, of the ego's synthetic and integrative functions — functions that are of course likewise essential and present in analyst and analysand. The poet expresses and resolves the paradoxes and reconciles the disparities so that the total statement through its imagery and connotations expresses more than at first appears. The analyst through his interventions often performs a similar task. The apparently irrelevant and disconnected phenomena are characterized, and their connections are noted in a synthesizing solution to a problem that might have been overlooked, misunderstood, or in other ways lost through resistances. In this way inner and outer experiences are integrated. Disparate experience is first indicated and then amalgamated in a new combination. These are the intentions and orientations of the analyst and of the poet, each in his own sphere of influence. These are the meanings and uses of paradox — that inner and outer reality are assimilated in an effort toward both reconciliation and defense. It must be added that the results of clarifying the paradox are not always so esthetically pleasing as in these distilled lines of poetry. Still, it can be said that in an analysis there are also moments of subjective pleasure and satisfaction, not dissimilar to an esthetic experience, when analyst or patient through their joint efforts have arrived at an integrated piece of understanding. At the risk of exposure to the genetic fallacy, can we juxtapose such experiences to the toddler's who has returned to his mother, or who has recovered his security blanket?

Paradox: Clinical Illustrations

A patient who had made considerable progress in the understanding and amelioration of his mood swings and problems with envy and competition was enabled at long last to purchase a new home for his family. After several days of inner turmoil following the family's actual move into the new residence he was able to say, with a manifest pleasure that he had usually denied himself, "I could be content to live there for the rest of my life!" And then, with great anxiety: "My God, I could die there!" Here was a paradox of daydreams fulfilled, but in conflict with fear of success, of reality consummated and illusion threatening.

I do not suggest that paradox is synonymous with conflict, nor that awareness or resolution of the paradox in this clinical instance is synonymous with resolution of the conflict. Paradox is concerned with the external and objective, but to the analyst it points to the patient's having both internalized and externalized, and thereby concealed himself and defended against his conflicts under a false but plausible appearance. The paradox in this depends on the fact that the subjective and objective are neither completely differentiated nor any longer fused. Illusion and reality were at this moment for this patient "separate but inter-related," in Winnicott's phrase (1953, p. 230).

With cool composure the patient was able soon to dismiss these incongruous but interrelated affective statements. Not so the analyst, who was alerted to the significance of the contradictions in terms of the patient's continuing problems with dependence, envy, and oedipal rivalry. I add the important fact for this analytic fragment that initially and momentarily the analyst did not grasp the implications of this combined statement by the patient of contented triumph and anxious concern about being enviable. In this, he was automatically engaged with the patient in disavowal; an attempted clarification or interpretation at that moment of heightened anxiety would have been premature and too stressful. This momentary trial identification or empathic mutuality with the patient places the incident into the context of dyadic commonality; as Winnicott stated concerning the transitional object and the baby: "We will never ask the question 'Did you conceive of this or was it presented to you from without?'" (1953, p. 239). The phenomenon of this mutuality was surely within the analyst insofar as it was achieved by the trial identification of empathy; it was as surely outside him, insofar as it was an empathically perceived state of mind of the patient's. It was not a cognitive, evaluative situation until after the fact. It was both between and within the two participants and it was neither a conscious, deliberate withholding of comment by the analyst nor a counterresistance.

In speaking of paradox as a perception, experience, and evaluation by the analyst's work ego, I am referring to a function that is integrative. It is a beginning clarification for the analyst of the nature of the problem. Paradox contains and accommodates the conflict, encompassing the intrapsychic, the projected, and the externalized. It also often contains those momentous, external factors that are constantly impinging on the person, but are not fully objectively perceived—the internalized social customs, values, morals, and ethics, as well as unstated, tacit influences of other persons.

The notable paradoxes confronting the analyst represent the human quandaries of being suspended between an internal and an external world, of maintaining oneself among contradictions and conflicts. One must make decisions and compromises and erect defenses in order to claim oneself from a primary or a transitional process that is subliminally intruding and encroaching upon one's sense of self.

When an analyst observes, for instance, that a person in a high executive position has been able to make sound decisions, even though he is in part motivated by unconscious fantasies and projective identifications, this is to state a paradox involving the patient's confused but effective use of what is inner and outer, self and not-self. His reality testing is ruled and limited by narcissistic fantasy, and yet his actions are for the most part not only effective but also ego syntonic. The inevitable subjective distress that may bring him to analytic treatment will become understandable only when his reality testing is scrutinized in the light of his transference. Indeed, the difficulties with his reality testing will be discernible only in the context of his slowly developing transference, though they are defended against recognition with all the strength of his intellectual argumentativeness. To recognize these disparities and anomalies as narcissistic transitional phenomena, as unfinished business from early development, is a first step toward ultimately analyzing them.

The paradoxes of psychoanalysis exist by means of the interposition between conscious self and outer reality of preconscious and unconscious processes. Schematically these are repositories or metaphors of the persisting, uncompleted, infantile developmental issues that remain the sources in adult life of incongruities and contradictions, as well as of imagination and creativity. The residues of incomplete separation-individuation and of unresolved traumas to narcissism—the monuments to the yearned-for contacts with the mother's body (Greenacre 1971, p. 208)—constitute the source of adult paradoxes of transitionalism. Blanck states it well: "The ideal developmental achievement, to be fully in the world and yet fully separate, is arrived at (*more or less*) only after conquest of the myriad developmental tasks which, to Mahler, culminate in success of the process of separation-individuation" (1976, p. 152, emphasis added).

An example from another field, by a well-known medical writer, may further illustrate the effects on the observer of certain incongruous, paradoxical patterns in nature. Lewis Thomas (1977) writes of what he calls "a mixup about selfness," describing the confusing life history of two mutually parasitic creatures, a sea slug and a jellyfish found only in the Bay of Naples, whose survivals depend exclusively on each other. He says, in an elaborate but suitable metaphor: "Sometimes there is such a mixup about selfness that two creatures, each attracted by the molecular configuration of the other, incorporate the two selves to make a single organism" (p. 1104). He concludes his essay, "The Medusa and the Snail," with these words: "The thought of these creatures gives me an odd feeling. They do not remind me of anything, really. I've never heard of such a cycle before. They are bizarre—that's it, unique. And at the same time, *like a vaguely remembered dream*, they remind me of the whole earth at once. *I cannot get my mind to stay still and think it through*" (p. 1105, emphasis added).

What Thomas describes here is a paradox of nature, reflected in the writer and the reader as a personal paradox—one, I surmise, that contains a ubiquitous conflict between a feared experience of the uncanny and a sought-after resolution of the problem that would have the calming and soothing effect of a cogent explanation. The uncanny is opposed to or conflicted with the soothing effect of the internalized transitional process. An unsophisticated observer of the medusa and the sea slug might be variously curious or repelled, but surely would fail to recognize the paradox with its evocation of primitive and conflicted feelings about selfness and symbiotic parasitism and the metaphoric reference to some forms of the human condition. Distilled and transmuted in the writing, Thomas evokes this uncanny effect in the reader.

Freud, in his study of "The Uncanny" (1919) points out that the uncanny "leads back to what is known of old and long familiar" (p. 220). The uncanny is something secretly familiar which has been repressed and has returned from the repressed. He discusses the fact that it is easier in fiction than in reality to produce an uncanny effect.

I suggest that, in the example above, aside from the necessary skills of the writer, what is essential for its effect is a degree of regressive dependence on the part of the reader in his responses, as described by Holland (1973). This is similar to the adaptive, controlled response of the analyst's work ego during the willing suspension of disbelief that is inherent in his evenly suspended attention. Further relevance to the analyst's work lies in the analogous disruption of the work ego's autonomy when anxieties are induced by the patient's own regressive affects. Such disruptive events impinge upon the work ego's automatic use of the intermediate area of experience entailed in empathic perception and integration, and this may result in an uncanny experience of varying intensity—an eccentric or a countertransference reaction, although these are not always experienced consciously as uncanny. The reader's response to the excerpts from Lewis Thomas's essay will similarly have been predicated on his own experiences with dependency conflicts. As a reader invested in psychoanalytic matters he will almost surely have had evoked in him the puzzling, tantalizingly unresolved, because anxiety-laden, issues of separation-individuation, with which every analyst is confronted through his work.

Freud observed the paradox that when we first encounter the neurosis in its full development it is not comprehensible to us, but that when we have come to understand it we no longer regard the patient as being ill; nor does the patient when he too begins to comprehend his illness. I submit the possibility that this initial incomprehensibility is related to a subject little discussed, but well-nigh ubiquitous in the experiences of analysts. I refer to the muted anxiety that is aroused when a new patient is to enter the consulting room—the eccentric reaction of subdued, "familiar uncanniness" when faced with a stranger who presents himself or herself dependently for assistance. In the seasoned analyst this reaction is minimal, a signal function, and perhaps not clearly within awareness. It vanishes as the problems begin to be clarified and understood. The paradox observed by Freud contains anxious, perhaps "uncanny" conflict, which in turn is mastered by the work ego in the course of its autonomous functions of problem solving.

The Ubiquity of Paradox in Psychoanalysis

The ubiquity of paradox in everyday life may be explained in terms of the ubiquity of inconsistency, contradiction, or conflict. The presence of self-contradictory, conflictual circumstances and experiences in human life has been part of folklore and literary tradition, and it had been conceptualized as paradox. The unsophisticated observer puzzles over incongruities and contradictions in his fellows as though he expected them to be fully consistent, rational, and uniform—in a word, as he imagines or wishes himself to be. The expectation of smooth, predictable consistency in others is a self-deception that is projected or externalized. The analyst, on the contrary, must study self-deception and its motivations in himself and in his analysands. The sometimes altered, regressive state of consciousness in which the work ego often functions is conducive to perceiving the many ways in which reality, fantasy, and illusion— often in the form of an anachronistic present or in other plausible admixtures of inner and outer reality—are in contradiction and conflict with each other as well as in congruence and harmony.

The opposition between the real and the illusional is so pervasive in the practice of psychoanalysis as to constitute a background against which the living figures depict themselves. This opposition is not at first recognized as such. Paradox appears when the initial fusion or confusion, the likeness between the two polarities, yields to the perception of differences, opposition, or contradiction with a feeling of unrest or puzzlement in either or both of the analytic pair. This was the case in the vignette of the young man and his new home and in the graphic example of the essay evocatively entitled, "The Medusa and the Snail."

I offer now a longer clinical vignette—an example of transference as paradox—and shall then discuss the altering effects of these phenomena on the analyst.

Transference and Paradox as Transitionalism

A basic paradox in psychoanalysis is that the perception of the inner and outer realities in which the patient lives is approached through the paths of illusion. Transference suffuses, distorts, defines, and, above all, informs the psychoanalytic situation. Extreme and bizarre examples of this, reminiscent of Lewis Thomas's comments about the mutual parasitism of the medusa and the snail, may be found among those narcissistically injured patients whose subjective and objective lives are organized around a no longer present parent.

The patient was a young, attractive divorcee who had recently come to Washington to take up a semiprofessional assignment. She was articulate and clear about her wish for treatment, though not very clear at first about the specifics of the discomfort that impelled her to seek therapy. She could not enjoy, she said; and men were either erratic, as her late father had been or solid and boring, like her former husband. She was upset, she said, about her recent divorce, which she had sought, and about a failed love affair with a married man, begun after separating from her husband. The lover had betrayed her with another woman, not his wife. She could offer little information about her childhood, because of a massive, incomplete amnesia extending back from about age fourteen. Her memories and feelings about childhood were all negative: Father, now dead some three years, had been angry, unstable, charming, seductive, provocative, and rejecting; Mother had been withdrawn or preoccupied with Father; she remembered Mother as playing solitaire by the hour. A succession of maids had been responsible for her. A brother was born when she was three, and he was an object of an intense and painful rivalry persisting to the present time.

The course of psychoanalytic psychotherapy was stormy. She lost and found jobs and lovers in bafflingly quick succession. The sessions were containers for her angry, reproachful, tearful complaints about her bad luck and the unfair, cruel treatment received from employers, lovers, and others. Nor were the sessions successful containers: so far as could be ascertained, the same behavior—provocative, ill-tempered, angrily dependent—prevailed throughout her life. It became a matter of considerable concern, for example, that the people on whom she was most dependent were those with whom she was — paradoxically — most ill tempered. The more she wanted narcissistic supplies, such as affection, a job, a landlord's consideration, the more malevolent she became. Gradually, another aspect of her behavior emerged: she was compliant, ingratiating, and deferential in a little-girl way that alternated with the little-girl tantrums. Withal, she was intelligent and able in her work, a fact that gradually began to assert itself in her changing mode of living and in her settling in with one relatively enduring and durable lover.

Not surprisingly, the analyst often found himself discouraged, antagonized, and helpless. Despite her reproaches, her insulting mistrust, and her proclamations of lack of therapeutic progress, she clung dependently to the treatment. The analyst became aware of this paradox of ambivalence and could begin to interpret the nature of her widely spread transference: She was engaged in perpetuating the image of her father by provoking his kind of behavior in others, while at the same time engaging in his kind of behavior herself. Thus, the strange combination of seductive and rejecting, vituperative and ingratiating behavior slowly came to be understood by her, and to be modified accordingly.

Lest this vignette become too discursive and lengthy, I am omitting description of other factors that contributed to this therapeutic change — the vicissitudes of interpretation of externalizing and of splitting (Kernberg 1976) and the reasonably steady analytic stance maintained amidst the buffetings of the work ego in the face of what was at best a tenuous treatment alliance (see chapter 4). Nor shall I describe all the other aspects of a transference that was suffused with rage, anxiety, and depression.

Her behavior continued in mitigated form to be projectively directed toward actualizing internal events that were all that desperately remained of the beloved and hated father. The illusional object (subjective object, Winnicott 1965, or self-object, Kohut 1971) and the illusional relationship were fiercely retained and asserted again and again. Subsequently, considerable working through of this theme of the transference led her to speak in a more sympathetic way of her mother and of what she had endured.

During the heights of her innumerable crises, this patient was utterly convinced of the reality of a transference subjectivity that she was externalizing and projecting. The analyst received the impression that it was reassuring to her to be in the grip of such emotion and fantasy, however painful. It was for this patient a reassuring disavowal of her father's death, and an assertion that he still lived.

Such transference enactments, however, are not always related to mourning; in my experience, they are related, in the absence of the death of the ambivalently regarded parent, to the patient's having experienced recurrent promises and disappointments at the hands of a domineering, depressive parent of either sex who had dealt ambivalently with the child and enforced a mutually parasitic dependence. Can the medusa and the snail learn to live apart?

Illusion, Transitionalism, and Signals Alerting the Work Ego

The vignette just reported illustrates the patient in her transference enactments disavowing her father's death and asserting his living presence. She was dramatically making herself at one with her father by playing out both roles, that of the seduced and fretful little girl and that of the provocative and frustrated father. I should interject that the patient was not psychotic, although at times of crisis her feelings of persecution bordered on the paranoid and early in treatment her grandiosity was from time to time out of contact with reality.

She sought the father imago in lovers, employers, and analyst. She almost literally sought him through inseparable merger. As might be expected, the sexual act was of primary, even primal, importance and had to be consummated in strict accord with her specifications, lest she suffer physical pain. Between lovers, she was deeply anxious and depressed and could not tolerate being physically alone.

It would be only partly true to say that the analyst first began to comprehend the transference with his recognition of what I have called the paradox of ambivalence. This was in any case an approximate, summarizing statement, resulting from a growing series of congruent impressions, dating from the first interview. The clinical picture of arrested mourning and primitive identifications with the lost, ambivalent object, together with the contradictory, confused, and confusing behavior led to continued unrest and puzzlement in the analyst. But even this is to describe in secondary-process terms phenomena that were basically and empathically affective and regressed. The analyst felt, though less keenly than she, what the patient felt—unrest, puzzlement, and anguish. These feelings were induced in him by the transference pressure; he also empathized with the patient as part of the work ego's function of collecting and collating data.

The transference was expressed as a metaphor of action and a paradoxical guardedness and striving toward an experience of a transitional phenomenon. An essential part of her transference behavior was her requirement that the analyst participate with her in her strivings. In fact, it was useful for the therapy that the analyst experience her anguished demands for a parental transitional object, so long as he did not enact the role with her. The clarifications of her paradoxical transference gave the work ego sustenance. The successful empathic integrations were effectively integrative to the analyst's self-esteem through rapprochement with the patient in the treatment alliance.

With accurate interpretations the patient complained: "My mind gets fogged." At other times she thought of sucking her thumb, or curling up on the couch. She constantly toyed with a piece of Kleenex, twisting it into elongated shapes and puncturing it. Aside from its genital symbolism, which she announced herself and then derided, this was her transitional object, as was the analyst, and as were her lovers. Each was intensely needed, abused and used, preserved beyond needfulness, and separated from reproachfully and sadly, as from the analyst at the end of the session. She lived amidst illusion, sometimes with no little success and skill.

I take the feelings of unrest and puzzlement as a paradigm of the triggering mechanism in the analyst, leading to a changeover from the attitude of evenly suspended attention to an exercise in problem solving and, eventually, to a verbal intervention. That which puzzled was the complexity of the paradoxes; the principle one of many was her seeking of oneness in multiplicity, her seeking of reunion with her father through a series of men. Such feelings of disquiet and puzzlement in the analyst are not always fully conscious: they are often of a quality that exists only on the periphery of awareness. Preconsciously or consciously, the unrest impels the work ego to a specific activity. When the analyst is in this way affectively separated from his patient by being unable to comprehend, he must take such opportunity as he can of listening further with evenly suspended attention. The problem in such instances is that with a minimal or absent treatment alliance, the work ego is hampered and empathy is correspondingly limited. Nevertheless, even when the treatment alliance is tenuous and minimal, such filtered attentiveness serves as a stimulus to empathic perceptions, a form of rapprochement in the course of the self-induced, controlled regression that ensues. The perception of paradoxical dissonance between the real and the illusional is in this way both a stimulus to action and a result of action taken by the work ego. Accurate perception of paradox in psychoanalysis requires that the unrest and puzzlement initiate a testing and shaping of inner responses to the outer sources, thereby construing the meaning. The analyzing functions are set in motion when a disequilibrium is experienced; they are initiated by disparity, dissonance, and paradox. Optimally there follows a perception by the work ego through the intermediate experience of empathy; by means of this the analyst is apprised of what is transpiring in his patient. Meaning is clarified. The process is similar with metaphor.

The paradox, to repeat, is between real and illusional, inner and outer, self and nonself: above all, there is paradox in the final fact that the analyst learns to know his patient other than cognitively by noting his own associations to what has been responsive in himself to the patient. Reductively speaking, this is a mother-child dyadic communication; more precisely, the comprehension of the patient takes place in a mode that approximates and takes its patterning from the transitionalism of the mother-child unit.

Paradox, as this applies to psychoanalysis, is a manifestation of an area of experiencing that represents one adult form of the transitional. The subjective and objective are not completely differentiated nor are they still fused; they are "separate but inter-related." The analytic task is to assist in their further development, and this involves the solving of the paradox.

Although we customarily speak of the solving or resolving of paradox, I must point out that this does not mean that the paradox no longer exists. It continues to exist, but now as meaningful rather than as enigmatic, puzzling, and defensive. The observer who has participated in the paradox, who has interacted with it, so to say, is able to extend and develop his thought and feeling when he is not under the stultifying influence of the prior rigid and puzzling incongruities. I have pointed this out in connection with paradoxes in poetry and in other imaginative literature, and compared this with the work of the analyst. Tolerance for paradox and its meaning are analogous to the tolerance for uncertainty and ambiguity that are essential to the successful work of the analyst. A much-quoted statement from a letter written by John Keats is apropos: For him, he says, the quality of a "Man of Achievement, especially in Literature, and which Shakespeare possessed so enormously . . . [is] when a man is capable of being in uncertainties, mysteries, doubts, without any irritable reaching after fact and reason."

Countertransference and Paradox

It is paradoxical that certain countertransference problems have something in common with those specific factors that also motivate a young man or woman to seek training in psychoanalysis (see chapter 1). Whether the motives are neurotic or valid do not concern us in this connection, so much as does the external plausibility of the actions, and the basic question of their analyzability.

For example, one young student of psychoanalysis consistently displayed a difficulty in his supervisory work. He was sensitively attuned to his patient, a distraught young married woman with preschool children; his trial identifications of empathy overcarried: he became excessively sympathetic and overidentified with her envy and resentment of her husband, a successful junior executive whose ambitions and business demands left him little awareness of his family. The therapist became as exclusively preoccupied as was the patient with the day-to-day realities of her discouraged, angry, self-defeating attitudes toward maintaining a family and home and toward social entertaining for her husband. In this way she barely avoided a depression that would have duplicated in many ways her mother's distress and withdrawal and would have required her to face her own feelings of deprivation and loss in childhood. The therapist unwittingly colluded with her in avoiding this; for him, this correlated with his own need to be chivalrous and protective of women. This in turn had its historical roots in his responsiveness to his own mother's injured narcissism and depressive reactions (see chapter 1) and her investment in her son for the fulfillment of her own frustrated personal ambitions. He projectively identified with his patient as he had with his mother, and as we may presume she had done with him. He feared "depriving" any woman—that is, causing her to be depressed. His work therefore consisted largely of supportive and mutually avoiding maneuvers, in a modified *folie à deux* that was predominantly comprised of plausible sadomasochistic manipulations by both patient and therapist.

Similar situations are frequent in the early learning phases of an analyst's development, and they are charged with paradoxes. To name a few from this vignette: the analyst is peculiarly satisfied but uneasy; what professes to be analytic is only supportive; what professes to be protective and supportive is revealed as sadomasochistic; the patient is not grateful but seductive and slyly bad tempered. On a deeper level is an uncanny paradox of living alluded to previously — one that entails the seeking out of that which one fears, of yearning after that which one abhors, and which ultimately has to do with conflicts of separation and individuation from the maternal imago. The student in this vignette is avoiding a paradox of the uncanny by seeking the spurious comfort and soothing effects of recreating an internal relationship with his depressive maternal imago. He is making of the patient a transitional object, and here I think it justifiable to equate the term to the *self-object* of Kohut (1971). The supervisor's and the training analyst's tasks were to assist in disclosing the repressed infantile complexes that had been revived and reconfirmed in the heat of the transference-countertransference impasse.

METAPHOR

Metaphor, according to the dictionary, is "a figure of speech in which a word or phrase literally denoting one kind of object or idea is used in place of another by way of suggesting a likeness or analogy between them." In his *Principles of Literary Criticism* (1925), I. A. Richards wrote: "A metaphor may be illustrative or diagrammatical, providing a concrete instance of a relation which would otherwise have to be stated in abstract terms. This is the most common scientific or prose use of metaphor" (p. 239). He continues, that metaphor is "the supreme agent by which disparate and hitherto unconnected things are brought together in poetry" (p. 240). We are confronted with the fact that metaphor is paradoxical.

It is useful to recognize that metaphors may be expressed in word or in action. An example of the former: the patient of the longer clinical vignette vigorously denied her penis envy and was one day considering whether she should have a tubal ligation or her lover should have a vasectomy. She concluded with characteristic ambiguity that, "I'm not cut out to have a baby." The metaphors of action will be recognized as those events ordinarily referred to as symptomatic actions, as acting out, or as enactments. I am not proposing that they be renamed, nor that the usual designations are inadequate. The term *metaphor of action* is intended as a heuristic and expository convenience. I offer two examples: (1) Over a period of a few years, a woman patient resistantly explored her fear of the "bad stranger," a haunting conception of hers that, through projections and externalizations, variously denoted a member of her family, a true stranger, a menace, or someone benevolent who might become menacing. Through this period of time the patient had insisted on herself closing the door between the consulting room and the waiting room, but frequently she did not securely latch it. On a few occasions she arrived at the wrong hour for her appointment, and on one such occasion she knocked on the consulting room door and was of course politely turned away. The primal scene correlates of these actions are irrelevant for the purposes of this illustration. The patient was eventually able to recognize an aspect of herself as the bad stranger, derived by identification with her mother as the envious aggressor. (2) A patient's father developed pulmonary carcinoma. Thereupon, the patient began to notice that he was himself markedly curtailing his smoking, but not in a conscious, deliberate fashion. The action was expiatory, identificatory, and symbolically sacrificial, as though to say, "I yield up so that my father may have; I abstain so that he may be well."

In a collection of essays, *Other Inquisitions, 1937–1952,* Jorge Luis Borges (1952) returns the word *inquisitions* to its basic meaning of inquiries or investigations (for application of these developments of the psychology of the question to psychoanalysis, see chapters 8 and 9). He tells us, in his first essay, of the contradictory feelings aroused in him on reading of the Chinese emperor who ordered the building of the Great Wall and decreed the burning of all the books that had been written before his time. This, he writes, "unaccountably satisfied and, at the same time, disturbed me." The paradox of his being satisfied and "at the same time" disturbed led him to inquire into the meanings of such vast destruction and construction by "a Caesar who ordered the most reverent of nations to burn its past," and who left the "tenacious Wall" as his "shadow." The book burning and the Great Wall were experienced by Borges as the metaphoric actions of this emperor's tyrannical rule and the stimuli to the writing of the essay.

Borges is a writer of exquisitely accurate intellectual expression who is at the same time concerned with the covert, even the occult, that stirs behind the plausible facade. He often writes about what analysts would refer to as primary or transitional processes, but always in terms that are thoroughly in the mode of secondary process. His literary predecessors include the nineteenth-century French Symbolists, yet his short stories are uncannily realistic. For me he illustrates uniquely and esthetically the fact that the interface connecting the writer and his reader lies in transitional processes (Winnicott 1953, Holland 1973) that are mutually evoked in the artistic paths that lead between fantasy and reality (Freud 1917). Similar processes are constituted in the psychoanalytic situation through the paradoxes, metaphors, and other data with which the analyst must cope.

Metaphor is a potent linguistic device for the communication of abstact and abstruse thought. Its value is that it tends to be explanatory, opening up new ways of thought and action. Its special quality is to suggest meaning from the interaction of disparate items. Paradox is thus implicit in metaphor, perhaps because the latter bridges unconscious processes, such as fantasies, with language and action (Arlow 1969), in the manner I have described for paradox.

The analyst's work ego is continually and creatively perceiving metaphor and paradox in the course of his work, while forming a view of the patient's inner and outer realities. Since Sharpe wrote of metaphor (1940), we have recognized that the patient's use of metaphor indicates where in his associations the presenting edge of affect may be found. At these times the work ego is stimulated to alertness by the evocative and apparently disparate imagery. The operative factor for the work ego in these matters lies in their dissonance and incongruity, which become signals indicating a fruitful area to explore. The metaphor expresses and combines discontinuity and incongruity. It is itself a paradox.

A paradigm of this interpenetration of paradox and metaphor is found in the familiar Oedipus myth. In psychoanalysis, the story of Oedipus has become a metaphor for both a developmental phase and the nuclear neurosis. In Sophocles' trilogy (Grene and Latimore

1954) ironies are numerous and interlocked with paradox. He depicts Oedipus as knowing and not knowing his fate, as evading it only to stumble into it (*Oedipus* = swelled foot), as rescuing Thebes, only to expose it to the wrath of Apollo. In the third play of the trilogy, the incestuous parricide is received peacefully into the bosom of the earth in the sacred grove of the Eumenides, the tamed, yet vengeful, personifications of parental curses. Above all, Oedipus had been determined to tear the veil from the unknown—to rediscover what he preconsciously knew. Through his indomitable questioning it can be deduced that he knew himself to be the culprit (see chapters 8 and 9).

The literature on metaphor is vast, both in its literary and psychoanalytic applications, and I can do no more than to select a few references. The fact of this huge bibliography attests not only to the importance of and interest in the subject but also to the fact that metaphor in many ways continues to present unsolved problems. Perhaps these problems derive from the inherent biosocial nature of language. For the psychoanalyst the problems are compounded by the fact that metaphor, like paradox and like transitional phenomena, tends to bridge and to participate in the multiple admixtures in everyday living of primary and secondary process, of conscious, preconscious, and unconscious factors, and in general of regressive elements obtruding on more mature developmental processes (Brenner 1968).

Sharpe pointed out that metaphor connects a present-day emotional state with a past "psycho-physical experience" (1940, p. 162, also chapter 5). She also observed that metaphor "fuses sense experience and thought in language" (p. 155) and that speech, correlated as it is in its origins with the acquisition of sphincter control, becomes a means of physical discharge, a way of expression and a metaphor itself.

Wright (1976) has compared symptom and metaphor, stating that the symptom is an abortive metaphor, stopping below the level of speech, while metaphor is a "paradigm of integration within the ego" (p. 98). Doubtless, language and metaphor are integrative or, more exactly, they require integrative psychic action for their efficient use. Thus, to accept a metaphor literally is to fall into madness or dream. The work ego, alerted to the analysand's use of metaphor, is likewise alerted to suspend defenses and should be ready to engage in evenly suspended attention and in integrative, problem-solving activity.

Sharpe (1940) suggested that, when the analysand employed metaphor, the analyst should respond at the appropriate moment in a similar mode. It is a clinical fact, often enough for it to be significant, that the analytic process is metaphorical. Language is at times a metaphoric, transitional phenomenon, and this is markedly so during the regressive transactions with which analysis abounds. Metaphor and paradox lead beyond the immediate experience toward implications, innovations, and even toward creativity. This superordinate synthesizing is involved in special aspects of the work of the analyst. As we have seen, empathy as an instrument of the work ego makes use of transitional phenomena; moreover, as I have demonstrated elsewhere (see chapter 5) empathy makes use of metaphoric correspondence between language, imagery, and subliminal or overt action on the part of the analysand and the corresponding internal and internalized process in the analyst. Metaphor, in word or action, is thereby employed to carry meaning in empathic communication; it is an intersystemic vehicle — intrapsychic as well as interpersonal or, in other words, interactional between and within the members of the analytic dyad (see clinical vignettes in chapter 5 and in Poland 1974). Metaphor is associated in these ways with the transitional phenomena that are part of the data with which the work ego operates.

IMPLICATIONS AND CONCLUSIONS

The work ego of the analyst in the course of its integrative problem-solving actions makes use of a variety of form and content derived from subjective and objective perceptions and evaluations. I have attempted here to define and to utilize as explanatory principles two classes of the work ego's data, paradox and metaphor. These are uniquely and traditionally appropriate phenomena and processes. Feelings, wishes, memories, images, and other internal and internalized processes are often illusional and transitional as they are manifested in the transference and reflected in the work ego.

Empathy is a mode of experiencing transitional phenomena. It is a way of mediating between and within systems that are interpersonal and/or intrapsychic, by means of intersystemic, synesthetic metaphoric correspondences of both verbal and nonverbal communication. The empathic experience, subtle and sophisticated as it is when fully integrated by the work ego, encompasses the regressive borderline between the illusional and the real. An intrapsychic phenomenon becomes the basis for an experience that is intimately interpersonal. Adult transitional processes are transformed or transmuted and integrated by the work ego from regressive experience associated with separation and loss into an experience that is more mature and adaptive—that is to say, a paradox is resolved through being clarified and having its meaning construed.

The paradox of "separation in intimacy" (Stone 1961) is essential to the patient's experience in analysis. For the analyst's work ego it is important as one of many dissonances, discontinuities, and gaps between the illusional and the real. These evoke in the work ego the sensitive curiosity and unrest that motivate the analyzing functions. This implies that the principle of abstinence is indirectly as necessary to the work ego's functions as it is to the analysand's developing analyzing functions.

Such paradoxes for the analyst, consisting of adult forms of transitionalism, are recognized as such when the opposition and contradiction are permitted to emerge out of the prior fusion and confusion—when psychoanalytic meaning is derived. This is a creatively perceptive action by a trained, motivated, and sensitive person who is disposed to operate in the service of another in the special syntax of psychoanalytic methodology. To recognize and to contain a paradox or a metaphor, if one is not to fall into the benign literalism and humor of a Lewis Carroll world or into a less benign madness, requires a special readiness for seeking and finding problems and resolutions in unconventional ways and places.

The paradox of a transitionalism between illusion and reality, fusion and opposition, self and nonself, inner and outer reality is a generalization of the special case that Winnicott described for the finding of the primal object (1965, p. 181): it must be created to be found, but must be found to be created. The language that naturally falls into place is that of metaphor and paradox.

Paradox and metaphor are rhetorical, literary devices which are also defensive and adaptive modes for controlling and managing incongruity; they reflect and enable processes that are central to the developmental psychology of the person. Imaginative literature, the source of these devices, has evolved to deal with the universals of living in subjective and detailed forms that lend verisimilitude for the reader, but that depend on the reader's compliance and involvement in a mutual process. In this way enlightenment and enjoyment may be achieved through delayed and vicarious mastery. Through its connection with transference, the analytic interpretation tends in the same direction, depending upon alliance with the analysand. Literature deals with oedipal and preoedipal matters in an often transitional mode that connects writer, reader, and the intermediary metaphoric narrative and characterizations. This is analogous and perhaps homologous to the processes connecting analyst, analysand, and the intermediary developments of transference and alliance within the psychoanalytic process and situation.

The analyst is polarized toward human dilemmas of living in an attempt to clarify them and to impart that understanding to the patient. His work ego is alerted by such phenomena, in a setting or a form that resonates with his own recognition of his psychic beginnings. Clinical judgment and evaluation in the tradition of his science and art afford his validation. There are many sources of this motivation (see chapter 1, Kohut 1971), and the mastery of these processes may be a continuing lifelong task. The return to unfinished tasks, whether of early childhood or not, is well known to analysts and to other students of human nature.

Provisionally I conclude that paradox and metaphor are adaptive and defensive processes focused on dilemmas and predicaments of living. They are directed against primitive affects deriving from the separation-individuation period of child development; they are closely linked with and expressive of adult forms of transitional processes associated with the stresses and conflicts of the same period. These constitute an important segment of the data from which the work ego draws its stimuli and information.

REFERENCES

Arlow, J. (1969). Unconscious fantasy and disturbance of conscious experience. *Psychoanalytic Quarterly* 38: 1–25.

Blanck, R. (1976). Book review: *The Psychological Birth of the Human Infant*, by M. S. Mahler, F. Pine, and A. Bergman. *Journal of the Philadelphia Association for Psychoanalysis* 3: 150–154.

Borges, J. L. (1952). *Other Inquisitions, 1937-1952*. New York: Simon and Schuster, 1964.

Brenner, C. (1968). Archaic features of ego functioning. *International Journal of Psycho-Analysis* 49: 426-430.

Brooks, C. (1939). *Modern Poetry and the Tradition*. New York: Oxford University Press, 1965.

Coppolillo, H. P. (1976). The transitional phenomenon revisited. *Journal of the American Academy of Child Psychiatry* 15: 36-48.

Empson, W. (1930). *Seven Types of Ambiguity*. New York: New Directions.

———(1935). *Poems*. London: Chatto and Windus.

Fliess, R. (1942). The metapsychology of the analyst. *Psychoanalytic Quarterly* 11: 211-227.

Freud, S. (1900). The interpretation of dreams (1). *Standard Edition* 4.

———(1910). Leonardo da Vinci and a memory of his childhood. *Standard Edition* 11: 59-137.

———(1911). Formulations on the two principles of mental functioning. *Standard Edition* 12: 218-226.

———(1912). Recommendations to physicians practising psycho-analysis. *Standard Edition* 12: 111-120.

———(1917). Introductory lectures on psycho-analysis: lecture 23. *Standard Edition* 16: 358-377.

———(1919). The "uncanny." *Standard Edition* 17: 217-252.

———(1923a). The ego and the id. *Standard Edition* 19: 3-68.

———(1923b). Two encyclopaedia articles: (A) psycho-analysis. *Standard Edition* 18: 234-254.

———(1925). Some additional notes on dream-interpretation as a whole: (C) the occult significance of dreams. *Standard Edition* 19: 135-140.

Greenacre, P. (1971). *Emotional Growth*. 2 vols. New York: International Universities Press.

Greenson, R. (1960). Empathy and its vicissitudes. *International Journal of Psycho-Analysis* 44: 418-424.

Grene, D. and Lattimore, R., eds. (1954). *Sophocles* 1. Chicago: The University of Chicago Press.

Holland, N. (1968). The Dynamics of Literary Response. New York: Oxford University Press.

———(1973). *Poems in Persons: An Introduction to the Psycho-analysis of Literature*. New York: Norton.

———(1975). *5 Readers Reading*. New Haven: Yale University Press.

Isakower, O. (1938). A contribution to the pathopsychology of phenomena associated with falling asleep. *International Journal of Psycho-Analysis* 19: 331–345.

Kernberg, O. (1976). *Object Relations Theory and Clinical Psychoanalysis*. New York: Jason Aronson.

Kohut, H. (1971). *The Analysis of The Self*. New York: International Universities Press.

Kumin, I. M. (1978). Developmental aspects of opposites and paradox. *International Review of Psycho-Analysis* 5: 477–478.

Langs, R. (1976). *The Therapeutic Interaction*. 2 vols. New York: Jason Aronson.

Lewin, B. D. (1954). Sleep, narcissistic neurosis, and the analytic situation. *Psychoanalytic Quarterly* 24: 169–199.

Loewald, E. (1976). The development and uses of humour in a four-year-old's treatment. *International Review of Psycho-Analysis* 3: 209–221.

Loewald, H. (1960). On the therapeutic action of psycho-analysis. *International Journal of Psycho-Analysis* 41: 16–33.

Mahler, M., Pine, F., Bergman, A. (1975). *The Psychological Birth of the Human Infant*. New York: Basic.

Malcove, L. (1975). The analytic situation: toward a view of the supervisory experience (and panel discussion). *Journal of the Philadelphia Association for Psychoanalysis* 2: 1–19.

Milner, M. (1957). *On Not Being Able to Paint*. New York: International Universities Press.

Poland, W. S. (1974). On empathy in analytic practice. *Journal of the Philadelphia Association for Psychoanalysis* 1: 284–297.

Richards, I. A. (1925). *Principles of Literary Criticism*. New York: Harcourt, Brace, and World.

Sharpe, E. F. (1940). Psycho-physical problems revealed in language: an examination of metaphor. In *Collected Papers on Psycho-Analysis*. London: Hogarth, 1950.

Stone, L. (1961). *The Psychoanalytic Situation*. New York: International Universities Press.

Thomas, L. (1977). Notes of a biology watcher: the medusa and the snail. *New England Journal of Medicine* 296: 1103–1105.

Tolpin, M. (1971). On the beginnings of a cohesive self. *Psychoanalytic Study of the Child* 26: 316–352.

Volkan, V. D. (1976). *Primitive Internalized Object Relations*. New York: International Universities Press.

———(1978). "Immortal" Ataturk: narcissism and creativity in a revolutionary leader. *Psychoanalytic Study of Society* 10.

Winnicott, D. W. (1953). Transitional objects and transitional phenomena. *Collected Papers.* New York: Basic Books, 1958.

———(1958). *Collected Papers.* New York: Basic Books.

———(1965). *The Maturational Processes and the Facilitating Environment.* New York: International Universities Press.

———(1967). The location of cultural experience. *International Journal of Psycho-Analysis* 48: 368–372.

Wright, K. J. T. (1976). Metaphor and symptom: a study of integration and its failure. *International Review of Psycho-Analysis* 3: 97–109.

SOURCE NOTES

Chapter 1 first appeared in the *British Journal of Medical Psychology* 42 (1969): 41–49. It is reprinted here with permission of Cambridge University Press.

Chapter 2 is reprinted, with permission, from the *International Journal of Psycho-Analysis* 54 (1973): 143–151. It was presented to the Washington Psychoanalytic Society on March 17, 1972.

Chapter 3 originally appeared in the *International Journal of Psycho-Analysis* 56 (1975): 147–154 and is reprinted by permission.

Chapter 4 is reprinted, with permission, from the *Journal of the Philadelphia Association for Psychoanalysis,* vol. 3, nos. 1 and 2, pp. 3–21.

Chapter 5 first appeared in the *Annual of Psychoanalysis,* vol. 4, and is reprinted by permission of the publisher, International Universities Press.

Chapters 6 and 7 appeared first in the *International Encyclopedia of Neurology, Psychiatry, Psychoanalysis, and Psychology,* published by Van Nostrand Reinhold and copyrighted by Aesculapius Publishers.

Chapter 8 is reprinted from the *Journal of the American Psychoanalytic Association* 2: 57–66. Additional material is included.

Chapter 9 is reproduced, with permission, from the *Journal of the American Psychoanalytic Association* 5: 302•324.

Chapter 10 originally appeared in the *International Journal of Psycho-Analysis* 45: 540•548. Additional material is included, which was published in *The Journal of The Philadelphia Association for Psychoanalysis,* 1979.

Chapter 11 first appeared in *Psychiatry* 22 (1959): 333•339. The article is reprinted by special permission of The William Alanson White Psychiatric Foundation, Inc. Additional material has been included with the original article.

Chapter 12 first appeared in the *International Journal of Psychoanalytic Psychotherapy* 7 (1978): 533–561.

INDEX